# F.M. Trollope

# *Paris & The Parisians in 1835*

# *VOL I*

© 2025, F.M. Trollope (domaine public)
Publisher : BoD · Books on Demand, 31 avenue Saint-Rémy,
57600 Forbach, bod@bod.fr
Print : Libri Plureos GmbH, Friedensallee 273,
22763 Hamburg (Allemagne)
ISBN : 978-2-3226-1388-5
Dépôt légal : Avril 2025

**LETTER I.**

Difficulty of giving a systematic account of what is doing in France.—Pleasure of revisiting Paris after long absence.—What is changed; what remains the same.

Paris, 11th April 1835.

My dear Friend,

In visiting Paris it certainly was my intention to describe in print what I saw and heard there; and to do this as faithfully as possible, I proposed to continue my old habit of noting in my journal all things, great and small, in which I took an interest. But the task frightens me. I have been here but a few days, and I already find myself preaching and prosing at much greater length than I approve: I already feel that I am involved in such a mizmaze of interesting subjects, that to give anything like an orderly and well-arranged digest of them, would beguile me into attempting a work greatly beyond my power to execute.

The very most I can hope to do will be but to "skim lightly over the surface of things;" and in addressing myself to you, I shall feel less as if I were about to be guilty of the presumption of writing "a work on France," than if I threw my notes into a less familiar form. I will then discourse to you, as well as I may, of such things as leave the deepest impression among the thousand sights and sounds in the midst of which I am now placed. Should it be our will hereafter that these letters pass from your [...] those of the public, I trust that nobody will be so unmerciful [...] ect that they shall make them acquainted with everything pa[...] and to come, "respecting the destinies of this remarkable coun[try...]

It must indeed be a bold pen that [...] write of "Young France," as it is at present the fashion to call it, w[ith] like a reasonable degree of order and precision, while still surrounded by all the startling novelties she has to show. To reason of what she has done, what she is doing, and—more difficult still—of what she is about to do, would require a steadier head than most persons can command, while yet turning and twisting in all directions to see what this Young France looks like.

In truth, I am disposed to believe that whatever I write about it will be much in the style of the old conundrum—

"I saw a comet rain down hail

I saw a cloud" &c.

And here you will remember, that though the things seen are stated in the most simple and veracious manner, much of the meaning is occult, depending altogether upon the stopping or pointing of the narrative. This stopping or pointing I must leave to you, or any other readers I may happen to have, and confine myself to the plain statement of "I saw;" for though it is sufficiently easy to see and to hear, I feel extremely doubtful if I shall always be able to understand.

It is just seven years and seven months since I last visited the capital of the "Great Nation." The interval is a long one, as a portion of human life; but how short does it appear when the events that it has brought forth are contemplated! I left the white banner of France floating gaily over her palaces, and I find it torn down and trampled in the dust. The renowned lilies, for so many ages the symbol of chivalric bravery, are everywhere erased; and it should seem that the once proud shield of St. Louis is soiled, broken, and reversed for ever.

But all this was old. France is grown young again; and I am assured that, according to the present condition of human judgment, everything is exactly as it should be. Knighthood, glory, shields, banners, faith, loyalty, and the like, are gone out of fashion; and they say it is only necessary to look about me a little, to perceive how remarkably well the present race of Frenchmen can do without them;—an occupation, it is added, which I shall find much more profitable and amusing than lamenting over the mouldering records of their ancient greatness.

The good sense of this remonstrance is so evident, that I am determined henceforth to profit by it; remembering, moreover, that, as an Englishwoman, I have certainly no particular call to mourn over the fading honours of my country's rival. So in future I shall turn my eyes as much as I can from the tri-coloured flag—(those three stripes are terribly false heraldry)—and only think of amusing myself; a business never performed anywhere with so much ease as at Paris.

Since I last saw it, I have journeyed half round the globe; but nothing I have met in all my wanderings has sufficed to damp the pleasure with which I enter again this gay, bright, noisy, restless city,—this city of the living, as beyond all others it may be justly called.

And where, in truth, can anything be found that shall make its air of ceaseless jubilee seem tame?—or its thousand depôts of all that is prettiest in art, lose by comparison with any other pretty things in the wide world? Where do all the externals of happiness meet the eye so readily?—or where can the heavy spirit so easily be roused to seek and find enjoyment? Cold, worn-out, and dead indeed must the heart be that does not awaken to some throb of pleasure when Paris, after long absence, comes again in sight! For though a throne has been overturned, the Tuileries still remain;—though the main stock of a right royal tree has been torn up, and a scion sprung from one of the roots, that had run, wildly enough, to a distance, has been barricaded in, and watered, and nurtured, and fostered into power and strength of growth to supply its place, the Boulevards, with their matchless aspect of eternal holiday, are still the same. No commotion, however violent, has yet been able to cause this light but precious essence of Parisian attractiveness to evaporate; and while the very foundations of society have been shaken round them, the old elms go on, throwing their flickering shadows upon a crowd that—allowing for some vagaries of the milliner and tailor—might be taken for the very same, and no other, which has gladdened the eye and enlivened the imagination since first their green boughs beckoned all that was fairest and gayest in Paris to meet together beneath them.

Whilst this is the case, and while sundry other enchantments that may be named in their turn continue to proclaim that Paris is Paris still, it would be silly quarrelling with something better than bread-and-butter, did we spend the time of our abode here in dreaming of what has been, instead of opening our eyes and endeavouring to be as much awake as possible to look upon all that is.

Farewell!

# LETTER II.

Absence of the English Embassy.—Trial of the Lyons Prisoners.—Church of the Madeleine.—Statue of Napoleon.

It may be doubtful, perhaps, whether the present period be more favourable or unfavourable for the arrival of English travellers at Paris. The sort of interregnum which has taken place in our embassy here deprives us of the centre round which all that is most gay among the English residents usually revolves; but, on the other hand, the approaching trial of the Lyons prisoners and their Parisian accomplices is stirring up from the very bottom all the fermenting passions of the nation. Every principle, however quietly and unobtrusively treasured,—every feeling, however cautiously concealed,—is now afloat; and the most careless observer may expect to see, with little trouble, the genuine temper of the people.

The genuine temper of the people?—Nay, but this phrase must be mended ere it can convey to you any idea of what is indeed likely to be made visible; for, as it stands, it might intimate that the people were of one temper; and anything less like the truth than this cannot easily be imagined.

The temper of the people of Paris upon the subject of this "atrocious trial," as all parties not connected with the government are pleased to call it, varies according to their politics,—from rage and execration to ecstasy and delight—from indifference to enthusiasm—from triumph to despair.

It will be impossible, my friend, to ramble up and down Paris for eight or nine weeks, with a note-book in my hand, without recurring again and again to a theme that meets us in every *salon*, murmurs through the corridors of every theatre, glares from the eyes of the republican, sneers from the lip of the doctrinaire, and in some shape or other crosses our path, let it lead in what direction it may.

This being inevitable, the monster must be permitted to protrude its horns occasionally; nor must I bear the blame should it sometimes appear to you a very tedious and tiresome monster indeed. Having announced that its appearance may be frequently expected, I will leave you for the present in the same state of expectation respecting it that we are in ourselves; and, while we are still safe from its threatened violence, indulge in a little peaceable examination of the still-life part of the picture spread out before me.

The first objects that struck me as new on re-entering Paris, or rather as changed since I last saw them, were the Column of the Place Vendôme, and the finished Church of the Madeleine. Finished indeed! Did Greece ever show any combination of stones and mortar more graceful, more majestic than this?

If she did, it was in the days of her youth; for, poetical association apart, and the unquestionably great pleasure of learned investigation set aside, no ruin can possibly meet the eye with such perfect symmetry of loveliness, or so completely fill and satisfy the mind, as does this modern temple.

Why might not our National Gallery have risen as noble, as simple, as beautiful as this?

As for the other novelty—the statue of the sometime Emperor of the French, I suspect that I looked up at it with rather more approbation than became an Englishwoman. But in truth, though the name of Napoleon brings with it reminiscences which call up many hostile feelings, I can never find myself in Paris without remembering his good, rather than his terrible actions. Perhaps, too, as one gazes on this brazen monument of his victories, there may be something soothing in the recollection that the bold standard he bore never for an instant wantoned on a British breeze.

However, putting sentiment and personal feeling of every kind apart, so much that is admirable in Paris owes its origin to him, that his ambition and his usurpations are involuntarily forgotten, and the use made of his ill-gotten power almost obliterates the lawless tyranny of the power itself. The appearance of his statue, therefore, on the top of the column formed of the cannon taken by the armies of France when fighting under his command, appeared to me to be the result of an arrangement founded upon perfect propriety and good taste.

When his effigy was torn down some twenty years ago by the avenging hands of the Allies, the act was one both of moral justice and of natural feeling; and that the rightful owners of the throne he had seized should never have replaced it, can hardly be matter of surprise: but that it should now again be permitted to look down upon the fitful fortunes of the French people, has something of historic propriety in it which pleases the imagination.

This statue of Napoleon offers the only instance I remember in which that most grotesque of European habiliments, a cocked-hat, has been immortalized in marble or in bronze with good effect. The original statue, with its flowing outline of Roman drapery, was erected by a feeling of pride; but this portrait of him has the every-day familiar look that could best satisfy affection. Instead of causing the eye to turn away as it does from some faithful portraitures of modern costume with positive disgust, this *chapeau à trois cornes,* and the well-known loose *redingote,* have that air of picturesque truth in them which is sure to please the taste even where it does not touch the heart.

To the French themselves this statue is little short of an idol. Fresh votive wreaths are perpetually hung about its pedestal; and little draperies of black crape, constantly renewed, show plainly how fondly his memory is still cherished.

While Napoleon was still among them, the halo of his military glory, bright as it was, could not so dazzle the eyes of the nation but that some portentous spots were discerned even in the very nucleus of that glory itself; but now that it shines upon them across his tomb, it is gazed at with an enthusiasm of devoted affection which mixes no memory of error with its regrets.

It would, I think, be very difficult to find a Frenchman, let his party be what it might, who would speak of Napoleon with disrespect.

I one day passed the foot of his gorgeous pedestal in company with a legitimate *sans reproche*, who, raising his eyes to the statue, said—"Notre position, Madame Trollope, est bien dure: nous avons perdu le droit d'être fidèles, sans avoir plus celui d'être fiers."

## LETTER III.

Slang.—Les Jeunes Gens de Paris.—La Jeune France.—Rococo.—Décousu.

I suppose that, among all people and at all times, a certain portion of what we call slang will insinuate itself into familiar colloquial intercourse, and sometimes even dare to make its unsanctioned accents heard from the tribune and the stage. It appears to me, I confess, that France is at present taking considerable liberties with her mother-tongue. But this is a subject which requires for its grave discussion a native critic, and a learned one too. I therefore can only venture distantly and doubtingly to allude to it, as one of the points at which it appears to me that innovation is visibly and audibly at work.

I know it may be said that every additional word, whether fabricated or borrowed, adds something to the riches of the language; and no doubt it does so. But there is a polished grace, a finished elegance in the language of France, as registered in the writings of her Augustan age, which may well atone for the want of greater copiousness, with which it has been sometimes reproached. To increase its strength, by giving it coarseness, would be like exchanging a high-mettled racer for a dray-horse. A brewer would tell you, that you gained in power what you lost in grace: it may be so; but there are many, I think, even in this age of operatives and utilitarians, who would regret the change.

This is a theme, however, as I have said before, on which I should not feel myself justified in saying much. None should pretend to examine, or at any rate to discuss critically, the niceties of idiom in a language that is not native to them. But, distinct from any such presumptuous examination, there are words and phrases lawfully within the reach of foreign observation, which strike me as remarkable at the present day, either from their frequent recurrence, or for something of unusual emphasis in the manner in which they are employed.

*Les jeunes gens de Paris* appears to me to be one of these. Translate it, and you find nothing but "the young men of Paris;" which should seem to have no more imposing meaning than "the young men of London," or of any other metropolis. But hear it spoken at Paris—Mercy on me! it sounds like a thunderbolt. It is not only loud and blustering, however; you feel that there is something awful—nay, mystical, implied by the phrase. It appears solemnly to typify the power, the authority, the learning—ay, and the wisdom too, of the whole nation.

*La Jeune France* is another of these cabalistic forms of speech, by which everybody seems expected to understand something great, terrible, volcanic, and sublime. At present, I confess that both of these, pronounced as they always are with a sort of mysterious emphasis, which seems to say that "more is meant than meets the ear," produce rather a paralysing effect upon me. I am conscious that I do not clearly comprehend all the meaning with which they are pregnant, and yet I am afraid to ask, lest the explanation should prove either more unintelligible or more alarming than even the words themselves. I hope, however, that ere long I shall grow more intelligent or less timid; and whenever this happens, and I conceive that I fully comprehend their occult meaning, I will not fail to transmit it faithfully to you.

Besides these phrases, and some others that I may perhaps mention hereafter as difficult to understand, I have learned a word quite new to me, and which I suspect has but very recently been introduced into the French language; at least, it is not to be found in the dictionaries, and I therefore presume it to be one of those happy inventions which are permitted from time to time to enrich the power of expression. How the Academy of former days might have treated it, I know not; but it seems to me to express a great deal, and might at this time, I think, be introduced very conveniently into our own language: at any rate, it may often help me, I think, as a very useful adjective. This new-born word is "*rococo*," and appears to me to be applied by the young and innovating to everything which bears the stamp of the taste, principles, or feelings of time past. That part of the French population to whom the epithet of *rococo* is thus applied, may be understood to contain all varieties of old-fashionism, from the gentle advocate for laced coats and diamond sword-knots, up to the high-minded venerable loyalist, who only loves his rightful king the better because he has no means left to requite his love. Such is the interpretation of *rococo* in the mouth of a doctrinaire: but if a republican speaks it, he means that it should include also every gradation of orderly obedience, even to the powers that be; and, in fact, whatever else may be considered as essentially connected either with law or gospel.

There is another adjective which appears also to recur so frequently as fully to merit, in the same manner, the distinction of being considered as fashionable. It is, however, a good old legitimate word, admirably expressive too, and at present of more than ordinary utility. This is "*décousu;*" and it seems to be the epithet now given by the sober-minded to all that smacks of the rambling nonsense of the new school of literature, and of all those fragments of opinions which hang so loosely about the minds of the young men who discourse fashionably of philosophy at Paris.

Were the whole population to be classed under two great divisions, I doubt if they could be more expressively designated than by these two appellations, the *décousu* and the *rococo*. I have already stated who it is that form the *rococo* class: the *décousu* division may be considered as embracing the whole of the ultra-romantic school of authors, be they novelists, dramatists, or poets; all shades of republicans, from the avowed eulogists of the "spirited Robespierre" to the gentler disciples of Lamennais; most of the schoolboys, and all the *poissardes* of Paris.

## LETTER IV.

Théâtre Français.—Mademoiselle Mars.—Elmire.—Charlotte Brown.— Extract from a Sermon.

It was not without some expectation of having "Guilty of rococoism" recorded against me, that I avowed, very soon after my arrival, the ardent desire I felt of turning my eyes from all that was new, that I might once again see Mars perform the part of Elmire in the "Tartuffe."

I was not quite without fear, too, that I was running some risk of effacing the delightful recollections of the past, by contemplating the change which seven years had made. I almost feared to let my children behold a reality that might destroy their *beau idéal* of the only perfect actress still remaining on the stage.

But "Tartuffe" was on the bills: it might not soon appear again; an early dinner was hastily dispatched, and once more I found myself before the curtain which I had so often seen rise to Talma, Duchenois, and Mars.

I perceived with great pleasure on reaching the theatre, that the Parisians, though fickle in all else, were still faithful in their adoration of

Mademoiselle Mars: for now, for perhaps the five hundredth representation of her Elmire, the barricades were as necessary, the *queue* as long and as full, as when, fifteen years ago, I was first told to remark the wonderful power of attraction possessed by an actress already greatly past the first bloom of youth and beauty. Were the Parisians as defensible in their ordinary love of change as they are in this singular proof of fidelity, it would be well. It is, however, strange witchery.

That the ear should be gratified, and the feelings awakened, by the skilful intonations of a voice the sweetest perhaps that ever blest a mortal, is quite intelligible; but that the eye should follow with such unwearied delight every look and movement of a woman, not only old—for that does sometimes happen at Paris—but one known to be so from one end of Europe to the other, is certainly a singular phenomenon. Yet so it is; and could you see her, you would understand why, though not how, it is so. There is still a charm, a grace, in every movement of Mademoiselle Mars, however trifling and however slight, which instantly captivates the eye, and forbids it to wander to any other object—even though that object be young and lovely.

Why is it that none of the young heads can learn to turn like hers? Why can no arms move with the same beautiful and easy elegance? Her very fingers, even when gloved, seem to aid her expression; and the quietest and least posture-studying of actresses contrives to make the most trifling and ordinary movement assist in giving effect to her part.

I would willingly consent to be dead for a few hours, if I could meanwhile bring Molière to life, and let him see Mars play one of his best-loved characters. How delicious would be his pleasure in beholding the creature of his own fancy thus exquisitely alive before him; and of marking, moreover, the thrill that makes itself heard along the closely-packed rows of the parterre, when his wit, conveyed by this charming conductor, runs round the house like the touch of electricity! Do you think that the best smile of Louis le Grand could be worth this?

Few theatrical pieces can, I think, be calculated to give less pleasure than that of "Charlotte Brown," which followed the "Tartuffe;" but as the part of Charlotte is played by Mademoiselle Mars, people will stay to see it. I repented however that I did not go, for it made me cross and angry.

Such an actress as Mars should not be asked to try a *tour de force* in order to make an abortive production effective. And what else can it be called, if her touching pathos and enchanting grace are brought before the public, to make them endure a platitude that would have been hissed into oblivion ere it had well seen light without her? It is hardly fair to expect that a performer should create as well as personate the chief character of a piece; but Mademoiselle

Mars certainly does nothing less, when she contrives to excite sympathy and interest for a low-born and low-minded woman, who has managed to make a great match by telling a great falsehood. Yet "Charlotte Brown" is worth seeing for the sake of a certain tragic look given by this wonderful actress at the moment when her falsehood is discovered. It is no exaggeration to say, that Mrs. Siddons never produced an expression of greater power.

It is long since I have seen any theatre so crowded.

I remember many years ago hearing what I thought an excellent sermon from a venerable rector, who happened to have a curate more remarkable for the conscientious manner in which he performed his duty to the parish, and the judicious selection of his discourses, than for the excellence of his original sermons. "It is the duty of a minister," said the old man, "to address the congregation which shall assemble to hear him with the most impressive and most able eloquence that it is within the compass of his power to use; and far better is it that the approved wisdom of those who have passed away be read from the pulpit, than that the weak efforts of an ungifted preacher should fall wearily and unprofitably on the ears of his congregation. The fact that his discourse is manuscript, instead of printed, will hardly console them for the difference."

Do you not think—with all reverence be it spoken—that the same reasoning might be very usefully addressed to the managers of theatres, not in France only, but all the world over? If it cost too much to have a good new piece, would it not be better to have a good old one?

## LETTER V.

Exhibition of Living Artists at the Louvre.—The Deluge.—Poussin and Martin.—Portraits.—Appearance of the company.

I have been so little careful about dates and seasons, as totally to have forgotten, or rather neglected to learn, that the period of our arriving at Paris was that of the Exhibition of Living Artists at the Louvre: and it is not easy to describe the feeling produced by entering the gallery, with the expectation of seeing what I had been used to see there, and finding what was, at least, so very different.

Nevertheless, the exhibition is a very fine one, and so greatly superior to any I had heretofore seen of the modern French school, that we soon had the consolation of finding ourselves amused, and I may say delighted, notwithstanding our disappointment.

But surely there never was a device hit upon so little likely to propitiate the feelings which generate applause, as this of covering up Poussin, Rubens, Raphael, Titian, and Correggio, by hanging before them the fresh results of modern palettes. It is indeed a most un-coquettish mode of extorting attention.

There are some pictures of the Louvre Gallery in particular, with which my children are well acquainted, either by engravings or description, whose eclipse produced a very sad effect. "The Deluge" of Poussin is one of these. Perhaps it may have been my brother's striking description of this picture which made it pre-eminently an object of interest to us. You may remember that Mr. Milton, in his elegant and curious little volume on the Fine Arts, written at Paris just before the breaking up of Napoleon's collection, says in speaking of it—"Colouring was unquestionably Poussin's least excellence; yet in this collection there is one of his pictures—the Deluge—in which the effect produced by the mere colouring is most singular and powerful. The air is burdened and heavy with water; the earth, where it is not as yet overwhelmed, seems torn to pieces by its violence: the very light of heaven is absorbed and lost." I give you this passage, because I remember no picture described with equal brevity, yet brought so powerfully before the imagination of the reader.

Can the place where one comes to look for this be favourable for hanging our illustrious countryman's representation of the same subject? It is doing him a most ungratifying honour; and were I Mr. Martin, or any other painter living, I would not consent to be exposed to the invidious comparisons which must inevitably ensue from such an injudicious arrangement.

How exceedingly disagreeable, for instance, must it be for the artists—who, I believe, not unfrequently indulge themselves by hovering under the incognito of apparent indifference near their favourite works—to overhear such remarks as those to which I listened yesterday in that part of the gallery where Le Sueur's St. Brunos hang!—"Certainly, the bows on that lady's dress are of a delicate blue," said the critic; "and so is the drapery of Le Sueur, which, for my sins, I happen to know is hid just under it.... Would one wish a better contrast to what it hides, than that unmeaning smile—that cold, smooth, varnished skin,—those lifeless limbs, and the whole unspeakable tameness of this thing, called *portrait d'une dame*?"

He spoke truly; yet was there but little point in what he said, for it might have referred with equal justice to many a pretty lady doomed to simper for ever in her gilded frame.

On the whole, however, portraits are much less oppressively predominating than with us; and among them are many whose size, composition, and exquisite style of finishing redeem them altogether from the odium of being *de trop* in the collection. I cannot but wish that this style of portrait-painting may find favour and imitation in England.

Lawrence is gone; and though Gérard on this side of the water, and indeed too many to rehearse on both, are left, whose portraitures of the human face are admirable; true to nature; true to art; true to expression,—true, even to the want of it; I am greatly inclined to believe that the enormous sums annually expended on these clever portraits contribute more to lower than to raise the art in popularity and in the genuine estimation of the public. The sums thus lavished may be termed patronage, certainly; but it is patronage that bribes the artist to the restraint, and often to the destruction, of his genius.

Is there, in fact, any one who can honestly deny that a splendid exhibition-room, crowded with ladies and gentlemen on canvass, as large as life, is a lounge of great tediousness and inanity?

We may feel some satisfaction in recognising at a glance the eyes, nose, mouth, and chin of many of our friends and acquaintance,—nay, our most critical judgment may often acknowledge that these familiar features are registered with equal truth and skill; but this will not prevent the exhibition from being very dull. Nor is the thing much mended when each portrait, or pair of portraits, has been withdrawn from the gaudy throng, and hung up for ever and for ever before the eyes of their family and friends. The fair lady, sweetly smiling in one division of the apartment, and the well-dressed gentleman looking *distingué* in another, contribute as little at home as they did when suspended on the walls of the academy to the real pleasure and amusement of the beholder.

At the exhibition this year at the Louvre are many exquisite full-length portraits in oil, of which the canvass measures from eighteen inches to a foot in height, and from a foot to ten inches in width. The composition and style of these beautiful little pictures are often such as to detain one long before them, even though one does not recognise in them the features of an acquaintance. Their unobtrusive size must prevent their ever being disagreeably predominant in the decoration of a room; while their delicate and elaborate finish, and the richness of their highly-studied composition, will well reward attention; and even the closest examination, when directed to them, either by politeness, affection, or connoisseurship, can never be disappointed.

The Catalogue of the exhibition notices all the pictures which have been either ordered or purchased by the king or any of the royal family; and the number is so considerable as to show plainly that the most liberal and widely-extended patronage of art is a systematic object with the government.

The gold medal of the year has been courteously bestowed upon Mr. Martin for his picture of the Deluge. Had I been the judge, I should have awarded it to Stuben's Battle of Waterloo. That the faculty of imagination is one of the highest requisites for a painter is most certain; and that Mr. Martin pre-eminently possesses it, not less so. But imagination, though it can do much, cannot do all; and common sense is at least equally important in the formation of a finished artist. The painter of the great day of Waterloo has both. His imagination has enabled him to dive into the very hearts and souls of the persons he has depicted. Passion speaks in every line; and common sense has taught him, that, however powerful—nay, vehement, might be the expression he sought to produce, it must be obtained rather by the patient and faithful imitation of Nature than by a bold defiance of her.

The Assassination of the Duc de Guise, by M. Delaroche, is an admirable and highly popular work. It requires some patient perseverance to contest inch by inch the slow approach to the place where this exquisite piece of finishing is hung—but it well rewards the time and labour. One or two lovely little pictures by Franquelin made me envy those who have power to purchase, and sigh to think that they will probably go into private collections, where I shall never see them more. There are, indeed, many pictures so very good, that I think it possible the judges may have relieved themselves from the embarrassment of declaring which was best, by politely awarding the palm to the stranger.

I could indulge myself, did I not fear to weary you, by dwelling much longer upon my agreeable recollections of this extensive exhibition—containing, by the way, 2,174 pictures,—and might particularise many very admirable works. Nevertheless, I must repeat, that thus hiding the precious labours of all schools, and of all ages of painting, by the promiscuous productions of the living artists of France during the last year, is a most injudicious device for winning for them the golden opinions of those who throng from all quarters of the world to visit the Louvre.

This exhibition reaches to about three-fourths of the gallery; and where it ceases, a grim curtain, suspended across it, conceals the precious labours of the Spanish and Italian schools, which occupy the farther end. Can anything be imagined more tantalising than this? And where is the living artist who could stand his ground against such cruel odds?

To render the effect more striking still, this dismal curtain is permitted so to hang as to leave a few inches between its envious amplitude and the rich wall —suffering the mellow browns of a well-known Murillo to meet and mock the eye. Certainly not all the lecturers of all the academies extant could point out a more effectual manner of showing the modern French artist wherein he chiefly fails: let us hope he will profit by it.

As I am writing of Paris, it must be almost superfluous to say that the admission to this collection is gratis.

I cannot quit the subject without adding a few words respecting the company, or at least a part of it, whose appearance, I thought, gave very unequivocal marks of the march of mind and of indecorum;—for a considerable sprinkling of very particularly greasy citizens and citizenesses made itself felt and seen at every point where the critical crowd was thickest. But—

"Sweetest nut hath sourest rind;"

and it were treason here, I suppose, to doubt that such a proportion of intellect and refinement lies hid under the soiled *blouse* and time-worn petticoat, as is at least equal to any that we may hope to find enveloped in lawn, and lace, and broadcloth.

It is an incontrovertible fact, I think, that when the immortals of Paris raised the barricades in the streets, they pulled them down, more or less, in society. But this is an evil which those who look beyond the present hour for their sources of joy and sorrow need not deeply lament. Nature herself—at least such as she shows herself, when man, forsaking the forest, agrees with his fellows to congregate in cities—Nature herself will take care to set this right again.

"Strength will be lord of imbecility;"

and were all men equal in the morning, they would not go to rest till some amongst them had been thoroughly made to understand that it was their lot to strew the couches of the rest. Such is the law of nature; and mere brute numerical strength will no more enable a mob to set it aside, than it will enable the ox or the elephant to send us to plough, or draw out our teeth to make their young one's toys.

For the present moment, however, some of the rubbish that the commotion of "the Ordonnances" stirred up may still be seen floating about on the surface; and it is difficult to observe without a smile in what chiefly consists the liberty which these immortals have so valiantly bled to acquire. We may truly say of the philosophical population of Paris, that "they are thankful for small matters;" one of the most remarkable of their newly-acquired rights being certainly the privilege of presenting themselves dirty, instead of clean, before the eyes of their magnates.

I am sure you must remember in days of yore,—that is to say, before the last revolution,—how very agreeable a part of the spectacle at the Louvre and in the Tuileries Gardens was constituted by the people,—not the ladies and gentlemen—they look pretty much the same everywhere; but by the careful coquetry of the pretty costumes, now a *cauchoise*, and now a *toque*,—the spruce neatness of the men who attended them,—nay, even by the tight and tidy trimness of the "wee things" that in long waist, silk apron, snow-white cap, and faultless *chaussure*, trotted beside them. All these added greatly to the pleasantness and gaiety of the scene. But now, till the fresh dirt (not the fresh gloss) of the Three Days' labour be worn off, dingy jackets, uncomely *casquettes*, ragged *blouses*, and ill-favoured round-eared caps, that look as if they did duty night and day, must all be tolerated; and in this toleration appears to consist at present the principal external proof of the increased liberty of the Parisian mob.

## LETTER VI.

Society.—Morality.—False Impressions and False Reports.—Observations from a Frenchman on a recent publication.

Much as I love the sights of Paris,—including as we must under this term all that is great and enduring, as well as all that is for ever changing and for ever new,—I am more earnestly bent, as you will readily believe, upon availing myself of all my opportunities for listening to the conversation within the houses, than on contemplating all the marvels that may be seen without.

Joyfully, therefore, have I welcomed the attention and kindness that have been offered me in various quarters; and I have already the satisfaction of finding myself on terms of most pleasant and familiar intercourse with a variety of very delightful people, many of them highly distinguished, and, happily for me, varying in their opinions of all things both in heaven and earth, from the loftiest elevation of the *rococo*, to the lowest profundity of the *décousu* school.

And here let me pause, to assure you, and any other of my countrymen and countrywomen whose ears I can reach, that excursions to Paris, be they undertaken with what spirit of enterprise they may, and though they may be carried through with all the unrestrained expense that English wealth can permit, yet without the power by some means or other of entering into good French society, they are nothing worth.

It is true, that there is something most exceedingly exhilarating to the spirits in the mere external novelty and cheerfulness of the objects which surround a stranger on first entering Paris. That indescribable air of gaiety which makes every sunshiny day look like a fête; the light hilarity of spirit that seems to pervade all ranks; the cheerful tone of voice, the sparkling glances of the numberless bright eyes; the gardens, the flowers, the statues of Paris,—all together produce an effect very like enchantment.

But "use lessens marvel;" and when the first delightful excitement is over, and we begin to feel weary from its very intensity, the next step is backward into rationality, low spirits, and grumbling.

From that moment the English tourist talks of nothing but wide rivers, magnificent bridges, prodigious *trottoirs,* unrivalled drains, and genuine port. It is at this stage that the traveller, in order to continue his enjoyment and bring it to perfection, should remit his examination of the exterior of noble *hôtels,* and endeavour to be admitted to the much more enduring enchantment which prevails within them.

So much has already been said and written on the grace and charm of the French language in conversation, that it is quite needless to dwell upon it. That *good things*can be said in no other idiom with equal grace, is a fact that can neither be controverted nor more firmly established than it is already. Happily, the art of expressing a clever thought in the best possible words did not die with Madame de Sévigné; nor has it yet been destroyed by revolution of any kind.

It is not only for the amusement of an hour, however, that I would recommend the assiduous cultivation of good French society to the English. Great and important improvements in our national manners have already arisen from the intercourse which long peace has permitted. Our dinner-tables are no longer disgraced by inebriety; nor are our men and women, when they form a party expressly for the purpose of enjoying each other's society, separated by the law of the land during half the period for which the social meeting has been convened.

But we have much to learn still; and the general tone of our daily associations might be yet farther improved, did the best specimens of Parisian habits and manners furnish the examples.

It is not from the large and brilliant parties which recur in every fashionable mansion, perhaps, three or four times in each season, that I think we could draw much improvement. A fine party at Lady A——'s in Grosvenor Square, is not more like a fine party at Lady B——'s in Berkeley Square, than a fine party in Paris is to one in London. There are abundance of pretty women, handsome men, satin, gauze, velvet, diamonds, chains, stars, moustaches, and imperials at both, with perhaps very little deserving the name of rational enjoyment in either.

I suspect, indeed, that we have rather the advantage on these crowded occasions, for we more frequently change the air by passing from one room to another when we eat our ices; and as the tulip-tinctured throng enjoy this respite from suffocation by detachments, they have often not only opportunity to breathe, but occasionally to converse also, for several minutes together, without danger of being dislodged from their standing-ground.

It is not, therefore, at the crowded roll-calls of all their acquaintance that I would look for anything rational or peculiar in the *salons* of Paris, but in the daily and constant intercourse of familiar companionship. This is enjoyed with a degree of pleasant ease—an absence of all pomp, pride, and circumstance, of which unhappily we have no idea. Alas! we must know by special printed announcement a month beforehand that our friend is "at home,"—that liveried servants will be in attendance, and her mansion blazing with light,—before we can dare venture to pass an evening hour in her drawing-room. How would a London lady stare, if some half-dozen—though perhaps among the most chosen favourites of her visiting-list—were to walk unbidden into her presence, in bonnets and shawls, between the hours of eight and eleven! And how strangely new would it seem, were the pleasantest and most coveted engagements of the week, formed without ceremony and kept without ostentation, to arise from a casual meeting at the beginning of it!

It is this ease, this habitual absence of ceremony and parade, this national enmity to constraint and tediousness of all kinds, which renders the tone of French manners so infinitely more agreeable than our own. And the degree in which this is the case can only be guessed at by those who, by some happy accident or other, possess a real and effective "open sesame!" for the doors of Paris.

With all the superabundance of vanity ascribed to the French, they certainly show infinitely less of it in their intercourse with their fellow-creatures than we do. I have seen a countess, whose title was of a dozen fair descents, open the external door of her apartment, and welcome the guests who appeared at it with as much grace and elegance as if a triple relay of tall fellows who wore her colours had handed their names from hall to drawing-room. Yet in this case there was no want of wealth. Coachman, footman, abigail, and doubtless all fitting etceteras, owned her as their sovereign lady and mistress. But they happened to have been sent hither and thither, and it never entered her imagination that her dignity could be compromised by her appearing without them. In short, the vanity of the French does not show itself in little things; and it is exactly for this reason that their enjoyment of society is stripped of so much of the anxious, sensitive, ostentatious, self-seeking etiquette which so heavily encumbers our own.

There are some among us, my friend, who might say of this testimony to the charm of French society, that there was danger in praising, and pointing out as an example to be followed, the manners of a people whose morality is considered as so much less strict than our own. Could I think that, by thus approving what is agreeable, I could lessen by a single hair's-breadth the interval which we believe exists between us in this respect, I would turn my approval to reproof, and my superficial praise to deep-dyed reprobation: but to any who should express such a fear, I would reply by assuring them that it would require a very different species of intimacy from any to which I had the honour of being admitted, in order to authorise, from personal observation, any attack upon the morals of Parisian society. More scrupulous and delicate refinement in *the tone of manners* can neither be found nor wished for anywhere; and I do very strongly suspect, that many of the pictures of French depravity which have been brought home to us by our travellers, have been made after sketches taken in scenes and circles to which the introductions I so strongly recommend to my countrywomen could by no possibility lead them. It is not of such that I can be supposed to speak.

Apropos of false impressions and false reports, I may repeat to you an anecdote which I heard yesterday evening. The little committee in which it was related consisted of at least a dozen persons, and it appeared that I was myself the only one to whom it was new.

"It is rather more than two years ago," said the speaker, "that we had amongst us an English gentleman, who avowed that it was his purpose to write on France, not as other men write—superficially, respecting truths that lie obvious to ordinary eyes—but with a research that should make him acquainted with all things above, about, and underneath. He professed this intention to more than one dear friend; and more than one dear friend took the trouble of tracing him in his chase after hidden truths. Not long after his arrival among us, this gentleman became intimately acquainted with a lady more celebrated for the variety of her friendships with men of letters than for the endurance of them. This lady received the attentions of the stranger with distinguished kindness, and, among other proofs of regard, undertook to purvey for him all sorts of private anecdotes, great and little, that from the mass he might form an average estimate of the people; assuring him at the same time, that no one in Paris was more *au fait* of its secret histories than herself. This," continued my informant, "might be, and I believe was, very particularly true; and the English traveller might have been justified in giving to his countrymen and countrywomen as much insight into such mysteries as he thought good for them: but when he published the venomous slanders of this female respecting persons not only of the highest honour, but of the most unspotted reputation, he did what will blast his name as long as his charlatan book is remembered." Such were the indignant words, and there was nothing in the tone with which they were uttered to weaken their expression.

I tell you the tale as I heard it; but I will not repeat much more that was said on the same subject, nor will I give any A..., B..., or C... hints as to the names so freely mentioned.

Some degree of respectability ought certainly to attach to those from whom important information is sought respecting the morals and manners of a country, when it is the intention of the inquirer that his observations and statements upon it should become authority to the whole civilized world.

The above conversation, however, was brought to a laughing conclusion by Madame C——, who, addressing her husband as he was seconding the angry eloquence I have repeated, said, "Calmez-vous donc, mon ami: après tout, le tableau fait par M. le Voyageur des dames Anglaises n'a rien à nous faire mourir de jalousie."

I suspect that neither you nor any other lady of England will feel disposed to contradict her.

Adieu!

## LETTER VII.

Alarm created by the Trial of the Lyons Prisoners.—Visits from a Republican and from a Doctrinaire: reassured by the promises of safety and protection received from the latter.

We have really had something very like a panic amongst us, from the rumours in circulation respecting this terrible trial, which is now rapidly approaching. Many people think that fearful scenes may be expected to take place in Paris when it begins.

The newspapers of all parties are so full of the subject, that there is little else to be found in them; and all those, of whatever colour, which are opposed to the government, describe the manner in which the proceedings are to be managed, as the most tyrannical exercise of power ever practised in modern Europe.

The legitimate royalists declare it to be illegal, inasmuch as the culprits have a right to be tried by a jury of their peers—the citizens of France; whereas it appears that this their chartered right is denied them, and that no other judge or jury is to be permitted in their case than the peers of France.

Whether this accusation will be satisfactorily answered, I know not; but there certainly does appear to be something rather plausible, at least, in the objection. Nevertheless, it is not very difficult to see that the 28th Article of the Charter may be made to answer it, which says,—

"The Chamber of Peers takes cognizance of high-treason, and of attempts against the safety of the state, *which shall be defined by law.*"

Now, though this *defining by law* appears, by what I can learn, to be an operation not yet quite completed, there seems to be something so very like high-treason in some of the offences for which these prisoners are to be tried, that the first clause of the article may do indifferently well to cover it.

The republican journals, pamphlets, and publications of all sorts, however, treat the whole business of their detention and trial as the most tremendous infringement of the newly-acquired rights of Young France; and they say— nay, they do swear, that crowned king, created peers, and placed ministers never dared to venture upon anything so tyrannical as this.

All that the unfortunate Louis Seize ever did, or suffered to be done—all that the banished Charles Dix ever threatened to do—never "roared so loud, and thundered in the index," as does this deed without a name about to be perpetrated by King Louis-Philippe the First.

At last, however, the horrible thing has been christened, and Procès Monstre is its name. This is a happy device, and will save a world of words. Before it received this expressive appellation, every paragraph concerning it began by a roundabout specification of the horrific business they were about to speak of; but since this lucky name has been hit upon, all prefatory eloquence is become unnecessary: *Procès Monstre!* simply *Procès Monstre!* expresses all it could say in two words; and whatever follows may safely become matter of news and narrative respecting it.

This news, and these narratives, however, still vary considerably, and leave one in a very vacillating state of mind as to what may happen next. One account states that Paris is immediately to be put under martial law, and all foreigners, except those attached to the different embassies, civilly requested to depart. Another declares all this to be a weak invention of the enemy; but hints that it is probable a pretty strong *cordon* of troops will surround the city, to keep watch day and night, lest *les jeunes gens* of the metropolis, in their mettlesome mood, should seek to wash out in the blood of their fellow-citizens the stain which the illegitimate birth of the monster has brought upon France. Others announce that a devoted body of patriots have sworn to sacrifice a hecatomb of National Guards, to atone for an abomination which many believe to originate with them.

Not a few declare that the trial will never take place; that the government, audacious as they say it is, dare do no more than hold up the effigy of the monster to frighten the people, and that a general amnesty will end the business. In truth, it would be a tedious task to record one half of the tales that are in circulation on this subject: but I do assure you, that listening to the awful note of preparation for all that is to be done at the Luxembourg is quite enough to make one nervous, and many English families have already thought it prudent to leave the city.

At one moment we were really worked into a state very nearly approaching terror by the vehement eloquence of a fiery-hot republican who paid us a visit. I ventured to lead to the terrible subject by asking him if he thought the approaching political trials likely to produce any result beyond their disagreeable influence on the convenience of the parties concerned; but I really repented my temerity when I saw the cloud which gathered on his brow as he replied:—

"Result! What do you call result, madam? Is the burning indignation of millions of Frenchmen a result? Are the execrations of the noble beings enslaved, imprisoned, tortured, trampled on by tyranny, a result? Are the groans of their wives and mothers—are the tears of their bereaved children—a result?—Yes, yes, there will be results enough! They are yet to come, but come they will; and when they do, think you that the next revolution will be one of three days? Do your countrymen think so? does Europe think so? There has been another revolution, to which it will more resemble."

He looked rather ashamed of himself, I thought, when he had concluded his tirade,—and well he might: but there was such a hideous tone of prophecy in this, that I actually trembled as I listened to him, and, all jesting apart, thoughts of passports to be signed and conveyances to be hired were arranging themselves very seriously in my brain. But before we went out for the evening, all these gloomy meditations were most agreeably dispersed by a visit from a staid old doctrinaire, who was not only a soberer politician, but one considerably more likely to know what he was talking about than the youth who had harangued us in the morning.

Anxious to have my fears either confirmed or removed, I hastened to tell him, half in jest, half in earnest, that we were beginning to think of taking an abrupt leave of Paris. "And why?" said he.

I stated very seriously my newly-awakened fears; at which he laughed heartily, and with an air of such unfeigned amusement, that I was cured at once.

"Whom can you have been listening to?" said he.

"I will not give up my authority," I replied with proper diplomatic discretion; "but I will tell you exactly what a gentleman who has been here this morning has been saying to us." And I did so precisely as I have repeated it to you;

upon which he laughed more heartily than before, and rubbing his hands as if perfectly delighted, he exclaimed, "Delicious! And you really have been fortunate enough to fall in with one of these *enfans perdus*? I really wish you joy. But do not set off immediately: listen first to another view of the case." I assured him that this was exactly what I wished to do, and very truly declared that he could do me no greater favour than to put me *au fait* of the real state of affairs.

"Willingly will I do so," said he; "and be assured I will not deceive you." Whereupon I closed the *croisée*, that no rattling wheels might disturb us, and prepared to listen.

"My good lady," he began with great kindness, "soyez tranquille. There is no more danger of revolution at this time in France than there is in Russia. Louis-Philippe is adored; the laws are respected; order is universally established; and if there be a sentiment of discontent or a feeling approaching to irritation among any deserving the name of Frenchmen, it is against these miserable *vauriens*, who still cherish the wild hope of disturbing our peace and our prosperity. But fear nothing: trust me, the number of these is too small to make it worth while to count them."

You will believe I heard this with sincere satisfaction; and I really felt very grateful, both for the information, and the friendly manner in which it was given.

"I rejoice to hear this," said I: "but may I, as a matter of curiosity, ask you what you think about this famous trial? How do you think it will end?"

"As all trials ought to end," he replied: "by bringing all such as are found guilty to punishment."

"Heaven grant it!" said I; "for the sake of mankind in general, and for that portion of it in particular which happen at the present moment to inhabit Paris. But do you not think that the irritation produced by these preparations at the Luxembourg is of considerable extent and violence?"

"To whatever extent this irritation may have gone," he answered gravely, "it is an undoubted fact,—undoubted in the quarter where most is known about the matter,—that the feeling which approves these preparations is not only of greater extent, but of infinitely deeper sincerity, than that which is opposed to it. What you have heard to-day is mere unmeaning bluster. The trial, I do assure you, is very popular. It is for the justification and protection of the National Guard;—and are we not all National Guards?"

"But are all the National Guards true?"

"Perhaps not. But be sure of this, that there are enough true to *égorger* without any difficulty those who are not."

"But is it not very probable," said I, "that the republican feeling may be quite strong enough to produce another disturbance, though not another revolution? And the situation of strangers would probably become very embarrassing, should this eventually lead to any renewed outbreakings of public enthusiasm."

"Not the least in the world, I do assure you: for, at any rate, all the enthusiasm, as you civilly call it, would only elicit additional proof of the stability and power of the government which we are now so happy as to enjoy. The enthusiasm would be speedily calmed, depend upon it."

"A peaceable traveller," said I, "can wish for no better news; and henceforward I shall endeavour to read and to listen with a tranquil spirit, let the prisoners or their partisans say what they may."

"You will do wisely, believe me. Rest in perfect confidence and security, and be assured that Louis-Philippe holds all the English as his right good friends. While this is the case, neither Windsor Castle nor the Tower of London itself could afford you a safer abode than Paris."

With this seasonable and very efficient encouragement, he left me; and as I really believe him to know more about the new-born politics of "Young France" than most people, I go on very tranquilly making engagements, with but few misgivings lest barricades should prevent my keeping them.

## LETTER VIII.

Eloquence of the Pulpit.—L'Abbé Cœur.—Sermon at St. Roch.—Elegant Congregation.—Costume of the younger Clergy.

There is one novelty, and to me a very agreeable one, which I have remarked since my return to this volatile France: this is the fashion and consideration which now attend the eloquence of her preachers.

Political economists assert that the supply of every article follows the demand for it in a degree nicely proportioned to the wants of the population; and it is upon this principle, I presume, that we must account for the present affluence of a talent which some few years ago could hardly be said to exist in France, and might perhaps have been altogether denied to it, had not the pages both of Fenelon and his eloquent antagonist, Bossuet, rendered such an injustice impossible.

It was, I think, about a dozen years ago that I took some trouble to discover if any traces of this glorious eloquence remained at Paris. I heard sermons at Notre Dame—at St. Roch—at St. Eustache; but never was a search after talent attended with worse success. The preachers were nought; they had the air, too, of being vulgar and uneducated men,—which I believe was, and indeed still is, very frequently the case. The churches were nearly empty; and the few persons scattered up and down their splendid aisles appeared, generally speaking, to be of the very lowest order of old women.

How great is now the contrast! Nowhere are we so certain of seeing a crowd of elegantly-dressed and distinguished persons as in the principal churches of Paris. Nor is it a crowd that mocks the eye with any tinsel pretensions to a rank they do not possess. Inquire who it is that so meekly and devoutly kneels on one side of you—that so sedulously turns the pages of her prayer-book on the other, and you will be answered by the announcement of the noblest names remaining in France.

Though the eloquence of the pulpit has always been an object of attention and interest to me in all countries, I hardly ventured on my first arrival here to inquire again if anything of the kind existed, lest I should once more be sent to listen to an inaudible mumbling preacher, and to look at the deaf and dozing old women who formed his congregation. But it has needed no inquiry to make us speedily acquainted with the fact, that the churches have become the favourite resort of the young, the beautiful, the high-born, and the instructed. Whence comes this change?

"Have you heard l'Abbé Cœur?" was a question asked me before I had been here a week, by one who would not for worlds have been accounted *rococo*. When I replied that I had not even heard of him, I saw plainly that it was decided I could know very little indeed of what was going on in Paris. "That is really extraordinary! but I engage you to go without delay. He is, I assure you, quite as much the fashion as Taglioni."

As the conversation was continued on the subject of fashionable preachers, I soon found that I was indeed altogether benighted. Other celebrated names were cited: Lacordaire, Deguerry, and some others that I do not remember, were spoken of as if their fame must of necessity have reached from pole to pole, but of which, in truth, I knew no more than if the gentlemen had been private chaplains to the princes of Chili. However, I set down all their names with much docility; and the more I listened, the more I rejoiced that the Passion-week and Easter, those most Catholic seasons for preaching, were before us, being fully determined to profit by this opportunity of hearing in perfection what was so perfectly new to me as popular preaching in Paris.

I have lost little time in putting this resolution into effect. The church of St.

Roch is, I believe, the most fashionable in Paris; it was there, too, that we were sure of hearing this celebrated Abbé Cœur; and both these reasons together decided that it was at St. Roch our sermon-seeking should begin: I therefore immediately set about discovering the day and hour on which he would make his appearance in the pulpit.

When inquiring these particulars in the church, we were informed, that if we intended to procure chairs, it would be necessary to come at least one good hour before the high mass which preceded the sermon should begin. This was rather alarming intelligence to a party of heretics who had an immense deal of business on their hands; but I was steadfast in my purpose, and, with a small detachment of my family, submitted to the preliminary penance of sitting the long silent hour in front of the pulpit of St. Roch. The precaution was, however, perfectly necessary, for the crowd was really tremendous; but, to console us, it was of the most elegant description; and, after all, the hour scarcely appeared much too long for the business of reviewing the vast multitude of graceful personages, waving plumes, and blooming flowers, that ceased not during every moment of the time to collect themselves closer and closer still about us.

Nothing certainly could be more beautiful than this collection of bonnets, unless it were the collection of eyes under them. The proportion of ladies to gentlemen was on the whole, we thought, not less than twelve to one.

"Je désirerais savoir," said a young man near me, addressing an extremely pretty woman who sat beside him,—"Je désirerais savoir si par hasard M. l'Abbé Cœur est jeune."

The lady answered not, but frowned most indignantly.

A few minutes afterwards, his doubts upon this point, if he really had any, were removed. A man far from ill-looking, and farther still from being old, mounted the tribune, and some thousands of bright eyes were riveted upon him. The silent and profound attention which hung on every word he uttered, unbroken as it was by a single idle sound, or even glance, showed plainly that his influence upon the splendid and numerous congregation that surrounded him must be very great, or the power of his eloquence very strong: and it was an influence and a power that, though "of another parish," I could well conceive must be generally felt, *for he was in earnest.* His voice, though weak and somewhat wirey, was distinct, and his enunciation clear: I did not lose a word.

His manner was simple and affectionate; his language strong, yet not intemperate; but he decidedly appealed more to the hearts of his hearers than to their understandings; and it was their hearts that answered him, for many of them wept plenteously.

A great number of priests were present at this sermon, who were all dressed in their full clerical habits, and sat in places reserved for them immediately in front of the pulpit: they were consequently very near us, and we had abundant opportunity to remark the traces of that *march of mind* which is doing so many wondrous works upon earth.

Instead of the tonsure which we have been used to see, certainly with some feeling of reverence—for it was often shorn into the very centre of crisped locks, while their raven black or shining chesnut still spoke of youth that scrupled not to sacrifice its comeliness to a feeling of religious devotion;—instead of this, we now saw unshaven crowns, and more than one pair of flourishing *favoris*, nourished, trained, and trimmed evidently with the nicest care, though a stiff three-cornered cowl in every instance hung behind the rich and waving honours of the youthful head.

The effect of this strange mixture is very singular. But notwithstanding this bold abandonment of priestly costume among the junior clergy, there were in the long double row of anointed heads which faced the pulpit some exceedingly fine studies for an artist; and wherever the offending Adam was subdued by years, nothing could be in better keeping than the countenances, and the sacred garb of those to whom they belonged. Similar causes will, I suppose, at all times produce similar effects; and it is therefore that among the twenty priests at St. Roch in 1835, I seemed to recognise the originals of many a holy head with which the painters of Italy, Spain, and Flanders have made me familiar.

The contrast furnished by the deep-set eyes, and the fine severe expression of some of these consecrated brows, to the light, airy elegance of the pretty women around them, was sufficiently striking; and, together with the mellow light of the shaded windows, and the lofty spaciousness of the noble church, formed a spectacle highly picturesque and impressive.

After the sermon was over, and while the gaily-habited congregation fluttered away through the different doors like so many butterflies hastening to meet returning sunshine, we amused ourselves by wandering round the church. It is magnificently large for a parish church; but, excepting in some of the little chapels, we found not much to admire.

That very unrighteous old churchman, the Abbé Dubois, has a fine monument there, restored from Les Petits Augustins; and a sort of marble medallion, bearing the head of the immortal Corneille—immortal despite M. Victor Hugo —is also restored, and placed against one of the heavy columns of, I think, the centre aisle. But we paused longest in a little chapel behind the altar—not the middle one, with its well-managed glory of crimson light, though that is very beautiful; but in the one to the right of it, which contains a sculptured Calvary. It is, I believe, only one of *les stations*, of which twelve are to be found in different parts of the church; but it has a charm—seen as we saw it, with a strong effect of accidental light, bringing forward the delicate figure of the adoring Magdalene, and leaving the Saviour in the dark shadow and repose of death—that sets at defiance all the connoisseurship of art, and taking from you all faculty to judge, leaves only the power to feel. Under these circumstances, whether quite delusive or not I hardly know, this group appeared to us one of exceeding beauty.

The high altar of St. Roch, and the extremity of the carpeted space enclosed round it, is most lavishly, beautifully, and fragrantly adorned with flowers of the choicest kind, all flourishing in the fullest bloom in boxes and vases. It is the only instance I remember in which the perfume of this most fair and holy decoration actually pervaded the church. They certainly offer the sweetest incense that can be found to breathe its grateful life and spirit out on any altar; and were it not for the graceful swinging of the censers, which very particularly pleases my eye, I would recommend to the Roman Catholic church henceforth an economy of their precious gums, and advise them to offer the incense of flowers in their stead.

Before we left the church, about a hundred and fifty boys and girls, from ten to fourteen years of age, assembled to be catechised by a young priest, who received them behind the Lady Chapel. His manner was familiar, caressing and kind, and his waving hair fell about his ears like the picture of a young St. John.

## LETTER IX.

Literature of the Revolutionary School.—Its low estimation in France.

Among many proofs of attentive kindness which I have received from my Paris friends, their care to furnish me with a variety of modern publications is not the least agreeable.

One fancies everywhere, that it is easy, by the help of a circulating library, to know tolerably well what is going on at Paris: but this is a mighty fond delusion; though sometimes, perhaps, our state may be the more gracious from our ignorance.

One gentleman, to whom I owe much gratitude for the active good-nature with which he seems willing to assist me in all my researches, has given me much curious information respecting the present state of literature and literary men in France.

In this department of human greatness, at least, those of the party which has lost power and place have a most decided pre-eminence. Would it be a pun to say that there is poetical justice in this?

The active, busy, bustling politicians of the hour have succeeded in thrusting everything else out of place, and themselves into it. One dynasty has been overthrown, and another established; old laws have been abrogated, and hundreds of new ones framed; hereditary nobles have been disinherited, and little men made great;—but amidst this plenitude of destructiveness, they have not yet contrived to make any one of the puny literary reputations of the day weigh down the renown of those who have never lent their voices to the cause of treason, regicide, rebellion, or obscenity. The literary reputations both of Châteaubriand and Lamartine stand higher, beyond all comparison, than those of any other living French authors: yet the first, with all his genius, has often suffered his imagination to run riot, and the last has only given to the public the leisure of his literary life. But both of them are men of honour and principle, as well as men of genius; and it comforts one's human nature to see that these qualities will keep themselves aloft, despite whatever squally winds may blow, or blustering floods assail them. That both Châteaubriand and Lamartine belong rather to the imaginative than to the *positif* class, cannot be denied; but they are renowned throughout the world, and France is proud of them.

The most curious literary speculations, however, suggested by the present state of letters in this country, are not respecting authors such as these: they speak for themselves, and all the world knows them and their position. The circumstance decidedly the most worthy of remark in the literature of France at the present time, is the effect which the last revolution appears to have produced. With the exception of history, to which both Thiers and Mignet have added something that may live, notwithstanding their very defective philosophy, no single work has appeared since the revolution of 1830 which has obtained a substantial, elevated, and generally acknowledged reputation for any author unknown before that period: not even among all the unbridled ebullitions of imagination, though restrained neither by decorum, principle, nor taste,—not even here (excepting from one female pen, which might become, were it the pleasure of the hand that wields it, the first now extant in the world of fiction,) has anything appeared likely to survive its author; nor is there any writer who during the same period has raised himself to that station in society, by means of his literary productions, which is so universally accorded to all who have acquired high literary celebrity in any country.

The name of M. Guizot was too well known before the revolution for these observations to have any reference to him; and however much he may have distinguished himself since July 1830, his reputation was made before. There are, however, little writers in prodigious abundance; and though as perfectly sure of the truth of what I have here stated as that I am alive to write it, I should expect a terrible riot about my ears, could such words be heard by the swarm of tiny geniuses that settle in clusters, some on the newspapers, some on the theatres, and some on the busy little printing-press of the tale-tellers—could they catch me, I am sure I should be stung to death.

How well I can fancy the clamour!... "Infamous libeller!" cries one; "have not I achieved a reputation? Do I not receive yearly some hundreds of francs for my sublime familiarity with sin and misery? and are not my works read by 'Young France' with ecstasy? Is not this fame?" "And I," says another,—"is it of such as I and my cotemporary fellow-labourers in the vast field of new-ploughed speculation that you speak?" "What call you reputation, woman?" says a third: "do not the theatres overflow when I send murder, lust, and incest on the stage, to witch the world with wondrous wickedness?" "And, I too," groans another,—"am I not famous? Are not my delicious tales of unschooled nature in the hands of every free-born youth and tender maid in this our regenerated Athens? Is not this fame, infamous slanderer?"

Were I obliged to answer all this, I could only say, "*Arrangez-vous, canaille!* If you call this fame, take it, try it, make the most of it, and see where you will be some dozen years hence."

Notwithstanding this extraordinary lack of great ability, however, there never, I believe, was any period in which the printing-presses of France worked so hard as at present. The revolution of 1830 seems to have set all the minor spirits in motion. There is scarcely a boy so insignificant, or a workman so unlearned, as to doubt his having the power and the right to instruct the world. "Every breathing soul in Paris took a part in this glorious struggle," says the recording newspaper;—"Yes, all!" echoes the smutched mechanic, snorting and snuffing the air with the intoxicating consciousness of imputed power; —"Yes!" answer the *galopins* one and all, "it is we, it is we!" And then, like the restless witches on the barren heath that their breath has blasted, the great reformers rouse themselves again, and looking from the mischief they have done to the still worse that remains behind, they mutter prophetically, "We'll do—we'll do—we'll do!"

To me, I confess, it is perfectly astonishing that any one can be found to class the writers of this restless *clique* as "the literary men of France." Yet it has been done; and it is not till the effects of the popular commotion which brought them into existence has fully subsided, that the actual state of French literature can be fairly ascertained.

Béranger was not the production of that whirlwind: but, in truth, let him sing what or when he will, the fire of genuine poetic inspiration must perforce flash across the thickest mist that false principles can raise around him. He is but a meteor perhaps, but a very bright one, and must shine, though his path lie amongst unwholesome exhalations and most dangerous pitfalls. But he cannot in any way be quoted as one of the new-born race whose claim to genuine fame I have presumed to doubt.

That flashes of talent, sparkles of wit, and bursts of florid eloquence are occasionally heard, seen, and felt even from these, is, however, certain: it could hardly be otherwise. But they blaze, and go out. The oil which feeds the lamp of revolutionary genius is foul, and such noxious vapours rise with the flame as must needs check its brightness.

Do not, however, believe me guilty of such presumption as to give you my own unsupported judgment as to the position which this "new school" (as the *décousu* folks always call themselves) hold in the public esteem. Such a judgment could be little worth if unsupported; but my opinion on this subject is, on the contrary, the result of careful inquiry among those who are most competent to give information respecting it.

When the names of such as are best known among this class of authors are mentioned in society, let the politics of the circle be what they may, they are constantly spoken of as a Paria caste that must be kept apart.

"Do you know —— ——?" has been a question I have repeatedly asked respecting a person whose name is cited in England as the most esteemed French writer of the age,—and so cited, moreover, to prove the low standard of French taste and principle.

"No, madam," has been invariably the cold reply.

"Or ——?"

"No. He is not in society."

"Or ——?"

"Oh no! His works live an hour (too long!) and are forgotten."

Should I therefore, my friend, return from France with an higher idea of its good taste and morality than I had when I entered it, think not that my own standard of what is right has been lowered, but only that I have had the pleasure of finding it differed much less than I expected from that of our agreeable and hardly-judged neighbours on this side the water. But I shall probably recur to this subject again; and so, for the present, farewell!

# LETTER X.

Lonchamps.—The "Three Hours' Agony" at St. Roch.—Sermons on the Gospel of Good-Friday.—Prospects of the Catholics.—O'Connell.

I dare say you may know, my friend, though I did not, that the Wednesday, Thursday, and Friday of Passion-week are yearly set apart by the Parisians for a splendid promenade in carriages, on horseback, and on foot, to a part of the Bois de Boulogne called Lonchamps. What the origin could be of so gay and brilliant an assemblage of people and equipages, evidently coming together to be stared at and to stare, on days so generally devoted to religious exercises, rather puzzled me; but I have obtained a most satisfactory explanation, which, in the hope of your ignorance, I will communicate. The custom itself, it seems, is a sort of religious exercise; or, at any rate, it was so at the time of its institution.

When the *beau monde* of Paris first adopted the practice of repairing to Lonchamps during these days of penitence and prayer, a convent stood there, whose nuns were celebrated for performing the solemn services appointed for the season with peculiar piety and effect. They sustained this reputation for many years; and for many years all who could find admittance within their church thronged to hear their sweet voices.

This convent was destroyed at *the* revolution (*par excellence*), but the horses and carriages of Paris still continue to move for evermore in the same direction when the last three days of Lent arrive.

The cavalcade assembled on this occasion forms an extremely pretty spectacle, rivalling a spring Sunday in Hyde Park as to the number and elegance of the equipages, and greatly exceeding it in the beauty and extent of the magnificent road on which they show themselves. Though the attending this congregation of wealth, rank, and fashion is still called "going to Lonchamps," the evolutions of the company, whether in carriages, on horseback, or on foot, are at present almost wholly confined to the noble avenue which leads from the entrance to the Champs Elysées up to the Barrière de l'Etoile.

From about three till six, the whole of this ample space is crowded; and I really had no idea that so many handsome, well-appointed equipages could be found collected together anywhere out of London. The royal family had several handsome carriages on the ground: that of the Duke of Orleans was particularly remarkable for the beauty of the horses, and the general elegance of the "turn-out."

The ministers of state, and all the foreign legations, did honour to the occasion; most of them having very complete equipages, chasseurs of various plumage, and many with a set of four beautiful horses really well harnessed. Many private individuals, also, had carriages which were handsome enough, together with their elegant lading, greatly to increase the general brilliancy of the scene.

The only individual, however, except the Duke of Orleans, who had two carriages on the ground, two feathered chasseurs, and twice two pair of richly-harnessed steeds, was a certain Mr. T——, an American merchant, whose vast wealth, and still more vast expenditure, is creating considerable consternation among his sober-minded countrymen in Paris. We were told that the exuberance of this gentleman's transatlantic taste was such, and such the vivacity of his inventive fancy, that during the three days of the Lonchamps promenade he appeared on the ground each day with different liveries; having, as it should seem, no particular family reasons for preferring any one set of colours to another.

The ground was sprinkled, and certainly greatly adorned, by many very elegant-looking Englishmen on horseback; the pretty caprioles, sleek skins, and well-managed capers of that prettiest of creatures, a high-bred English saddle-horse, being as usual among the most attractive parts of the show. Nor was there any deficiency of Frenchmen, with very handsome *montures,* to complete the spectacle; while the ample space under the trees on either side was crowded with thousands of smart pedestrians; the whole scene being one vast moving mass of pomp and pleasure.

Nevertheless, the weather on the first of the three days was very far from favourable: the wind was so bitterly cold that I countermanded the carriage I had ordered, and instead of going to Lonchamps, we actually sat shivering over the fire at home; indeed, before three o'clock, the ground was perfectly covered with snow. The next day promised something better, and we ventured to emerge: but the spectacle was really vexatious; many of the carriages being open, and the shivering ladies attired in all the light and floating drapery of spring costume. For it is at Lonchamps that all the fashions of the coming season are exhibited; and no one can tell, however fashion-wise they be, what bonnet, scarf or shawl, or even what prevailing colour, is to be worn in Paris throughout the year, till this decisive promenade be over. Accordingly the milliners had done their duty, and, in fact, had far outstripped the spring. But it was sad to see the beautiful bunches of lilac, and the graceful, flexible laburnums—each a wonder of art—twisted and tortured, bending and breaking, before the wind. It really seemed as if the lazy Spring, vexed at the pretty mimicry of blossoms she had herself failed to bring, sent this inclement blast on purpose to blight them. Everything went wrong. The tender tinted ribbons were soon dabbled in a driving sleet; while feathers, instead of wantoning, as it was intended they should do, on the breeze, had to fight a furious battle with the gale.

It was not therefore till the following day—the last of the three appointed—that Lonchamps really showed the brilliant assemblage of carriages, horsemen, and pedestrians that I have described to you. Upon this last day, however, though it was still cold for the season—(England would have been ashamed of such a 17th of April)—the sun did come forth, and smiled in such a sort as greatly to comfort the pious pilgrims.

We remained, like all the rest of Paris, driving up and down in the midst of the pretty crowd till six, when they gradually began to draw off, and all the world went home to dinner.

The early part of this day, which was Good-Friday, had been very differently passed. The same beautiful and solemn music which formerly drew all Paris to the Convent in the Bois de Boulogne is now performed in several of the churches. We were recommended to hear the choir of St. Roch; and it was certainly the most impressive service at which I was ever present.

There is much wisdom in thus giving to music an important part in the public ceremonies of religion. Nothing commands and enchains the attention with equal power: the ear may be deaf to eloquence, and the thoughts may often grovel earthward, despite all the efforts of the preacher to lead them up to heaven; but few will find it possible to escape from the effect of music; and when it is of such a character as that performed in the Roman Catholic church on Good-Friday, it can hardly be that the most volatile and indifferent listener should depart unmoved.

This service was advertised as "The Three Hours' Agony." The crowd assembled to listen to it was immense. It is impossible to speak too highly of the composition of the music; it is conceived in the very highest tone of sublimity; and the deeply effective manner of its performance recalled to me an anecdote I have heard of some young organist, who, having accompanied an anthem in a manner which appeared greatly superior to that of the usual performer, was asked if he had not made some alteration in the composition. "No," he replied, "I have not; but I always read the words when I play."

So, I should think, did those who performed the services at St. Roch on Good-Friday; and nothing can be imagined more touching and effective than the manner in which the whole of these striking ceremonies were performed and arranged there.

The awful gospel of the day furnished a theme for the impassioned eloquence of several successive preachers; one or two of whom were wonderfully powerful in their manner of recounting the dreadful narrative. They were all quite young men; but they went through the whole of the appalling history with such deep solemnity, such strength of imagery and vehemence of eloquence, as to produce prodigious effect.

At intervals, while the exhausted preachers reposed, the organ, with many stringed instruments, and a choir of exquisite voices, performed the same gospel, in a manner that made one's whole soul thrill and quiver within one. The suffering—the submission—the plaintive yet sublime "It is finished!" and the convulsive burst of indignant nature that followed, showing itself in thunder, hail, and earthquake, were all brought before the mind with most miraculous power. I have been told since, that the services at Notre Dame on that day were finer still; but I really find some difficulty in believing that this is possible.

During these last and most solemn days of Lent, I have been endeavouring by every means in my power to discover how much fasting, of any kind, was going on. If they fast at all, it is certainly performed in most strict obedience to the very letter of the gospel: for, assuredly, they "appear not unto men to fast." Everything goes on as gaily as if it were the season of the carnival. The *restaurans* reek with the savoury vapour of a hundred dishes; the theatres are opened, and as full as the churches; invitations cease not; and I can in no direction perceive the slightest symptom of being among a Roman Catholic population during a season of penitence.

And yet, contradictory as the statement must appear, I am deeply convinced that the clergy of the church of Rome feel more hope of recovered power fluttering at their hearts now, than they have done at any time during the last half-century. Nor can I think they are far wrong in this. The share which the Roman Catholic priests of this our day are said to have had in the Belgian revolution, and the part, more remarkable still, which the same race are now performing in the opening scenes of the fearful struggle which threatens England, has given a new impulse to the ambition of Rome and of her children. One may read it in the portly bearing of her youthful priests,—one may read it in the deep-set meditative eye of those who are older. It is legible in their brand-new vestments of gold and silver tissue; it is legible in the costly decorations of their renovated altars; and deep, deep, deep is the policy which teaches them to recover with a gentle hand that which they have lost by a grasping one. How well can I fancy that, in their secret synods, the favourite text is, "No man putteth a piece of new cloth unto an old garment; for that which is put in to fill it up, taketh from the garment, and the rent is made worse." Were they a whit less cautious, they must fail at once; but they tickle their converts before they think of convincing them. It is for this that the pulpits are given to young and eloquent men, who win the eye and ear of their congregations long before they find out to what point they wish to lead them. But while the young men preach, the old men are not idle: there are rumours of new convents, new monasteries, new orders, new miracles, and of new converts, in all directions. This wily, worldly, tranquil-seeming, but most ambitious sect, having in many quarters joined themselves to the cause of democracy, sit quietly by, looking for the result of their work, and watching, like a tiger that seems to dose, for the moment when they may avenge themselves for the long fast from power, during which they have been gnawing their heart-strings.

But they now hail the morning of another day. I would that all English ears could hear, as mine have done, the prattle that prophesies the downfall of our national church as a thing certain as rain after long drought! I would that English ears could hear, as mine have done, the name of O'Connell uttered as that of a new apostle, and his bold bearding of those who yet raise their voices in defence of the faith their fathers gave them, triumphantly quoted in proof of the growing influence both of himself and his popish creed,—which are in truth one and inseparable! But forgive me!—all this has little to do with my subject, and it is moreover a theme I had much better not meddle with. I cannot touch it lightly, for my heart is heavy when I turn to it; I cannot treat it powerfully, for, alas! I have no strength but to lament.

"Hé! que puis-je au milieu de ce peuple abattu?

Benjamin est sans force, et Juda sans vertu."

## LETTER XI.

Trial Chamber at the Luxembourg.—Institute.—M. Mignet.—Concert Musard.

As a great and especial favour, we have been taken to see the new chamber that has been erected at the Luxembourg for the trial of the political prisoners. The appearance of the exterior is very handsome, and though built wholly of wood, it corresponds perfectly, to all outward seeming, with the old palace. The rich and massive style of architecture is imitated to perfection: the heavy balustrades, the gigantic bas-reliefs, are all vast, solid, and magnificent; and when it is stated that the whole thing has been completed in the space of two months, one is tempted to believe that Alladdin has turned doctrinaire, and rubbed his lamp most diligently in the service of the state.

The trial-chamber is a noble room; but from the great number of prisoners, and greater still of witnesses expected to be examined, the space left for the public is but small. Prudence, perhaps, may have had as much to do with this as necessity: nor can we much wonder if the peers of France should desire to have as little to do with the Paris mob upon this occasion as possible.

I remarked that considerable space was left for passages, ante-rooms, surroundings, and outposts of all sorts;—an excellent arrangement, the wisdom of which cannot be questioned, as the attendance of a large armed force must be indispensable. In fact, I believe it ever has been and ever will be found, that troops furnish the only means of keeping a remarkably free people in order.

It was, however, very comforting and satisfactory to hear the manner in which the distinguished and agreeable individual who had procured us the pleasure of seeing this building discoursed of the business which was to be carried on there.

There is a quiet steadiness and confidence in their own strength among these doctrinaries, that seems to promise well for the lasting tranquillity of the country; nor does it impeach either their wisdom or sincerity, if many among them adhere heart and hand to the government, though they might have better liked a white than a tri-coloured banner to wave over the palace of its head. Whatever the standers-by may wish or feel about future struggles and future changes, I think it is certain that no Frenchman who desires the prosperity of his country can at the present moment wish for anything but a continuance of the tranquillity she actually enjoys.

If, indeed, democracy were gaining ground,—if the frightful political fallacies, among which the very young and the very ignorant are so apt to bewilder themselves, were in any degree to be traced in the policy pursued by the existing government,—then would the question be wholly changed, and every honest man in full possession of his senses would feel himself called upon to stay the plague with all his power and might. But the very reverse of all this is evidently the case; and it may be doubted if any sovereign in Europe has less taste for license and misrule than King Louis-Philippe. Be very sure that it is not to him that the radicals of any land must look for patronage, encouragement, or support: they will not find it.

After quitting the Luxembourg, we went to the *bureau* of the secretary at the Institute, to request tickets for an annual sitting of the five Academies, which took place yesterday. They were very obligingly accorded—(O that our institutions, our academies, our lectures, were thus liberally arranged!)—and yesterday we passed two very agreeable hours in the place to which they admitted us.

I wish that the Polytechnic School, when they took a fancy for changing the ancient *régimes* of France, had included the uniform of the Institute in their proscriptions. The improvement would have been less doubtful than it is respecting some other of their innovations: for what can be said in defence of a set of learned academicians, varying in age from light and slender thirty to massive and protuberant fourscore, wearing one and all a fancy blue dress-coat "embroidered o'er with leaves of myrtle"? It is really a proof that very good things were said and done at this sitting, when I declare that my astonishment at the Corydon-like costume was forgotten within the first half-hour.

We first witnessed the distribution of the prizes, and then heard one or two members speak, or rather read their compositions. But the great fête of the occasion was hearing a discourse pronounced by M. Mignet. This gentleman is too celebrated not to have excited in us a very earnest wish to hear him; and never was expectation more agreeably gratified. Combined with the advantages of a remarkably fine face and person, M. Mignet has a tone of voice and play of countenance sufficient of themselves to secure the success of an orator. But on this occasion he did not trust to these: his discourse was every way admirable; subject, sentiment, composition, and delivery, all excellent.

He had chosen for his theme the history of Martin Luther's appearance before the Diet at Worms; and the manner in which he treated it surprised as much as it delighted me. Not a single trait of that powerful, steadfast, unbending character, which restored light to our religion and freedom to the mind of man, escaped him: it was a mental portrait, painted with the boldness of outline, breadth of light, and vigour of colouring, which mark the hand of a consummate master.

But was it a Roman Catholic who pronounced this discourse?—Were they Roman Catholics who filled every corner of the theatre, and listened to him with attention so unbroken, and admiration so undisguised? I know not. But for myself, I can truly declare, that my Protestant and reformed feelings were never more gratified than by listening to this eloquent history of the proudest moment of our great apostle's life, pronounced in the centre of Cardinal Mazarin's palace. The concluding words of the discourse were as follows:

"Sommé pendant quatre ans de se soumettre, Luther, pendant quatre ans, dit non. Il avait dit non au légat; il avait dit non au pape; il dit non à l'empereur. Dans ce non héroïque et fécond se trouvait la liberté du monde."

Another discourse was announced to conclude the sitting of the day. But when M. Mignet retired, no one appeared to take his place; and after waiting for a few minutes, the numerous and very fashionable-looking crowd dispersed themselves.

I recollected the anecdote told of the first representation of the "Partie de Chasse de Henri Quatre," when the overture of Mehul produced such an effect, that the audience would not permit anything else to be performed after it. The piece, therefore, was *remise*,—and so was the harangue of the academician who was to have followed M. Mignet.

You will confess, I think, that we are not idle, when I tell you that, after all this, we went in the evening to *Le Concert Musard*. This is one of the pastimes to which we have hitherto had no parallel in London. At half-past seven o'clock, you lounge into a fine, large, well-lighted room, which is rapidly filled with company: a full and good orchestra give you during a couple of hours some of the best and most popular music of the season; and then you lounge out again, in time to dress for a party, or eat ices at Tortoni's, or soberly to go home for a domestic tea-drinking and early rest. For this concert you pay a franc; and the humble price, together with the style of toilet (every lady wearing a bonnet and shawl), might lead the uninitiated to suppose that it was a recreation prepared for the *beau monde* of the Faubourg; but the long line of private carriages that occupies the street at the conclusion of it, shows that, simple and unpretending as is its style, this concert has attractions for the best company in Paris.

The easy *entrée* to it reminded me of the theatres of Germany. I remarked many ladies coming in, two or three together, unattended by any gentleman. Between the acts, the company promenaded round the room, parties met and joined, and altogether it appeared to us a very agreeable mode of gratifying that French necessity of amusing one's self out of one's own house, which seems contagious in the very air of Paris.

## LETTER XII.

Easter-Sunday at Notre Dame.—Archbishop.—View of Paris.—Victor Hugo. —Hôtel Dieu.—Mr. Jefferson.

It was long ago decided in a committee of the whole house, that on Easter-Sunday we should attend high mass at Notre Dame. I shall not soon forget the spectacle that greeted us on entering. Ten thousand persons, it was said, were on that day assembled in the church; and its dimensions are so vast, that I have no doubt the statement was correct, for it was crowded from floor to roof. The effect of the circular gallery, that at mid-height encompasses the centre aisle, following as it does the graceful sweep of the chapel behind the altar, and filled row after row with gaily-dressed company up, as it seemed, almost to the groining of the roof, was beautiful. The chairs on this occasion were paid for in proportion to the advantageousness of the position in which they stood, and by disbursing an extra franc or two we obtained very good places. The mass was performed with great splendour. The dresses of the archbishop and his train were magnificent; and when this splendid, princely-looking personage, together with his court of dignitaries and priests, paraded the Host round the church and up the crowded aisle spite of the close-wedged throng, they looked like a stream of liquid gold, that by its own weight made way through every obstacle. The archbishop is a mild and amiable-looking man, and ceased not to scatter blessings from his lips and sprinkle safety from his fingers'-ends upon the admiring people, as slowly and gracefully he passed among them.

The latter years of this prelate's life have been signalized by some remarkable changes. He has seen the glories and the penitences of his church alike the favourite occupation of his king;—he has seen that king and his highest nobles walking in holy procession through the streets of Paris;—he has seen that same king banished from his throne and his country, a proscribed and melancholy exile, while the pomp and parade of his cherished faith were forbidden to offend the people's eyes by any longer pouring forth its gorgeous superstitions into the streets;—he has seen his own consecrated palace razed to its foundation, and its very elements scattered to the winds:—and now, this self-same prelate sees himself again well received at the court whence Charles Dix was banished; and, stranger still, perhaps, he sees his startled flock once more assembling round him, quietly and silently, but steadily and in earnest; while he who, within five short years, was trembling for his life, now lifts his head again, and not only in safety, but, with all his former power and pride of place, is permitted to

"Chanter les *oremus*, faire des processions,

Et répandre à grands flots les bénédictions."

It is true, indeed, that there are no longer any Roman Catholic processions to be seen in the streets of Paris; but if we look within the churches, we find that the splendour concentrated there, has lost nothing of its impressive sumptuousness by thus changing the scene of its display.

The service of this day, as far as the music was concerned, was in my opinion infinitely less impressive than that of Good-Friday at St. Roch. This doubtless arose in a great degree from the style of composition; but I suspect, moreover, that my imagination was put out of humour by seeing about fifty fiddlers, with every appearance of being (what they actually were) the orchestra of the opera, performing from a space enclosed for them at the entrance of the choir. The singing men and boys were also stationed in the same unwonted and unecclesiastical place; and though some of those hired for the occasion had very fine Italian voices, they had all the air of singing without "reading the words;" and, on the whole, my ear and my fancy were disappointed.

Victor Hugo's description of old Paris as seen from the towers of Notre Dame sent us labouring to their summit. The state of the atmosphere was very favourable, and I was delighted to find that the introduction of coal, rapid as its progress has lately been, has not yet tinged the bright clear air sufficiently to prevent this splendid panorama from being distinctly seen to its remotest edge. That impenetrable mass of dun, dull smoke, that we look down upon whenever a mischievous imp of curiosity lures us to the top of any dome, tower, or obelisk in London, can hardly fail of making one remember every weary step which led to the profitless elevation; but one must be tired indeed to remember fatigue while looking down upon the bright, warm, moving miniature spread out below the towers of Notre Dame.

What an intricate world of roofs it is!—and how mystically incomprehensible are the ins and outs, the bridges and the islands, of the idle Seine! A raft, caught sight of at intervals, bearing wood or wine; a floating wash-house, with its line of bending naïads, looking like a child's toy with figures all of a row; and here and there a floating-bath,—are all this river shows of its power to aid and assist the magnificent capital which has so strangely chosen to stretch herself along its banks. When one thinks of the forest of masts which we see covering whole miles of extent in London, it seems utterly unintelligible how that which is found needful for the necessities of one great city should appear so perfectly unnecessary for another.

Victor Hugo's picture of the scene he has fancied beneath the towers of Notre Dame in the days of his Esmeralda is sketched with amazing spirit; though probably Paris was no more like the pretty panorama he makes of it than Timbuctoo. I heartily wish, however, that he would confine himself to the representation of still-life, and let his characters be all of innocent bricks and mortar: for even though they do look shadowy and somewhat doubtful in the distance, they have infinitely more nature and truth than can be found among all his horrible imaginings concerning his fellow-creatures.

His description of the old church itself, too, is delicious: for though it has little of architectural reality or strict graphic fidelity about it, there is such a powerful air of truth in every word he says respecting it, that one looks out and about upon the rugged stones, and studies every angle, buttress, and parapet, with the lively interest of old acquaintance.

I should like to have a legend, as fond and lingering in its descriptions, attached to some of our glorious and mysterious old Gothic cathedrals at home. This sort of reading gives a pleasure in which imagination and reality are very happily blended; and I can fancy nothing more agreeable than following an able romancer up and down, through and amongst, in and out, the gloomy, shadowy, fanciful, unintelligible intricacies of such a structure. How well might Winchester, for instance, with its solemn crypts, its sturdy Saxon strength, its quaintly-coffined relics of royal bones, its Gothic shrines, its monumental splendour, and its stately magnitude, furnish forth the material for some such spirit-stirring record!

Having spent an hour of first-rate interest and gratification in wandering inside and outside of this very magnificent church, we crossed the Place, or *Parvis*, of Notre Dame, to see the celebrated hospital of the Hôtel Dieu. It is very particularly large, clean, airy, and well-ordered in every way; and I never saw sick people look less miserable than some scores of men and women did, tucked snugly up in their neat little beds, and most of them with a friend or relative at their side to console or amuse them.

The access to the wards of this building is as free as that into a public bazaar; but there is one caution used in the admission of company which, before I understood it, puzzled me greatly. There are three doors at the top of the fine flight of steps which leads to the building. The centre one is used only as an exit; at the other two are placed guards, one a male, the other a female. Through these side-doors all who enter must pass—the men on one side, the women on the other; and all must submit to be pretty strictly examined, to see that they are conveying nothing either to eat or drink that might be injurious to the invalids.

The covered bridge which opens from the back part of the Hôtel Dieu, connecting *l'Isle de la Cité* with the left bank of the Seine, with its light glass roof, and safe shelter from wind, dust, or annoyance of any kind, forms a delightful promenade for the convalescent.

The evening of this day we spent at a *soirée*, where we met, among many other pleasant persons, a very sensible and gentlemanlike American. I had the pleasure of a long conversation with him, during which he said many things extremely worth listening to. This gentleman has held many distinguished diplomatic situations, appears to have acquired a great deal of general information, and moreover to have given much attention to the institutions and character of his own country.

He told me that Jefferson had been the friend of his early life; that he knew his sentiments and opinions on all subjects intimately well, and much better than those who were acquainted with them no otherwise than by his published writings. He assured me most positively that Jefferson was NOT a democrat in principle, but believed it expedient to promulgate the doctrine, as the only one which could excite the general feeling of the people, and make them hang together till they should have acquired strength sufficient to be reckoned as one among the nations. He said, that Jefferson's ulterior hope for America was, that she should, after having acquired this strength, give birth to men distinguished both by talent and fortune; that when this happened, an enlightened and powerful aristocracy might be hoped for, without which HE KNEW that no country could be really great or powerful.

As I am assured that the word of this gentleman may be depended on, these observations—or rather, I should say, statements—respecting Jefferson appear to me worth noting.

## LETTER XIII.

"Le Monomane."

As a distinguished specimen of fashionable horror, I went last night to the Porte St. Martin to see "The Monomane," a drama in five acts, from the pen of a M. Duveyrier. I hardly know whether to give you a sketch of this monstrous outrage against common sense or not; but I think I will do so, because I flatter myself that no one will be silly enough to translate it into English, or import it in any shape into England; and, therefore, if I do not tell you something about it, you may chance to die without knowing to what prodigious lengths a search after absurdity may carry men.

But first let me mention, as not the least extraordinary part of the phenomenon, that the theatre was crowded from floor to roof, and that Shakspeare was never listened to with attention more profound. However, it does not follow that approval or admiration of any kind was either the cause or the effect of this silent contemplation of the scene: no one could be more devoted to the business of the hour than myself, but most surely this was not the result of approbation.

If I am not very clear respecting the plot, you must excuse me, from my want of habitual expertness in such an analysis; but the main features and characters cannot escape me.

An exceedingly amiable and highly intellectual gentleman is the hero of this piece; a part personated by a M. Lockroi with a degree of ability deserving a worthier employment. This amiable man holds at Colmar the office of *procureur du roi*; and, from the habit of witnessing trials, acquires so vehement a passion for the shedding of blood on the scaffold, that it amounts to a mania. To illustrate this singular trait of character, M. Balthazar developes his secret feelings in an opening speech to an intimate friend. In this speech, which really contains some very good lines, he dilates with much enthusiasm on the immense importance which he conceives to attach to the strict and impartial administration of criminal justice. No man could deliver himself more judge-like and wisely; but how or why such very rational and sober opinions should lead to an unbounded passion for blood, is very difficult to understand.

The next scene, however, shows the *procureur du roi* hugging himself with a kind of mysterious rapture at the idea of an approaching execution, and receiving with a very wild and mad-like sort of agony some attempts to prove the culprit innocent. The execution takes place; and after it is over, the innocence of the unfortunate victim is fully proved.

The amiable and excellent *procureur du roi* is greatly moved at this; but his repentant agony is soon walked off by a few well-trod melodramatic turns up and down the stage; and he goes on again, seizing with ecstasy upon every opportunity of bringing the guilty to justice.

What the object of the author can possibly be in making out that a man is mad solely because he wishes to do his duty, I cannot even guess. It is difficult to imagine an honest-minded magistrate uttering more common-place, uncontrovertible truths upon the painful duties of his station, than does this unfortunate gentleman.

M. Victor Hugo, speaking of himself in one of his prefaces, says, "Il (Victor Hugo) continuera donc fermement; et chaque fois qu'il croira nécessaire de faire bien voir à tous, dans ses moindres détails, une idée utile, une idée sociale, une idée humaine, il posera le théâtre déssus comme un verre grossissant."

It strikes me that M. Duveyrier, the ingenious author of the Monomane, must work upon the same principle, and that in this piece he thinks he has put a magnifying-glass upon "une idée sociale."

But I must return to my analysis of this drama of five mortal acts.—After the execution, the real perpetrator of the murder for which the unfortunate victim of legal enthusiasm has innocently suffered appears on the scene. He is brought sick or wounded into the house of a physician, with whom the *procureur du roi* and his wife are on a visit. Balthazar sees the murderer conveyed to bed in a chamber that opens from that of his friend the doctor. He then goes to bed himself with his wife, and appears to have fallen asleep without delay, for we presently see him in this state come forth from his chamber upon a gallery, from whence a flight of stairs descends upon the stage. We see him walk down these stairs,—take some instrument out of a case belonging to the doctor,—enter the apartment where the murderer has been lodged,—return,—replace the instrument,—wash his bloody hands and wipe them upon a hand-towel,—then reascend the staircase and enter his lady's room at the top of it; all of which is performed in the silence of profound sleep.

The attention which hung upon the whole of this long silent scene was such, that one might have supposed the lives of the audience depended upon their not waking this murderous sleeper by any sound; and the applause which followed the mute performance, when once the awful *procureur du roi* was again safely lodged in his chamber, was deafening.

The following morning it is discovered that the sick stranger has been murdered; and instantly the *procureur du roi*, with his usual ardour in discovering the guilty, sets most ably to work upon the investigation of every circumstance which may throw light upon this horrible transaction. Everything, particularly the case of instruments, of which one is bloody, and the hand-towel found in his room, stained with the same accusing dye—all tends to prove that the poor innocent physician is the murderer: he is accordingly taken up, tried, and condemned.

This unfortunate young doctor has an uncle, of the same learned profession, who is addicted to the science of animal magnetism. This gentleman having some suspicion that Balthazar is himself the guilty person, imagines a very cunning device by which he may be made to betray himself if guilty. He determines to practise his magnetism upon him in full court while he is engaged in the duties of his high office, and flatters himself that he shall be able to throw him into a sleep or trance, in which state he may *par hasard* let out something of the truth.

This admirable contrivance answers perfectly. The attorney-general does fall into a most profound sleep the moment the old doctor begins his magnetising manœuvres, and in this state not only relates aloud every circumstance of the murder, but, to give this confession more sure effect, he writes it out fairly, and sets his name to it, being profoundly asleep the whole time.

And here it is impossible to avoid remarking on the extreme ill fortune which attends the sleeping hours of this amiable attorney-general. At one time he takes a nap, and kills a man without knowing anything of the matter; and then, in a subsequent state of oblivion, he confesses it, still without knowing anything of the matter.

As soon as the unfortunate gentleman has finished the business for which he was put to sleep, he is awakened, and the paper is shown to him. He scruples not immediately to own his handwriting, which, sleeping or waking, it seems, was the same; but testifies the greatest horror and astonishment at the information the document contains, which was quite as unexpected to himself as to the rest of the company.

His high office, however, we must presume, exempts him from all responsibility; for the only result of the discovery is an earnest recommendation from his friends, particularly the old and young doctors, that he should travel for the purpose of recovering his spirits.

There is a little episode, by the way, from which we learn, that once, in one of his alarming slumbers, this amiable but unfortunate man gave symptoms of wishing to murder his wife and child; in consequence of which, it is proposed by the doctors that this tour for the restoration of his spirits should be made without them. To this separation Balthazar strongly objects, and tells his beautiful wife, with much tenderness, that he shall find it very dull without her.

To this the lady, though naturally rather afraid of him, answers with great sweetness, that in that case she shall be extremely happy to go with him; adding tenderly, that she would willingly die to prove her devotion.

Nothing could be so unfortunate as this expression. At the bare mention of his hobby-horse, *death*, his malady revives, and he instantly manifests a strong inclination to murder her,—and this time without even the ceremony of going to sleep.

Big with the darling thought, his eyes rolling, his cheek pale, his bristling hair on end, and the awful genius of Melodrame swelling in every vein, Balthazar seats himself on the sofa beside his trembling wife, and taking the comb out of her (Mademoiselle Noblet's) beautiful hair, appears about to strangle her in the rope of jet that he pulls out to its utmost length, and twists, and twists, and twists, till one really feels a cold shiver from head to foot. But at length, at the very moment when matters seem drawing to a close, the lady throws herself lovingly on his bosom, and his purpose changes, or at least for a moment seems to change, and he relaxes his hold.

At this critical juncture the two doctors enter. Balthazar looks at them wildly, then at his wife, then at the doctors again, and finally tells them all that he must beg leave to retire for a few moments. He passes through the group, who look at him in mournful silence; but as he approaches the door, he utters the word 'poison,' then enters, and locks and bolts it after him.

Upon this the lady screams, and the two doctors fly for a crow-bar. The door is burst open, and the *procureur du roi* comes forward, wide awake, but having swallowed the poison he had mentioned.

This being "the last scene of all that ends this strange eventful history," the curtain falls upon the enthusiastic attorney-general as he expires in the arms of his wife and friends.

We are always so apt, when we see anything remarkably absurd abroad, to flatter ourselves with the belief that nothing like it exists at home, that I am almost afraid to draw a parallel between this inconceivable trash, and the very worst and vilest piece that ever was permitted to keep possession of the stage in England, lest some one better informed on the subject than myself should quote some British enormity unknown to me, and so prove my patriotic theory false.

Nevertheless, I cannot quit the subject without saying, that as far as my knowledge and belief go, English people never did sit by hundreds and listen patiently to such stuff as this. There is no very atrocious vice, no terrific wickedness in the piece, as far as I could understand its recondite philosophy; but its silliness surely possesses the silliness of a little child. The grimaces, the dumb show, the newly-invented passions, and the series of impossible events, which drag through these five longsome acts, seem to show a species of anomaly in the human mind that composed the piece, to which I imagine no parallel can be found on record.

Is this the result of the march of mind?—is it the fruit of that universal diffusion of knowledge which we are told is at work throughout the world, but most busily in France?... I shall never understand the mystery, let me meditate upon it as long as I will. No! never shall I understand how a French audience, lively, witty, acute, and prone to seize upon whatever is ridiculous, can thus sit night after night with profound gravity, and the highest apparent satisfaction, to witness the incredible absurdity of such a piece as "Le Monomane."

There is one way, and one way only, in which the success of this drama can be accounted for intelligibly. May it not be, that "LES JEUNES GENS," wanton in their power, have determined in merry mood to mystify their fellow-citizens by passing a favourable judgment upon this tedious performance? And may they not now be enjoying the success of their plot in ecstasies of private laughter, at seeing how meekly the dutiful Parisians go nightly to the Porte St. Martin, and sit in obedient admiration of what it has pleased their youthful tyrants to denominate "a fine drama"?

But I must leave off guessing; for, as the wise man saith, "the finding out of parables is a wearisome labour of the mind."

Some critic, speaking of the new school of French dramatists, says that "they have heaved the ground under the feet of Racine and Corneille." If this indeed be so, the best thing that the lovers of tragedy can do is to sit at home and wait patiently till the earth settles itself again from the shock of so deplorable an earthquake. That it will settle itself again, I have neither doubt nor fear. Nonsense has nothing of immortality in its nature; and when the storm which has scattered all this frothy scum upon us shall have fairly blown over and passed away, then I suspect that Corneille and Racine will still find solid standing-ground on the soil of France;—nay, should they by chance find also that their old niches in the temple of her great men remain vacant, it is likely enough that they may be again invited to take possession of them; and they may keep it too perhaps for a few more hundred years, with very little danger that any greater than they should arrive to take their places.

## LETTER XIV.

The Gardens of the Tuileries.—Legitimatist.—Republican—Doctrinaire.—Children.—Dress of the Ladies.—Of the Gentlemen.—Black Hair.—Unrestricted Admission.—Anecdote.

Is there anything in the world that can be fairly said to resemble the Gardens of the Tuileries? I should think not. It is a whole made up of so many strongly-marked and peculiar features, that it is not probable any other place should be found like it. To my fancy, it seems one of the most delightful scenes in the world; and I never enter there, though it is long since the enchantment of novelty made any part of the charm, without a fresh feeling of enjoyment.

The *locale* itself, independent of the moving throng which for ever seems to dwell within it, is greatly to my taste: I love all the detail of its embellishment, and I dearly love the bright and happy aspect of the whole. But on this subject I know there are various opinions: many talk with distaste of the straight lines, the clipped trees, the formal flower-beds, the ugly roofs,—nay, some will even abuse the venerable orange-trees themselves, because they grow in square boxes, and do not wave their boughs in the breeze like so many ragged willow-trees.

But I agree not with any one of these objections; and should think it as reasonable, and in as good taste, to quarrel with Westminster Abbey because it did not look like a Grecian temple, as to find fault with the Gardens of the Tuileries because they are arranged like French pleasure-grounds, and not like an English park. For my own part, I profess that I would not, if I had the power, change even in the least degree a single feature in this pleasant spot: enter it at what hour or at what point I will, it ever seems to receive me with smiles and gladness.

We seldom suffer a day to pass without refreshing our spirits by sitting for a while amidst its shade and its flowers. From the part of the town where we are now dwelling, the gate opposite the Place Vendôme is our nearest entrance; and perhaps from no point does the lively beauty of the whole scene show itself better than from beneath the green roof of the terrace-walk, to which this gate admits us.

To the right, the dark mass of unshorn trees, now rich with the flowers of the horse-chesnut, and growing as boldly and as loftily as the most English-hearted gardener could desire, leads the eye through a very delicious "continuity of shade" to the magnificent gate that opens upon the Place Louis-Quinze. To the left is the widely-spreading façade of the Tuileries Palace, the ungraceful elevation of the pavilion roofs, well nigh forgotten, and quite atoned for by the beauty of the gardens at their feet. Then, just where the shade of the high trees ceases, and the bright blaze of sunshine begins, what multitudes of sweet flowers are seen blushing in its beams! An universal lilac bloom seems at this season to spread itself over the whole space; and every breeze that passes by, comes to us laden with perfume. My daily walk is almost always the same,—I love it so well that I do not like to change it. Following the shady terrace by which we enter to the point where it sinks down to the level of the magnificent esplanade in front of the palace, we turn to the right, and endure the splendid brightness till we reach the noble walk leading from the gateway of the centre pavilion, through flowers, statues, orange-trees, and chesnut-groves, as far as the eye can reach, till it reposes at last upon the lofty arch of the Barrière de l'Etoile.

This *coup-d'œil* is so beautiful, that I constantly feel renewed pleasure when I look upon it. I do indeed confess myself to be one of those "who in trim gardens take their pleasure." I love the studied elegance, the carefully-selected grace of every object permitted to meet the pampered eye in such a spot as this. I love these fondly-nurtured princely exotics, the old orange-trees, ranged in their long stately rows; and better still do I love the marble groups, that stand so nobly, sometimes against the bright blue sky, and sometimes half concealed in the dark setting of the trees. Everything seems to speak of taste, luxury, and elegance.

Having indulged in a lingering walk from the palace to the point at which the sunshine ceases and the shade begins, a new species of interest and amusement awaits us. Thousands of chairs scattered just within the shelter of this inviting covert are occupied by an interminable variety of pretty groups.

I wonder how many months of constant attendance there, it would take before I should grow weary of studying the whole and every separate part of this bright picture? It is really matchless in beauty as a spectacle, and unequalled in interest as a national study. All Paris may in turn be seen and examined there; and nowhere is it so easy to distinguish specimens of the various and strongly-marked divisions of the people.

This morning we took possession of half a dozen chairs under the trees which front the beautiful group of Pelus and Aria. It was the hour when all the newspapers are in the greatest requisition; and we had the satisfaction of watching the studies of three individuals, each of whom might have sat as a model for an artist who wished to give an idea of their several peculiarities. We saw, in short, beyond the possibility of doubt, a royalist, a doctrinaire, and a republican, during the half-hour we remained there, all soothing their feelings by indulging in two sous' worth of politics, each in his own line.

A stiff but gentleman-like old man first came, and having taken a journal from the little octagon stand—which journal we felt quite sure was either "La France" or "La Quotidienne"—he established himself at no great distance from us. Why it was that we all felt so certain of his being a legitimatist I can hardly tell you, but not one of the party had the least doubt about it. There was a quiet, half-proud, half-melancholy air of keeping himself apart; an aristocratical cast of features; a pale care-worn complexion; and a style of dress which no vulgar man ever wore, but which no rich one would be likely to wear to-day. This is all I can record of him: but there was something pervading his whole person too essentially loyal to be misunderstood, yet too delicate in its tone to be coarsely painted. Such as it was, however, we felt it quite enough to make the matter sure; and if I could find out that old gentleman to be either doctrinaire or republican, I never would look on a human countenance again in order to discover what was passing within.

The next who approached us we were equally sure was a republican: but here the discovery did little honour to our discernment; for these gentry choose to leave no doubt upon the subject of their *clique,* but contrive that every article contributing to the appearance of the outward man shall become a symbol and a sign, a token and a stigma, of the madness that possesses them. He too held a paper in his hand, and without venturing to approach too nearly to so alarming a personage, we scrupled not to assure each other that the journal he was so assiduously perusing was "Le Réformateur."

Just as we had decided what manner of man it was who was stalking so majestically past us, a comfortable-looking citizen approached in the uniform of the National Guard, who sat himself down to his daily allowance of politics with the air of a person expecting to be well pleased with what he finds, but nevertheless too well contented with himself and all things about him to care over-much about it. Every line of this man's jocund face, every curve of his portly figure, spoke contentment and well-being. He was probably one of that very new race in France, a tradesman making a rapid fortune. Was it possible to doubt that the paper in his hand was "Le Journal des Débats?" was it possible to believe that this man was other than a prosperous doctrinaire?

Thus, on the neutral ground furnished by these delightful gardens, hostile spirits meet with impunity, and, though they mingle not, enjoy in common the delicious privileges of cool shade, fresh air, and the idle luxury of an *al fresco* newspaper, in the midst of a crowded and party-split city, with as much certainty of being unchallenged and uninterrupted as if each were wandering alone in a princely domain of his own.

Such, too, as are not over splenetic may find a very lively variety of study in watching the ways of the little dandies and dandiesses who, at some hours of the day, swarm like so many hummingbirds amidst the shade and sunshine of the Tuileries. Either these little French personages are marvellously well-behaved, or there is some superintending care which prevents screaming; for I certainly never saw so many young things assembled together who indulged so rarely in that salutary exercise of the lungs which makes one so often tremble at the approach of

"Soft infancy, that nothing can, but cry."

The costumes of these pretty creatures contribute not a little to the amusement; it is often so whimsical as to give them the appearance of miniature maskers. I have seen little fellows beating a hoop in the full uniform of a National Guard; others waddling under the mimicry of kilted Highlanders; and small ladies without number in every possible variety of un-babylike apparel.

The entertainment to be derived from sitting in the Tuileries Gardens and studying costume is, however, by no means confined to the junior part of the company. In no country have I ever seen anything approaching in grotesque habiliments to some of the figures daily and hourly met lounging about these walks. But such vagaries are confined wholly to the male part of the population; it is very rare to see a woman outrageously dressed in any way; and if you do, the chances are five hundred to one that she is not a Frenchwoman. An air of quiet elegant neatness is, I think, the most striking characteristic of the walking costume of the French ladies. All the little minor finishings of the female toilet appear to be more sedulously cared for than the weightier matters of the pelisse and gown. Every lady you meet is *bien chaussée,bien gantée*. Her ribbons, if they do not match her dress, are sure to accord with it; and for all the delicate garniture that comes under the care of the laundress, it should seem that Paris alone, of all the earth, knows how to iron.

The whimsical caprices of male attire, on the contrary, defy anything like general remark; unless, indeed, it be that the air of Paris appears to have the quality of turning all the *imperials, favoris,* and *moustaches* which dwell within its walls to jetty blackness. At a little distance, the young men have really the air of having their faces tied up with black ribbon as a cure for the mumps; and, handsome as this dark *chevelure* is generally allowed to be, the heavy uniformity of it at present very considerably lessens its striking effect. When every man has his face half covered with black hair, it ceases to be a very valuable distinction. Perhaps, too, the frequent advertisements of compositions infallible in their power of turning the hair to any colour except "what pleases God," may tend to make one look with suspicious eyes at these once fascinating southern decorations; but, at present, I take it to be an undoubted fact, that a clean, close-shaven, northern-looking gentleman is valued at a high premium in every *salon* in Paris.

It is not to be denied that the "glorious and immortal days" have done some injury to the general appearance of the Tuileries Gardens. Before this period, no one was permitted to enter them dressed in a *blouse,* or jacket, or *casquette*; and no one, either male or female, might carry bundles or baskets through these pretty regions, sacred to relaxation and holiday enjoyment. But liberty and unseemly sordidness of attire being somehow or other jumbled together in the minds of the sovereign mob,—not sovereign either—the mob is only vice-regal in Paris as yet;—but the mob, however, such as it is, has obtained, as a mark of peculiar respect and favour to themselves, a new law or regulation, by which it is enacted that these royal precincts may become like unto Noah's ark, and that both clean and unclean beasts may enter here.

Could one wish for a better specimen of the sort of advantage to be gained by removing the restraint of authority in order to pamper the popular taste for what they are pleased to call freedom? Not one of the persons who enter the gardens now, were restricted from entering them before; only it was required that they should be decently clad;—that is to say, in such garments as they were accustomed to wear on Sunday or any other holiday; the only occasions, one should imagine, on which the working classes could wish to profit by permission to promenade in a public garden: but the obligation to appear clean in the garden of the king's palace was an infringement on their liberty, so that formality is dispensed with; and they have now obtained the distinguished and ennobling privilege of being as dirty and ill-dressed as they like.

The power formerly intrusted to the sentinel, wherever there was one stationed, of refusing the *entrée* to all persons not properly dressed, gave occasion once to a saucy outbreaking of French wit in one of the National Guard, which was amusing enough. This civic guardian was stationed at the gates of a certain *Mairie* on some public occasion, with the usual injunction not to permit any person "*mal-mise*" to enter. An *incroyable* presented himself, not dressed in the fashion, but immoderately beyond it. The sentinel looked at him, and lowered his piece across the entrance, pronouncing in a voice of authority—

"You cannot enter."

"Not enter?" exclaimed the astonished beau, looking down at the exquisite result of his laborious toilet; "not enter?—forbid me to enter, sir?—impossible! What is it you mean? Let me pass, I say!"

The imperturbable sentinel stood like a rock before the entrance: "My orders are precise," he said, "and I may not infringe them."

"Precise? Your orders precise to refuse me?"

"Oui, monsieur, précis, de refuser qui que ce soit que je trouve mal-mis."


**LETTER XV.**

Street Police.—Cleaning Beds.—Tinning Kettles.—Building Houses.—Loading Carts.—Preparing for the Scavenger.—Want of Drains.—Bad Pavement.—Darkness.

My last letter was of the Tuileries Gardens; a theme which furnished me so many subjects of admiration, that I think, if only for the sake of variety, I will let the smelfungus vein prevail to-day. Such, then, being my humour,—or my ill-humour, if you will,—I shall indulge it by telling you what I think of the street-police of Paris.

I will not tell you that it is bad, for that, I doubt not, many others may have done before me; but I will tell you that I consider it as something wonderful, mysterious, incomprehensible, and perfectly astonishing.

In a city where everything intended to meet the eye is converted into graceful ornament; where the shops and coffee-houses have the air of fairy palaces, and the markets show fountains wherein the daintiest naïads might delight to bathe;—in such a city as this, where the women look too delicate to belong wholly to earth, and the men too watchful and observant to suffer the winds of heaven to visit them too roughly;—in such a city as this, you are shocked and disgusted at every step you take, or at every gyration that the wheels of your chariot can make, by sights and smells that may not be described.

Every day brings my astonishment on this subject to a higher pitch than the one which preceded it; for every day brings with it fresh conviction that a very considerable portion of the enjoyment of life is altogether destroyed in Paris by the neglect or omission of such a degree of municipal interference as might secure the most elegant people in the world from the loathsome disgust occasioned by the perpetual outrage of common decency in their streets.

On this branch of the subject it is impossible to say more; but there are other points on which the neglect of street-police is as plainly, though less disgustingly, apparent; and some of these I will enumerate for your information, as they may be described without impropriety; but when they are looked at in conjunction with the passion for graceful decoration, so decidedly a characteristic of the French people, they offer to our observation an incongruity so violent, as to puzzle in no ordinary degree whoever may wish to explain it.

You cannot at this season pass through any street in Paris, however pre-eminently fashionable from its situation, or however distinguished by the elegance of those who frequent it, without being frequently obliged to turn aside, that you may not run against two or more women covered with dust, and probably with vermin, who are busily employed in pulling their flock mattresses to pieces in the street. There they stand or sit, caring for nobody, but combing, turning, and shaking the wool upon all comers and goers; and, finally, occupying the space round which many thousand passengers are obliged to make what is always an inconvenient, and sometimes a very dirty *détour*, by poking the material, cleared from the filth, which has passed into the throats of the gentlemen and ladies of Paris, back again into its checked repository.

I have within this half-hour passed from the Italian Boulevard by the Opera-house, in the front of which this obscene and loathsome operation was being performed by a solitary old crone, who will doubtless occupy the place she has chosen during the whole day, and carry away her bed just in time to permit the Duke of Orleans to step from his carriage into the Opera without tumbling over it, but certainly not in time to prevent his having a great chance of receiving as he passes some portion of the various animate and inanimate superfluities which for so many hours she has been scattering to the air.

A few days ago I saw a well-dressed gentleman receive a severe contusion on the head, and the most overwhelming destruction to the neatness of his attire, in consequence of a fall occasioned by his foot getting entangled in the apparatus of a street-working tinker, who had his charcoal fire, bellows, melting-pot, and all other things necessary for carrying on the tinning trade in a small way, spread forth on the pavement of the Rue de Provence.

When the accident happened, many persons were passing, all of whom seemed to take a very obliging degree of interest in the misfortune of the fallen gentleman; but not a syllable either of remonstrance or remark was uttered concerning the invasion of the highway by the tinker; nor did that wandering individual himself appear to think any apology called for, or any change in the arrangement of his various chattels necessary.

Whenever a house is to be built or repaired in London, the first thing done is to surround the premises with a high paling, that shall prevent any of the operations that are going on within it from annoying in any way the public in the street. The next thing is to arrange a footpath round this paling, carefully protected by posts and rails, so that this unavoidable invasion of the ordinary foot-path may be productive of as little inconvenience as possible.

Were you to pass a spot in Paris under similar circumstances, you would fancy that some tremendous accident—a fire, perhaps, or the falling in of a roof—had occasioned a degree of difficulty and confusion to the passengers which it was impossible to suppose could be suffered to remain an hour unremedied: but it is, on the contrary, permitted to continue, to the torment and danger of daily thousands, for months together, without the slightest notice or objection on the part of the municipal authorities. If a cart be loading or unloading in the street, it is permitted to take and keep a position the most inconvenient, in utter disregard of any danger or delay which it may and must occasion to the carriages and foot-passengers who have to travel round it.

Nuisances and abominations of all sorts are without scruple committed to the street at any hour of the day or night, to await the morning visit of the scavenger to remove them: and happy indeed is it for the humble pedestrian if his eye and nose alone suffer from these ejectments; happy, indeed, if he comes not in contact with them, as they make their unceremonious exit from window or door. "*Quel bonheur!*" is the exclamation if he escapes; but a look, wholly in sorrow and nowise in anger, is the only helpless resource should he be splashed from head to foot.

On the subject of that monstrous barbarism, a gutter in the middle of the streets expressly formed for the reception of filth, which is still permitted to deform the greater portion of this beautiful city, I can only say, that the patient endurance of it by men and women of the year one thousand eight hundred and thirty-five is a mystery difficult to understand.

It really appears to me, that almost the only thing in the world which other men do, but which Frenchmen cannot, is the making of sewers and drains. After an hour or two of very violent rain last week, that part of the Place Louis-Quinze which is near the entrance to the Champs Elysées remained covered with water. The Board of Works having waited for a day or two to see what would happen, and finding that the muddy lake did not disappear, commanded the assistance of twenty-six able-bodied labourers, who set about digging just such a channel as little boys amuse themselves by making beside a pond. By this well-imagined engineering exploit, the stagnant water was at length conducted to the nearest gutter; the pickaxes were shouldered, and an open muddy channel left to adorn this magnificent area, which, were a little finishing bestowed upon it, would probably be the finest point that any city in the world could boast.

Perhaps it will hardly be fair to set it amongst my complaints against the streets of Paris, that they have not yet adopted our last and most luxurious improvement. I cannot but observe, however, that having passed some weeks here, I feel that the Macadamised streets of London ought to become the subject of a metropolitan jubilee among us. The exceeding noise of Paris, proceeding either from the uneven structure of the pavement, or from the defective construction of wheels and springs, is so violent and incessant as to appear like the effect of one great continuous cause,—a sort of demon torment, which it must require great length of use to enable one to endure without suffering. Were a cure for this sought in the Macadamising of the streets, an additional advantage, by the bye, would be obtained, from the difficulties it would throw in the way of the future heroes of a barricade.

There is another defect, however, and one much more easily remedied, which may fairly, I think, come under the head of defective street-police. This is the profound darkness of every part of the city in which there are not shops illuminated by the owners of them with gas. This is done so brilliantly on the Boulevards by the *cafés* and*restaurans*, that the dim old-fashioned lamp suspended at long intervals across the *pavé* is forgotten. But no sooner is this region of light and gaiety left, than you seem to plunge into outer darkness; and there is not a little country town in England which is not incomparably better lighted than any street in Paris which depends for its illumination upon the public regulations of the city.

As it is evident that gas-pipes must be actually laid in all directions in order to supply the individuals who employ it in their houses, I could in no way understand why these most dismal *réverbères*, with their dingy oil, were to be made use of in preference to the beautiful light which almost outblazes that of the sun; but I am told that some unexpired contract between Paris and her lamplighters is the cause of this. Were the convenience of the public as sedulously studied in France as in England, not all the claims of all the lamplighters in the world, let it cost what it might to content them, would keep her citizens groping in darkness when it was so very easy to give them light.

But not to dwell ungratefully upon the grievances which certainly disfigure this city of delight, I will not multiply instances; yet I am sure I may assert, without fear of contradiction or reproach, that such a street-police as that of

London would be one of the greatest civic blessings that King Philippe could possibly bestow upon his *"belle ville de Paris."*

## LETTER XVI.

Preparations for the Fête du Roi.—Arrival of Troops.—Champs Elysées.—Concert in the Garden of the Tuileries.—Silence of the People.—Fireworks.

May 2, 1835.

For several days past we have been watching the preparations for the King's fête, which though not quite equal to those in the days of the Emperor, when all the fountains in Paris ran wine, were on a large and splendid scale, and if more sober, were perhaps not less princely. Temporary theatres, ball-rooms, and orchestras in the Champs Elysées—magnificent fireworks on the Pont Louis-Seize—preparations for a full concert immediately in front of the Tuileries Palace, and arrangement of lamps for general illuminations, but especially in the Gardens, were the chief of these; but none of them struck us so much as the daily-increasing number of troops. National Guards and soldiers of the line divided the streets between them; and as a grand review was naturally to make a part of the day's pageantry, there would have been nothing to remark in this, were it not that the various parties into which the country is divided perpetually leads people to suppose that King Philippe finds it necessary to act on the defensive.

Numberless are the hints, as you may imagine, on this theme that have been thrown out on the present occasion; and it is confidently asserted in some quarters, that the reviewing of large bodies of troops is likely to become a very fashionable and frequent, if not a very popular, amusement here. If, indeed, a show of force be necessary to ensure the tranquillity of this strife-worn land, the government certainly do right in displaying it; but if this be not the case, there is some imprudence in it, for the effect much resembles that of

"A rich armour, worn in heat of day,

That scalds with safety."

Yesterday, then, being marked in the calendar as sacred to St. Jacques and St. Philippe, was kept as the fête of the present King of the French. The weather was brilliant, and everything looked gay, particularly around the courtly region of the Tuileries, Champs Elysées, and all parts near or between them.

Being assured by a philosophical looker-on upon all such assemblings of the people as are likely to show forth indications of their temper, that the humours of the Champs Elysées would display more of this than I could hope to find elsewhere, I was about to order a carriage to convey us there; but my friend stopped me.

"You may as well remain at home," said he; "from a carriage you will see nothing but a mob: but if you will walk amongst them, you may perhaps find out whether they are thinking of anything or nothing."

"Anything?—or nothing?" I repeated. "Does the *anything* mean a revolution? Tell me truly, is there any chance of a riot?"

Instead of answering, he turned to a gentleman of our party who was just returned from the review of the troops by the king.

"Did you not say you had seen the review?" he demanded.

"Yes; I am just come from it."

"And what do you think of the troops?"

"They are very fine troops,—remarkably fine men, both the National Guards and the troops of the line."

"And in sufficient force, are they not, to keep Paris quiet if she should feel disposed to be frolicsome?"

"Certainly—I should think so."

It was therefore determined, leaving the younger part of the females behind us however in case of the worst, that we should repair to the Champs Elysées.

No one who has not seen a public fête celebrated at Paris can form an idea of the scene which the whole of this extensive area presents: it makes me giddy even to remember it. Imagine a hundred swings throwing their laughing cargoes high into the air; a hundred winged ships flying in endless whirl, and bearing for their crews a *tête-à-tête* pair of holiday sweethearts: imagine a hundred horses, each with two prancing hoofs high poised in air, coursing each other in a circle, with nostrils of flame; a hundred mountebanks, chattering and gibbering their inconceivable jargon, some habited as generals, some as Turks,—some offering their nostrums in the impressive habit of an Armenian Jew, and others rolling head-over-heels upon a stage, and presenting a dose with the grin of Grimaldi. We stopped more than once in our progress to watch the ways of one of these animals when it had succeeded in fascinating its prey: the poor victim was cajoled and coaxed into believing that none of woman born could ever taste of evil more, if he would but trust to the one only true, sure, and certain specific.

At all sides of us, as we advanced, we were skirted by long lines of booths, decked with gaudy merchandise, rings, clasps, brooches, buckles, most tempting to behold, and all to be had for five sous each. It is pretty enough to watch the eager glances and the smirking smiles of the damsels, with the yielding, tender looks of the fond boys who hover round these magazines of female trumpery. Alas! it is perhaps but the beginning of sorrow!

In the largest open space afforded by these Elysian fields were erected two theatres, the interval between them holding, it was said, twenty thousand spectators. While one of these performed a piece, pantomimic I believe, the other enjoyed a *relâche* and reposed itself: but the instant the curtain of one fell, that of the other rose, and the ocean of heads which filled the space between them turned, and undulated like the waves of the sea, ebbing and flowing, backwards and forwards, as the moon-struck folly attracted them.

Four ample *al fresco* enclosures prepared for dancing, each furnished with a very respectable orchestra, occupied the extreme corners of this space; and notwithstanding the crowd, the heat, the sunshine, and the din, this exercise, which was carried on immediately under them, did not, I was told, cease for a single instant during the whole of that long summer-day. When one set of fiddlers were tired out, another succeeded. The activity, gaiety, and universal good-humour of this enormous mob were uniform and uninterrupted from morning to night.

These people really deserve fêtes; they enjoy them so heartily, yet so peaceably.

Such were the great and most striking features of the jubilee; but we hardly advanced a single step through the throng which did not exhibit to us some minor trait of national and characteristic revelry. I was delighted to observe, however, throughout the whole of my expedition, that, according to our friend's definition, "*nobody was thinking of anything.*"

But what pleased me incomparably more than all the rest was the temperate style of the popular refreshments. The young men and the old, the time-worn matron and the dainty damsel, all alike slaked their thirst with iced lemonade, which was furnished in incredible quantities by numberless ambulant cisterns, at the price of one sou the glass. Happily this light-hearted, fête-loving population have no gin-palaces to revel in.

But hunger was to be satisfied as well as thirst; and here the *friand* taste of the people displayed itself by dozens of little chafing-dishes lodged at intervals under the trees, each with its presiding old woman, who, holding a frying-pan, for ever redolent of onions, over the coals, screamed in shrill accents the praises of her *saucisses* and her *foie*. This was the only part of the business that was really disagreeable: the odour from these *al fresco* kitchens was not, I confess, very pleasant; but everything else pleased me exceedingly. It was the first time I ever saw a real mob in full jubilee; and I did not believe it possible I could have been so much amused, and so not at all frightened. Even before one of these terribly odoriferant kitchens, I could not help pausing for a moment as I passed, to admire the polite style in which an old woman who had taken early possession of the shade of a tree for her *restaurant* defended the station from the wheelbarrow of a merchant of gingerbread who approached it.

"Pardon, monsieur!... Ne venez pas, je vous prie, déranger mon établissement."

The two grotesque old figures, together with their fittings up, made this dignified address delightful; and as it was answered by a bow, and the respectful drawing back of the wheelbarrow, I cannot but give it the preference over the more energetic language which a similar circumstance would be likely to produce at Bartholomew Fair.

Altogether we were infinitely amused by this excursion; but I think I never was more completely fatigued in my life. Nevertheless, I contrived to repose myself sufficiently to join a large party to the Tuileries Gardens in the evening, where we were assured that *two hundred thousand persons* were collected. The crowd was indeed very great, and the party soon found it impossible to keep together; but about three hours afterwards we had the satisfaction of assembling in safety at the same pleasant mansion from which we set out.

The attraction which during the early part of the evening chiefly drew together the crowd was the orchestra in front of the palace. A large military band were stationed there, and continued playing, while the thousands and tens of thousands of lamps were being lighted all over the gardens.

During this time, the king, queen, and royal family appeared on the balcony. And here the only fault which I had perceived in this pretty fête throughout the day showed itself so strongly as to produce a very disagreeable effect. From first to last, it seemed that the cause of the jubilee was forgotten; not a sound of any kind greeted the appearance of the royal party. That so gay and demonstrative a people, assembled in such numbers, and on such an occasion, should remain with uplifted heads, gazing on the sovereign, without a sound being uttered by any single voice, appeared perfectly astonishing. However, if there were no bravoes, there was decidedly no hissing.

The scene itself was one of enchanting gaiety. Before us rose the illuminated pavilions of the Tuileries: the bright lights darting through the oleanders and myrtles on the balcony, showed to advantage the royal party stationed there. On every side were trees, statues, flowers, brought out to view by unnumbered lamps rising in brilliant pyramids among them, while the inspiring sounds of martial music resounded in the midst. The *jets d'eau*, catching the artificial light, sprang high into the air like arrows of fire, then turned into spray, and descended again in light showers, seeming to shed delicious coolness on the crowd; and behind them, far as the eye could reach, stretched the suburban forest, sparkling with festoons of lamps, that seemed drawn out, "fine by degrees and beautifully less," up to the Barrière de l'Etoile. The scene itself was indeed lovely; and if, instead of the heavy silence with which it was regarded, a loud heartfelt cheering had greeted the *jour de fête* of a long-loved king, it would have been perfect.

The fireworks, too, were superb; and though all the theatres in Paris were opened gratis to the public, and, as we afterwards heard, completely filled, the multitudes that thronged to look at them seemed enough to people a dozen cities. But it is so much the habit of this people, old and young, rich and poor, to live out of doors, that a slight temptation "bye common" is sufficient to draw forth every human being who is able to stand alone: and indeed, of those who are not, thousands are deposited in chairs, and other thousands in the arms of mothers and nurses.

The Pont Louis-Seize was the point from which all the fireworks were let off. No spot could have been better chosen: the terraces of the Tuileries looked down upon it; and the whole length of the quays, on both sides of the river, as far as the *Cité*, looked up to it, and the persons stationed on them must have seen clearly the many-coloured fires that blazed there.

One of the prettiest popular contrivances for creating a shout when fireworks are exhibited here, is to have rockets, sending up tri-coloured balls, blue, white, and red, in rapid succession, looking, as I heard a young republican say, "like winged messengers, from their loved banner up to heaven." I could not help remarking, that if the messengers repeated faithfully all that the tri-coloured banner had done, they would have strange tales to tell.

The *bouquet*, or last grand display that finished the exhibition, was very fanciful and very splendid: but what struck me as the prettiest part of the whole show, was the Chamber of Deputies, the architecture of which was marked by lines of light; and the magnificent flight of steps leading to it having each one its unbroken fencing of fire, was perhaps intended as a mystical type of the ordeal to be passed in a popular election before this temple of wisdom could be entered.

How very delightful was the abounding tea of that hot lamp-lit night!... And how very thankful was I this morning, at one o'clock, to feel that the *fête du roi* was peaceably over, and I ready to fall soundly to sleep in my bed!

## LETTER XVII.

Political chances.—Visit from a Republican.—His high spirits at the prospects before him.—His advice to me respecting my name.—Removal of the Prisoners from Ste. Pélagie.—Review.—Garde de Paris.—The National Guard.

We are so accustomed, in these our luckless days, to hear of *émuetes* and rumours of *émuetes*, here, there, and everywhere, that we certainly grow nerve-hardened, and if not quite callous, at least we are almost reckless of the threat. But in this city the business of getting up riots on the one hand, and putting them down on the other, is carried on in so easy and familiar a manner, that we daily look for an account of something of the kind as regularly as for our breakfast bread; and I begin already to lose in a great degree my fear of disagreeable results, in the interest with which I watch what is going on.

The living in the midst of all these different parties, and listening first to one and then to another of them, is to a foreigner much like the amusement derived by an idle spectator from walking round a card-table, looking into all the hands, and then watching the manner in which each one plays his game.

It has so often happened here, as we all know, that when the game has appeared over, and the winner in possession of the stake he played for, they have on a sudden shuffled the cards and begun again, that people seem always looking out for new chances, new bets, new losses, and new confusion. I can assure you, that it is a game of considerable movement and animation which is going on at Paris just now. The political trials are to commence on Tuesday next, and the republicans are as busy as a nest of wasps when conscious that their stronghold is attacked. They have not only been upon the alert, but hitherto in great spirits at the prospect before them.

The same individual whose alarming communications on this subject I mentioned to you soon after we came here, called on me again a few days ago. I never saw a man more altered in the interval of a few weeks: when I first saw him here, he was sullen, gloomy, and miserable-looking in the extreme; but at his last visit he appeared gay, frolicsome, and happy. He was not disposed, however, to talk much on politics; and I am persuaded he came with a fixed determination not to indulge our curiosity by saying a word on the subject. But "out of the fulness of the heart the mouth speaketh;" and this gentleman did not depart without giving us some little intimation of what was passing in his.

Observe, that I do no treason in repeating to you whatever this young man said in my hearing; for he assured me the first time I ever saw him, that he knew me to be "*une absolutiste enragée*;" but that, so far from fearing to speak freely before me, there was nothing that would give him so much pleasure as believing that I should publish every word he uttered on the subject of politics. I told him in return, that if I did so, it should be without mentioning his name; for that I should be truly sorry to hear that he had been consigned to Ste. Pélagie as a rebel on my evidence. So we understand each other perfectly.

On the morning in question, he began talking gaily and gallantly concerning the pleasures of Paris, and expressed his hope that we were taking care to profit by the present interval of public tranquillity.

"Is this interval of calm likely to be followed by a storm?" said one of the party.

"Mais ... que sais-je?... The weather is so fine now, you know.... And the opera? en vérité, c'est superbe!... Have you seen it yet?"

"Seen what?"

"Eh! mais, 'La Juive'! ... à présent il n'y a que cela au monde.... You read the journals?"

"Yes; Galignani's at least."

"Ah! ah!" said he, laughing; "c'est assez pour vous autres."

"Is there any interesting news to-day in any of the papers?"

"Intéressante? ... mais, oui ... assez.... Cependant...." And then again he rattled on about plays, balls, concerts, and I know not what.

"I wish you would tell me," said I, interrupting him, "whether you think, that in case any popular movement should occur, the English would be molested, or in any way annoyed."

"Non, madame—je ne le crois pas—surtout les femmes. Cependant, si j'étais vous, Madame Trollope, je me donnerai pour le moment le nom d'O'Connell."

"And that, you think, would be accepted as a passport through any scene of treason and rebellion?" said I.

He laughed again, and said that was not exactly what he meant; but that O'Connell was a name revered in France as well as at Rome, and might very likely belong one day or other to a pope, if his generous wishes for an Irish republic were too dear to his heart to permit him ever to accept the title of king.

"An Irish republic? ... perhaps that is just what is wanted," said I. But not wishing to enter into any discussion on the niceties of speech, I waived the compliments he began to pay me on this liberal sentiment, and again asked him if he thought anything was going on amongst the friends of the prisoners that might impede the course of justice.

Though not aware of the quibble with which I had replied to him, he answered me by another, saying with energy—

"No! ... never!... They will never do anything to impede the course of justice."

"Will they do anything to assist it?" said I.

He sprang from his chair, gave a bound across the room, as if to hide his glee by looking out of the window, and when he showed his face again, said with much solemnity—"They will do their duty."

The conversation continued for some time longer, wavering between politics and dissipation; and though we could not obtain from him anything approaching to information respecting what might be going on among his hot-headed party, yet it seemed clear that he at least hoped for something that would lead to important results.

The riddle was explained a very few hours after he left us. The political prisoners, most of whom were lodged in the prison of Ste. Pélagie, have been removed to the Luxembourg; and it was confidently hoped and expected by the republicans that enough malcontents would be found among the citizens of Paris to get up a very satisfactory *émeute* on the occasion. But never was hope more abortive: not the slightest public sensation appears to have been excited by this removal; and I am assured that the whole republican party are so bitterly disappointed at this, that the most sanguine among them have ceased for the present to anticipate the triumph of their cause. I suspect, therefore, that it will be some time before we shall receive another visit from our riot-loving friend.

Meanwhile preparations are going on in a very orderly and judicious style at the Luxembourg. The trial-chamber and all things connected with it are completed; tents have been pitched in the gardens for the accommodation of the soldiers, and guards stationed in such a manner in all directions as to ensure a reasonable chance of tranquillity to the peaceable.

We have attended a review of very fine troops in the Place du Carrousel, composed of National Guards, troops of the line, and that most superb-looking body of municipal troops called *La Garde de Paris*. These latter, it seems, have performed in Paris since the revolution of 1830 the duties of that portion of the police formerly called *gendarmerie*; but the name having fallen into disrepute in the capital—(*les jeunes gens, par exemple,* could not bear it)—the title of *Garde de Paris* has been accorded to them instead, and it is now only in the provinces that *gendarmes* are to be found. But let them be called by what name they may, I never saw any corps of more superb appearance. Men and horses, accoutrements and discipline, all seem perfect. It is amusing to observe how slight a thread will sometimes suffice to lead captive the most unruly spirits.

"What is there in a name?"

Yet I have heard it asserted with triumphant crowings by some of the revolutionary set, that, thanks to their valour! the odious system was completely changed—that *gendarmes* and *mouchards* no longer existed in Paris—that citizens would never again be tormented by their hateful *surveillance*—and, in short, that Frenchmen were redeemed from thraldom now and for evermore; so now they have *La Garde de Paris*, just to take care of them: and if ever a set of men were capable of performing effectually the duties committed to their charge, I think it must be this well-drilled stalworth corps.

The appearance of a large body of the National Guard too, when brought together, as at a review, in full military style, is very imposing. The eye at once sees that they are not ordinary troops. All the appointments are in excellent order; and the very material of which their uniform is made, being so much less common than usual, helps to produce this effect. Not to mention that the uniform itself, of dark blue, with the delicately white pantaloons, is peculiarly handsome on parade; much more so, I think, though perhaps less calculated for a battle-field, than the red lower garments by which the troops of the French line are at present distinguished.

The king looks well on horseback—so do his sons. The whole staff, indeed, was gay and gallant-looking, and in style as decidedly aristocratic as any prince need desire. Shouts of "*Vive le Roi!*" ran cheerily and lustily along the lines; and if these may be trusted as indications of the feelings of the soldiery towards King Philippe, he may, I think, feel quite indifferent as to whatever other vows may be uttered concerning him in the distance.

But in this city of contradictions one can never sit down safely to ruminate upon any one inference or conclusion whatever; for five minutes afterwards you are assured by somebody or other that you are quite wrong, utterly mistaken, and that the exact contrary of what you suppose is the real fact. Thus, on mentioning in the evening the cordial reception given by the soldiers to the king in the morning, I received for answer—"Je le crois bien, madame; les officiers leur commandent de le faire."

We remained a good while on the ground, and saw as much as the confinement of a carriage would permit. Like all reviews of well-dressed, well-appointed troops, it was a gay and pretty spectacle; and notwithstanding the caustic reprimand for my faith in empty sounds which I have just repeated to you, I am still of opinion that King Philippe had every reason to be contented with his troops, and with the manner in which he was received by them.

Every hour that one remains at Paris increases, I think, one's conviction of the enormous power and importance of the National Guard. Our volunteer corps, in the season of threatenings and danger, gave us unquestionably an immense accession of strength; and had the threatener dared to come, neither his legions nor his eagles, his veterans nor his victories, would have saved him from utter destruction. He knew this, and he came not: he knew that the little island was bristling from her centre to her shore with arms raised to strike, by the impulse of the heart and soul, and not by conscription; he knew this, and wisely came not.

Our volunteers were armed men—armed in a cause that warmed their blood; and it is sufficient to establish their importance, that History must record the simple fact, that Napoleon looked at them and turned away. But, great as was the power of this critical show of volunteer strength among us, as a permanent force it was trifling when compared to the present National Guard of France. Not only are their numbers greater—Paris alone has eighty thousand of them,—but their discipline is perfect, and their practical habits of being on duty keep them in such daily activity, that a tocsin sounded within their hearing would suffice to turn out within an hour nearly the whole of this force, not only completely armed, equipped, and in all respects fit for service—not only each one with his quarters and rations provided, but each one knowing and feeling the importance of the duty he is upon as intimately as the general himself; and each one, in addition to all other feelings and motives which make armed men strong, warmed with the consciousness that it is his own stronghold, his own property, his own castle, as well as his own life, that he is defending.

This force will save France from devouring her own vitals, if anything can do it.

Among all the novelties produced by the ever-growing experience of men, and of which so many have ripened in these latter days, I doubt if any can be named more rationally calculated to fulfil the purpose for which it is intended than this organization of a force formed of the industrious and the orderly part of a community to keep in check the idle and disorderly,—and that, without taxing the state, compromising their professional usefulness, or sacrificing their personal independence, more than every man in his senses would be willing to do for the purpose of keeping watch and ward over all that he loves and values on earth.

The more the power of such a force as this increases, the farther must the country where it exists be from all danger of revolution. Such men are, and must be, conservatives in the strongest sense of the word; and though it may certainly be possible for some who may be rebel to the cause of order to get enrolled among them, the danger of the enterprise will unquestionably prevent its frequent recurrence. The wolf might as safely mount guard in the midst of armed shepherds and their dogs, as demagogues and agitators place themselves in the ranks of the National Guard of Paris.

## LETTER XVIII.

First Day of the Trials.—Much blustering, but no riot.—All alarm subsided.—Proposal for inviting Lord B——m to plead at the Trial.—Society.—Charm of idle conversation.—The Whisperer of good stories.

6th May 1835.

The monster is hatched at last! The trials began yesterday, and we are all rejoicing exceedingly at having found ourselves alive in our beds this morning. What will betide us and it, as its scales or its plumes push forth and gather strength from day to day, I know not; but "sufficient for the day is the evil thereof;" and I do assure you in very sober earnest, that when Galignani's paper arrived this morning, the party round the breakfast-table was greatly comforted by finding that nothing more alarming than a few republican demands on the part of the prisoners, and a few monarchical refusals on the part of the court, took place.

This interchange of hostilities commenced by some of the accused refusing to answer when their names were called;—then followed a demand for free admission to the chamber, during the trials, for the mothers, wives, and all other females belonging to the respective families of the prisoners;—and next, a somewhat blustering demand for counsel of their own choosing; the body of legal advocates, who, by general rule and common usage, are always charged with the defence of prisoners, not containing, as it should seem, orators sufficiently of their own *clique* to content them.

This was of course stoutly refused by the court, after retiring, however, for a couple of hours to deliberate upon it—a ceremony I should hardly have supposed necessary. The company of the ladies, too, was declined; and as, upon a moderate computation, their numerical force could not have amounted to less than five hundred, this want of gallantry in the Peers of France must be forgiven in favour of their discretion.

The gentleman, however, who was appointed, as he said, by the rest, to request the pleasure of their society, declared loudly that the demand for it should be daily renewed. This reminds one of the story of the man who punished his wife for infidelity by making her sit to hear the story of her misdeeds rehearsed every day of her life, and pretty plainly indicates that it is the plan of the accused to torment their judges as much as they conveniently can.

One of the prisoners named the celebrated Abbé de Lamennais, author of "Les Paroles d'un Croyant," as his advocate. The *procureur-général* remarked, that it was for the interest of the defence that the rule for permitting lawyers only to plead should be adhered to.

Next came a demand from one of the accused, in the name of all the rest, that permission for free and unrestrained intercourse between the prisoners of Lyons, Paris, and Marseilles should be allowed. This was answered only by the announcement that "the court was adjourned;" an intimation which produced an awful clamour; and as the peers quitted the court, they were assailed with vehement cries of "We protest! ... we protest!... We will make no defence!... We protest! ... we protest!" And so ended the business of the day.

I believe that the government, and all those who are sufficiently connected with it to know anything of the real state of the case, were perfectly aware that no public movement was likely to take place at this stage of the business. Every one seems to know that the restless spirits, the desperate adventurers engaged in the extensive plot now under investigation, consider their trial as the best occasion possible for a political *coup de théâtre*, and that nothing would have disturbed their performance more than a riot before the curtain rose.

Everything like panic seems now to have subsided, even among those who are farthest from the centre of action; and all the effects of this mighty affair apparently visible at present are to be seen on the faces of the republicans, who, according to their wont, strut about wherever they are most likely to be looked at, and take care that each one of their countenances shall be

"Like to a book where men may read strange matters."

I thank Heaven, nevertheless, that this first day is so well over. I had heard so over-much about it, that it became a sort of nightmare to me, from which I now feel happily relieved. It is quite clear, that if the out-of-door agitators should think proper to make any attempts to produce disturbance, the government feels quite equal to the task of making them quiet again, and of insuring that peaceable security to the country for which she has so long languished in vain.

The military force employed at the Luxembourg is, however, by no means large. One battalion of the first legion of National Guards was in the court of the palace, and about four hundred troops of the line occupied the garden. But though no show of force is unnecessarily displayed, every one has the comfort of knowing that there is enough within reach should any necessity arise for employing it.

I was told the other day, that when Lord B———m was in Paris, he was so kind as to visit M. Armand Carrel in prison; and that, on the strength of this proof of sympathy and affection, it has been suggested to the prisoners at the Luxembourg, that they should despatch a deputation of their friends to wait upon his lordship, requesting the aid of his eloquence in pleading their cause against the tyrants who so unjustifiably hold them in durance.

The proposal, it seems, was very generally approved; but nevertheless, it was at last negatived on the representation of a person who had once heard his lordship argue in the French language. This is the more to be regretted by the friends of these suffering victims, since their choice of defenders is to be restricted to members of the bar: and this restriction, narrow-minded and severe as it is, would not exclude his lordship; a legal advocate being beyond all question a legal advocate all the world over.

It was not till we had sent out in one or two directions to ascertain if all things were quiet, that we ventured to keep an engagement which we had made for last night to pass the *soirée* at Madame de L*****'s. I should have been sorry to have lost it; for the business of the morning appeared to have awakened the spirits and set everybody talking. There are few things I like better than listening to a full, free flow of Paris talk; particularly when, as in this instance, the party is small and in a lively mood.

It appears as if there were nothing like caution or reserve here in any direction. Among those whom I have had the satisfaction of occasionally meeting are some who figure amongst the most important personages of the day; but their conversation is as gaily unrestrained as if they had nothing to do but to amuse themselves. These, indeed, are not likely to commit themselves; but I have known others less secure, who have appeared to permit every thought that occurred to them to meet the ear of whoever chose to listen. In short, whatever restraint the police, which by its nature is very phœnix-like, may endeavour to put upon the periodical press, its influence certainly does not as yet reach the lips, which open with equal freedom for the expression of faith, scepticism, loyalty, treason, philosophy, and wit.

In an intercourse so transient as mine is likely to be with most of the acquaintance I have formed here,—an intercourse consisting chiefly, as to the manner of it, of evening visits through a series of *salons*,—amusement is naturally more sought than information: and were it otherwise, I should, with some few exceptions, have reaped disappointment instead of pleasure; for it is evident that the same feeling which leads the majority of persons you meet in society here, to speak freely, prevents them from saying anything seriously. So that, after talking for an hour or two upon subjects which one should think very gravely important, a light word, a light laugh, ends the colloquy, and very often leaves me in doubt as to the real sentiments of those to whom I have been listening.

But if not always successful in obtaining information, I never fail in finding amusement. Rarely, even for a moment, does conversation languish; and a string of lively nothings, or a startling succession of seemingly bold, but really unmeaning speculations, often make me imagine that a vast deal of talent has been displayed; yet, when memory sets to work upon it, little remains worth recording. Nevertheless, there is talent, and of a very charming kind too, in this manner of uttering trifles so that they may be mistaken for wit.

I know some few in our own dear land who have also this happy gift; and, as a matter of grace and mere exterior endowment, I question if it be not fairly worth all the rest. But I believe we have it in about the same proportion that we have good actors of genteel comedy, compared to the number which they can boast of the same class here. With us this easy, natural style of mimicking real life is a rare talent, though sometimes possessed in great perfection; but with them it seems more or less the birthright of all.

So is it with the gift of that bright colloquial faculty which bestows such indescribable grace upon the airy nothings uttered in French drawing-rooms. To listen to it, is very like quaffing the sparkling, frothy beverage native to their sunny hills;—French talk is very like champagne. The exhilaration it produces is instantaneous: the spirits mount, and something like wit is often struck out even from dull natures by merely coming in contact with what is so brilliant.

I could almost venture to assert that the effect of this delightful inspiration might be perceived by any one who had gained admission to French society even if they did not understand the language. Let an observing eye, well accustomed to read the expression so legibly, though so transiently written in the countenances of persons in conversation,—let such a one only see, if he cannot hear, the effect produced by the hits and flashes of French eloquence. Allow me another simile, and I will tell you that it is like applying electricity to a bunch of feathers tied together and attached to the conductor by a thread: first one, then another starts, flies off, mounts, and drops again, as the bright spark passes lightly, gracefully, capriciously, yet still all making part of one circle.

Of course, I am not speaking now of large parties; these, as I think I have said before, are wonderfully alike in all lands, and nothing approaching to conversation can possibly take place at any of them. It is only where the circle is restricted to a few that this sort of effect can be produced; and then, the impulse once given by a piquant word, seemingly uttered at random, every one present receives a share of it, and contributes in return all the lively thoughts to which it has given birth.

But there was one gentleman of our party yesterday evening who had a most provoking trick of attracting one's attention as if on purpose to disappoint it. He was not quite like Molière's Timante, of whom Célimène says,

"Et, jusques au bonjour, il dit tout à l'oreille;"

but in the midst of pleasant talk, in which all were interested, he said aloud—

"*Par exemple!* I heard the very best thing possible to-day about the King. Will you hear it, Madame B...?"

This question being addressed to a decided doctrinaire, the answer was of course a reproachful shake of the head; but as it was accompanied by half a smile, and as the lady bent her fair neck towards the speaker, she, and she only, was made acquainted with "the best of all possible things," conveyed in a whisper.

At another time he addressed himself to the lady of the house; but as he spoke across the circle, he not only fixed her attention, but that of every one else.

"Madame!" said he coaxingly, "will you let me tell you a little word of treason?"

"Comment?—de la trahison?... Apropos de quoi, s'il vous plaît?... Mais c'est égal—contez toujours."

On receiving this answer, the whisperer of good stories got up from the depth of his arm-chair—an enterprise of some difficulty, for he was neither rapid nor light in his movements,—and deliberately walking round the chairs of all the party, he placed himself behind Madame de L*****, and whispered in her ear what made her colour and shake her head again; but she laughed too, telling him that she hated timid politics, and had no taste for any *trahisons* which were not "*hautement prononcées*."

This hint sent him back to his place; but it was taken very good-humouredly, for, instead of whispering any more, he uttered aloud sundry odds and ends of gossip, but all so well dressed up in lively wording, that they sounded very like good stories.

# LETTER XIX.

Victor Hugo.—Racine.

I have again been listening to some curious details respecting the present state of literature in France. I think I have before stated to you, that I have uniformly heard the whole of the *décousu* school of authors spoken of with unmitigated contempt,—and that not only by the venerable advocates for the *bon vieux temps*, but also, and equally, by the distinguished men of the present day—distinguished both by position and ability.

Respecting Victor Hugo, the only one of the tribe to which I allude who has been sufficiently read in England to justify his being classed by us as a person of general celebrity, the feeling is more remarkable still. I have never mentioned him or his works to any person of good moral feeling and cultivated mind, who did not appear to shrink from according him even the degree of reputation that those who are received as authority among our own critics have been disposed to allow him. I might say, that of him France seems to be ashamed.

Again and again it has happened to me, when I have asked the opinions of individuals as to the merit of his different plays, that I have been answered thus:—

"I assure you I know nothing about it: I never saw it played."

"Have you read it?"

"No; I have not. I cannot read the works of Victor Hugo."

One gentleman, who has heard me more than once persist in my inquiries respecting the reputation enjoyed by Victor Hugo at Paris as a man of genius and a successful dramatic writer, told me, that he saw that, in common with the generality of foreigners, particularly the English, I looked upon Victor Hugo and his productions as a sort of type or specimen of the literature of France at the present hour. "But permit me to assure you," he added gravely and earnestly, "that no idea was ever more entirely and altogether erroneous. He is the head of a sect—the high-priest of a congregation who have abolished every law, moral and intellectual, by which the efforts of the human mind have hitherto been regulated. He has attained this pre-eminence, and I trust that no other will arise to dispute it with him. But Victor Hugo is NOT a popular French writer."

Such a judgment as this, or the like of it, I have heard passed upon him and his works nine times out of ten that I have mentioned him; and I consider this as a proof of right feeling and sound taste, which is extremely honourable, and certainly more than we have lately given our neighbours credit for. It pleased me the more perhaps because I did not expect it. There is so much meretricious glitter in the works of Victor Hugo,—nay, so much real brightness now and then,—that I expected to find at least the younger and less reflective part of the population warm in their admiration of him.

His clinging fondness for scenes of vice and horror, and his utter contempt for all that time has stamped as good in taste or feeling, might, I thought, arise from the unsettled spirit of the times; and if so, he could not fail of receiving the meed of sympathy and praise from those who had themselves set that spirit at work.

But it is not so. The wild vigour of some of his descriptions is acknowledged; but that is all of praise that I ever heard bestowed upon Victor Hugo's theatrical productions in his native land.

The startling, bold, and stirring incidents of his disgusting dramas must and will excite a certain degree of attention when seen for the first time, and it is evidently the interest of managers to bring forward whatever is most likely to produce this effect; but the doing so cannot be quoted as a proof of the systematic degradation of the theatre. It is moreover a fact, which the play-bills themselves are alone sufficient to attest, that after Victor Hugo's plays have had their first run, they are never brought forward again: not one of them has yet become what we call a stock-play.

This fact, which was first stated to me by a person perfectly *au fait* of the subject, has been subsequently confirmed by many others; and it speaks more plainly than any recorded criticism could do, what the public judgment of these pieces really is.

The romance of "Notre Dame de Paris" is ever cited as Victor Hugo's best work, excepting some early lyrical pieces of which we know nothing. But even this, though there are passages of extraordinary descriptive power in it, is always alluded to with much more of contempt than admiration; and I have heard it ridiculed in circles, whose praise was fame, with a light pleasantry more likely to prove an antidote to its mischief than all the reprobation that sober criticism could pour out upon it.

But may not this champion of vice—this chronicler of sin, shame, and misery—quote Scripture and say, "A prophet is not without honour, save in his own country"? For I have seen a criticism in an English paper (The Examiner) which says, "*The* Notre Dame *of Victor Hugo must take rank with the best romances by the author of* Waverley.... *It transcends them in vigour, animation, and familiarity with the age.*"

In reply to the last point here mentioned, in which our countryman has given the superiority to Victor Hugo over Sir Walter Scott, a very strong testimony against its correctness has reached me since I have been in Paris. An able lawyer, and most accomplished gentleman and scholar, who holds a distinguished station in the Cour Royale, took us to see the Palais de Justice. Having shown us the chamber where criminal trials are carried on, he observed, that this was the room described by Victor Hugo in his romance; adding,—"He was, however, mistaken here, as in most places *where he affects a knowledge of the times of which he writes.* In the reign of Louis the Eleventh, no criminal trials ever took place within the walls of this building; and all the ceremonies as described by him resemble much more a trial of yesterday than of the age at which he dates his tale."

The vulgar old adage, that "there is no accounting for taste," must, I suppose, teach us to submit patiently to the hearing of any judgments and opinions which it is the will and pleasure of man to pronounce; but it does seem strange that any can be found who, after bringing Sir Walter Scott and Victor Hugo into comparison, should give the palm of superiority to the author of "Notre Dame de Paris."

Were the faults of this school of authors only of a literary kind, few persons, I believe, would take the trouble to criticise them, and their nonsense would die a natural death as soon as it was made to encounter the light of day: but such productions as Victor Hugo's are calculated to do great injury to human nature. They would teach us to believe that all our gentlest and best affections can only lead to crime and infamy. There is not, I truly believe, a single pure, innocent, and holy thought to be found throughout his writings: Sin is the muse he invokes—he would

"Take off the rose

From the fair forehead of an innocent love,

And set a blister there;"

Horror is his handmaid; and "thousands of liveried *monsters* lackey him," to furnish the portraits with which it is the occupation of his life to disgust the world.

Can there, think you, be a stronger proof of a diseased intellect among the *décousu* part of the world, than that they not only admire this man's hideous extravagances, but that they actually believe him to be ... at least they say so ... a second Shakspeare!... A Shakspeare!

To chastise as he deserves an author who may be said to defy mankind by the libels he has put forth on the whole race, requires a stouter and a keener weapon than any a woman can wield; but when they prate of Shakspeare, I feel that it is our turn to speak. How much of gratitude and love does every woman owe to him! He, who has entered deeper into her heart than ever mortal did before or since his day, how has he painted her?—As Portia, Juliet, Constance, Hermione;—as Cordelia, Volumnia, Isabella, Desdemona, Imogene!

Then turn and see for what we have to thank our modern painter. Who are his heroines?—Lucrèce Borgia, Marion de Lorme, Blanche, Maguelonne, with I know not how many more of the same stamp; besides his novel heroine, whom Mr. Henry Lytton Bulwer calls "the most delicate female ever drawn by the pen of romance"—The Esmeralda! ... whose sole accomplishments are dancing and singing in the streets, and who ... delicate creature! ... being caught up by a horseman in a midnight brawl, throws her arms round his neck, swears he is very handsome, and thenceforward shows the delicate tenderness of her nature, by pertinaciously doting upon him, without any other return or encouragement whatever than an insulting caress bestowed upon her one night when he was drunk ... "delicate female!"

But this is all too bad to dwell upon. It is, however, in my estimation a positive duty, when mentioning the works of Victor Hugo, to record a protest against their tone and tendency; and it is also a duty to correct, as far as one can, the erroneous impression existing in England respecting his reputation in France.

Whenever his name is mentioned in England, his success is cited as a proof of the depraved state, moral and intellectual, of the French people. And such it would be, were his success and reputation such as his partisans represent them to be. But, in point of fact, the manner in which he is judged by his own countrymen is the strongest possible evidence that neither a powerful fancy, a commanding diction, nor an imagination teeming with images of intense passion, can suffice to ensure an author any exalted reputation in France at the present day if he outrages good feeling and good taste.

Should any doubt the correctness of this statement, I can only refer them to the source from whence I derived the information on which it is founded,—I can only refer them to France herself. There is one fact, however, which may be ascertained without crossing the Channel;—namely, that when one of their reviews found occasion to introduce an article upon the modern drama, the editors acquitted themselves of the task by translating the whole of the able article upon that subject which appeared about a year and a half ago in the Quarterly, acknowledging to what source they were indebted for it.

Were the name and the labours of Victor Hugo confined to his own country, it would now be high time that I should release you from him; but it is an English critic who has said, that he has heaved the ground from under the feet of Racine; and you must indulge me for a few minutes, while I endeavour to bring the two parties together before you. In doing this, I will be generous; for I will introduce M. Hugo in "Le Roi s'amuse," which, from the circumstance (the happiest, I was assured, that ever befel the author) of its being withdrawn by authority from the Théâtre Français, has become infinitely more celebrated than any other he has written.

It may be remarked by the way, that a few more such acts of decent watchfulness over the morals and manners of the people may redeem the country from the stigma it now bears of being the most licentious in its theatre and its press in the world.

The first glorious moment of being forbidden at the Français appears almost to have turned the lucky author's brain. His preface to "Le Roi s'amuse," among many other symptoms of insanity has the following:—

"Le premier mouvement de l'auteur fut de douter.... L'acte était arbitraire au point d'être incroyable.... L'auteur ne pouvait croire à tant d'insolence et de folie.... Le ministre avait en effet, de son droit divin de ministre, intimé l'ordre.... Le ministre lui avait pris sa pièce, lui avait pris son droit, lui avait pris sa chose. Il ne restait plus qu'à le mettre, lui poëte, à la Bastille.... Est-ce qu'il y a eu en effet quelque chose qu'on a appelé la révolution de Juillet?... Que peut être le motif d'une pareille mesure?... Il parait que nos faiseurs de censure se prétendent scandalisés dans leur morale par 'Le Roi s'amuse;' le nom seul du poëte inculpé aurait dû être une suffisante réfutation (!!!)... Cette pièce a révolté la pudeur des gendarmes; la brigade Léotaud y était, et l'a trouvé obscène; le bureau des mœurs s'est voilé la face; M. Vidocq a rougi.... Holà, mes maîtres! Silence sur ce point!... Depuis quand n'est-il plus permis à un roi de courtiser sur la scène une servante d'auberge?... Mener un roi dans un mauvais lieu, cela ne serait pas même nouveau non plus.... L'auteur veut l'art chaste, et non l'art prude.... Il est profondément triste de voir comment se termine la révolution de Juillet...."

Then follows a *précis* of the extravagant and hateful plot, in which the heroine is, as usual, "une fille séduite et perdue;" and he sums it up thus pompously: —"Au fond d'un des ouvrages de l'auteur il y a la fatalité—au fond de celui-ci il y a la providence."

I wish much that some one would collect and publish in a separate volume all M. Victor Hugo's prefaces; I would purchase it instantly, and it would be a fund of almost inexhaustible amusement. He assumes a tone in them which, all things considered, is perhaps unequalled in the history of literature. In another part of the one from which I have given the above extracts, he says—

"Vraiment, le pouvoir qui s'attaque à nous n'aura pas gagné grand' chose à ce que nous, hommes d'art, nous quittions notre tâche consciencieuse, tranquille, sincère, profonde; notre tâche sainte...." What on earth, if it be not insanity, could have put it into Mr. Hugo's head that the manufacturing of his obscene dramas was "une tâche sainte"?

The principal characters in "Le Roi s'amuse" are François Premier; Triboulet, his pander and buffoon; Blanche, the daughter of Triboulet, "la fille séduite," and heroine of the piece; and Maguelonne, another Esmeralda.

The interest lies in the contrast between Triboulet pander and Triboulet père. He is himself the most corrupt and infamous of men; and because he is humpbacked, makes it both his pastime and his business to lead the king his master into every species of debauchery: but he shuts up his daughter to preserve her purity; and the poet has put forth all his strength in describing the worship which Triboulet père pays to the virtue which he passes his life as Triboulet pander in destroying.

Of course, the king falls in love with Blanche, and she with him; and Triboulet pander is made to assist in carrying her off in the dark, under the belief that she was the wife of a nobleman to whom also his majesty the king was making love.

When Triboulet père and pander finds out what he has done, he falls into a terrible agony: and here again is a *tour de force*, to show how pathetically such a father can address such a daughter.

He resolves to murder the king, and informs his daughter, who is passionately attached to her royal seducer, of his intention. She objects, but is at length brought to consent by being made to peep through a hole in the wall, and seeing his majesty King Francis engaged in making love to Maguelonne.

This part of the plot is brought out shortly and pithily.

BLANCHE (*peeping through the hole in the wall*).

Et cette femme! ... est-elle affrontée! ... oh!...

TRIBOULET.

Tais-toi;

Pas de pleurs. Laisse-moi te venger!

BLANCHE.

Hélas!—Faites—

Tout ce que vous voudrez.

TRIBOULET.

Merci!

This *merci*, observe, is not said ironically, but gravely and gratefully. Having arranged this part of the business, he gives his daughter instructions as to what she is to do with herself, in the following sublime verses:—

TRIBOULET.

Écoute. Va chez moi, prends-y des habits d'homme,
Un cheval, de l'argent, n'importe quelle somme;
Et pars, sans t'arrêter un instant en chemin,
Pour Evreux, où j'irai te joindre après-demain.
—Tu sais ce coffre auprès du portrait de ta mère;
L'habit est là,—je l'ai d'avance exprès fait faire.

Having dismissed his daughter, he settles with a gipsy-man named Saltabadil, who is the brother of Maguelonne, all the details of the murder, which is to be performed in their house, a small cabaret at which the foul weather and the fair Maguelonne induce the royal rake to pass the night. Triboulet leaves them an old sack in which they are to pack up the body, and promises to return at midnight, that he may himself see it thrown into the Seine.

Blanche meanwhile departs; but feeling some compunctious visitings about the proposed murder of her lover, returns, and again applying her ear to the hole in the wall, finds that his majesty is gone to bed in the garret, and that the brother and sister are consulting about his death. Maguelonne, a very "delicate female," objects too; she admires his beauty, and proposes that his life shall be spared if any stranger happens to arrive whose body may serve to fill the sack. Blanche, in a fit of heroic tenderness, determines to be that stranger; exclaiming,

"Eh bien! ... mourons pour lui!"

But before she knocks at the door, she kneels down to say her prayers, particularly for forgiveness to all her enemies. Here are the verses, making part of those which have overthrown Racine:—

BLANCHE.

Oh! Dieu, vers qui je vais,
Je pardonne à tous ceux qui m'ont été mauvais:
Mon père et vous, mon Dieu! pardonnez-leurs de même
Au roi François Premier, que je plains et que j'aime.

She knocks, the door opens, she is stabbed and consigned to the sack. Her father arrives immediately after as by appointment, receives the sack, and prepares to drag it towards the river, handling it with revengeful ecstasy, and exclaiming—

Maintenant, monde, regarde-moi:
Ceci, c'est un bouffon; et ceci, c'est un roi.

At this triumphant moment he hears the voice of the king, singing as he walks away from the dwelling of Maguelonne.

TRIBOULET.

Mais qui donc m'a-t-il mis à sa place, le traître!

He cuts open the sack; and a flash of lightning very melodramatically enables him to recognise his daughter, who revives, to die in his arms.

This is beyond doubt what may be called "a tragic situation;" and I confess it does seem very hard-hearted to laugh at it: but the *pas* that divides the sublime from the ridiculous is not distinctly seen, and there is something vulgar and ludicrous, both in the position and language of the parties, which quite destroys the pathetic effect.

It must be remembered that she is dressed in the "habit d'homme" of which her father says so poetically—

Je l'ai d'avance exprès fait faire.

Observe, too, that she is still in the sack; the stage directions being, "Le bas du corps, qui est resté vêtu, est caché dans le sac."

BLANCHE.

Où suis-je?

TRIBOULET.

Blanche! que t'a-t-on fait? Quel mystère infernal!
Je crains en te touchant de te faire du mal
...Ah! la cloche du bac est là sur la muraille:
Ma pauvre enfant, peux-tu m'attendre un peu, que j'aille
Chercher de l'eau....

A surgeon arrives, and having examined her wound, says,

Elle est morte.
Elle a dans le flanc gauche une plaie assez forte:
Le sang a dû causer la mort en l'étouffant.

TRIBOULET.

J'ai tué mon enfant! J'ai tué mon enfant!

(*Il tombe sur le pavé.*)

FIN.

All this is very shocking; but it is not tragedy,—and it is not poetry. Yet it is what we are told has heaved the earth from under Racine!

After such a sentence as this, it must be, I know, *rococo* to name him; but yet I would say, in his own words,

D'adorateurs zélés à peine un petit nombre

Ose des premiers temps nous retracer quelque ombre;

Le reste....

Se fait initier à ces honteux mystères,

Et blasphème le nom qu'ont invoqué leurs pères.

As I profess myself of the *petit nombre,* you must let me recall to your memory some of the fragments of that noble edifice which Racine raised over him, and which, as they say, has now perished under the mighty power of Victor Hugo. It will not be lost time to do this; for look where you will among the splendid material of this uprooted temple, and you will find no morsel that is not precious; nothing that is not designed, chiseled, and finished by the hand of a master.

Racine has not produced dramas from ordinary life; it was not his object to do so, nor is it the end he has attained. It is the tragedy of heroes and demi-gods that he has given us, and not of cut-purses, buffoons, and street-walkers.

If the language of Racine be poetry, that of M. Hugo is not; and wherever the one is admired, the other must of necessity be valueless. It would be endless to attempt giving citations to prove the grace, the dignity, the majestic flow of Racine's verse; but let your eye run over "Iphigénie," for instance,—there also the loss of a daughter forms the tragic interest,—and compare such verses as those I have quoted above with any that you can find in Racine.

Hear the royal mother, for example, describe the scene that awaits her:

Un prêtre environné d'une foule cruelle

Portera sur ma fille une main criminelle,

Déchirera son sein, et d'un œil curieux

Dans son cœur palpitant consultera les dieux;

—Et moi—qui l'amenai triomphante, adorée,

Je m'en retournerai, seule, et désespérée.

Surely this is of a better fabric than—

Tu sais ce coffre auprès du portrait de ta mère;

L'habit est là,—je l'ai d'avance exprès fait faire.

I have little doubt but that the inspired author, when this noble phrase, "exprès fait faire," suggested itself, felt ready to exclaim, in the words of Philaminte and Bélise—

Ah! que cet "exprès fait" est d'un goût admirable!

C'est à mon sentiment un endroit impayable;

J'entends là-dessous un million de mots.—

—Il est vrai qu'il dit plus de choses qu'il n'est gros.

But to take the matter seriously, let us examine a little the ground upon which this school of dramatic writers found their claim to superiority over their classic predecessors. Is it not that they declare themselves to be more true to nature? And how do they support this claim? Were you to read through every play that M. Hugo has written—(and may you long be preserved from so great annoyance!)—I doubt if you would find a single personage with whom you could sympathise, or a single sentiment or opinion that you would feel true to the nature within you.

It would be much less difficult, I conceive, so strongly to excite the imagination by the majestic eloquence of Racine's verses as to make you conscious of fellow-feeling with his sublime personages, than to debase your very heart and soul so thoroughly as to enable you to fancy that you have anything in common with the corrupt creations of Victor Hugo.

But even were it otherwise—were the scenes imagined by this new Shakspeare more like the real villany of human nature than those of the noble writer he is said to have set aside, I should still deny that this furnished any good reason for bringing such scenes upon the stage. Why should we make a pastime of looking upon vulgar vice? Why should the lowest passions of our nature be for ever brought out in parade before us?

"It is not and it cannot be for good."

The same reasoning might lead us to turn from the cultured garden, its marble terraces, its velvet lawns, its flowers and fruits of every clime, that we might take our pleasure in a bog—and for all consolation be told, when we slip and flounder about in its loathsome slime, that it is more natural.

I have written you a most unmerciful letter, and it is quite time that I should quit the theme, for I get angry—angry that I have no power to express in words all I feel on this subject. Would that for one short hour or so I had the pen which wrote the "Dunciad!"—I would use it—heartily—and then take my leave by saying,

"Rentre dans le néant, dont je t'ai fait sortir."

## LETTER XX.

Versailles.—St. Cloud.

The Château de Versailles, that marvellous *chef-d'œuvre* of the splendid taste and unbounded extravagance of Louis le Grand, is shut up, and has been so for the last eighteen months. This is a great disappointment to such of our party as have never seen its interminable chambers and their gorgeous decorations. The reason assigned for this unwonted exclusion of the public is, that the whole of this enormous pile is filled with workmen; not, however, for the purpose of restoring it as a palace for the king, but of preparing it as a sort of universal museum for the nation. The buildings are in fact too extensive for a palace; and splendid as it is, I can easily believe no king of modern days would wish to inhabit it. I have sometimes wondered that Napoleon did not take a fancy to its vastness; but, I believe, he had no great taste in the upholstering line, and preferred converting his millions into the sinews of war, to the possession of all the carving and gilding in the world.

If this projected museum, however, should be *monté* with science, judgment and taste, and on the usual scale of French magnificence, it will be turning the costly whim of *le Grand Monarque* to excellent account.

The works which are going on there, were mentioned at a party the other evening, when some one stated that it was the intention of the King to convert one portion of the building into a gallery of national history, that should contain pictures of all the victories which France had ever won.

The remark made in reply amused me much, it was so very French.—"Ma foi!... Mais cette galerie-là doit être bien longue—et assez ennuyeuse pour les étrangers."

Though the château was closed to us, we did not therefore give up our purposed expedition to Versailles: every object there is interesting, not only from its splendour, but from the recollections it revives of scenes with whose history we are all familiar. Not only the horrors of the last century, but all the regal glories of the preceding one, are so well known to everybody, that there must have been a prodigious deal of gossip handed down to us from France, or we never could feel so much better acquainted with events which have passed at Versailles than with any scenes that have occurred at an equal distance of time at Windsor.

But so it is; and the English go there not merely as strangers visiting a palace in a foreign land, but as pilgrims to the shrine of the princes and poets who have left their memory there, and with whose names and histories they are as familiar as if they belonged to us.

The day we passed among the royal spectres that never fail to haunt one at this palace of recollections, was a mixture of sunshine and showers, and our meditations seemed to partake of the vicissitude.

It is said that the great Louis reared this stupendous dwelling in which to pass the gilded hours of his idleness, because from St. Germain's he could see the plain of St. Denis, over which his funeral array was to pass, and the spire that marked the spot where his too precious dust was to be laid. Happy was it for him that the scutcheoned sepulchre of St. Denis was the most distant and most gloomy point to which his prophetic glance could reach! Could the great king have looked a little farther, and dreamed of the scenes which were destined to follow this dreaded passage to his royal tomb, how would he have blessed the fate which permitted him to pass into it so peacefully!

It is quite wonderful to see how much of the elaborate decoration and fine finishing of this sumptuous place remains uninjured after being visited by the most ferocious mob that ever collected together. Had they been less intent on the savage object of their mission, it is probable that they would have sated their insane rage in destroying the palace itself, and the costly decorations of its singular gardens. Though far inferior in all ways either to the gardens of the Elector of Hesse Cassel at Wilhelmshöhe, or to those of the Grand Duke of Baden at Schwetzingen, those of Versailles are still highly interesting from many causes, and have so much of majesty and pomp about them, that one cannot look upon them without feeling that only the kings of the earth could ever have had a master's right to take their pleasure therein.

Before we entered upon the orderly confusion of groves, statues, temples, and water-works through which it is necessary to be led, we made our grey-headed guide lead us round and about every part of the building while we listened to his string of interesting old stories about Louis Seize, and Marie Antoinette, and Monsieur, and le Comte d'Artois, (for he seemed to have forgotten that they had borne any other titles than those he remembered in his youth,) all of whom seemed to retain exactly the same place in his imagination that they had occupied some fifty years ago, when he was assistant to the keeper of the *orangerie*. He boasted, with a vanity as fresh as if it had been newly born, of the honours of that near approach to royalty which he had formerly enjoyed; recounted how the Queen called one of the orange-trees her own, because she fancied its blossoms sweeter than all the rest; and how from such a broad-leafed double-blossoming myrtle he had daily gathered a *bouquet* for her majesty, which was laid upon her toilet exactly at two o'clock. This old man knew every orange-tree, its birth and history, as well as a shepherd knows his flock. The venerable father of the band dates his existence from the reign of François Premier, and truly he enjoys a green old age. The one surnamed Louis le Grand, who was twin brother, as he said, to that mighty monarch, looks like a youth beside it—and you are told that it has not yet attained its full growth.

Oh! could those orange-trees but speak! could they recount to us the scenes they have witnessed; could they describe to us all the beauties over whom they have shed their fragrant flowers—all the heroes, statesmen, poets, and princes who have stepped in courtly paces beneath their shade; what a world of witty wickedness, of solemn warning, and of sad reflection, we should have!

But though the orange-trees were mute, our old man talked enough for them all. He was a faithful servant to the old *régime*: and indeed it should seem that there is something in the air of Versailles favourable alike to orange-trees and loyalty; for never did I hear, while wandering amidst their aristocratic perfume, one word that was not of sound orthodox legitimate loyalty to the race for whose service they have for so many hundred years lived and bloomed. And still they blossom on, unscathed by revolution, unblighted though an usurper called them his;—happier in this than many of those who were once privileged to parade their dignity beneath their royal shade. The old servitors still move among these venerable vegetable grandees with the ceremonious air of courtiers, offering obsequious service, if not to the king himself, at least to his cousin-germans; and I am persuaded there is not one of these old serving-men, who wander about Versailles like ghosts revisiting the scenes of former happiness, who would not more humbly pull off his hat to François Premier or Louis le Grand in the greenhouse, than to any monarch of a younger race.

Napoleon has left less trace of himself and his giant power at Versailles than anywhere else; and the naïads and hamadryads still lift their sculptured heads with such an eternity of stately grace, as makes one feel the evanescent nature of the interlude that was played among them during the empire. It is of the old race of Bourbon that the whole region is redolent. "There," said our old guide, "is the range of chambers that was occupied by the Queen ... those were the King's apartments ... there were the royal children ... there Monsieur ... and there the Comte d'Artois."

Then we were led round to the fatal balcony which overhangs the entrance. It was there that the fallen Marie Antoinette stood, her young son in her arms, and the doomed King her husband beside her, when she looked down upon the demons drunk with blood, who sought her life. I had heard all this hateful, but o'er-true history, more than once before on the same spot, and shortening the frightful detail, I hastened to leave it, though I believe the good old man would willingly have spent hours in dwelling upon it.

The day had been named as one on which the great waters were to play. But, little as Nature has to do with this pretty exhibition, she interfered on this occasion to prevent it. There was no water. The dry winter would, they told us, probably render it impossible to play them during the whole summer.

Here was another disappointment; but we bore it heroically, and after examining and much admiring the numberless allegories which people the grounds, and to the creation of which, a poet must have been as necessary as a sculptor, we adjourned to the Trianons, there to meditate on all the ceaseless vicissitudes of female influence from Maintenon to Josephine. It is but a sad review, but it may serve well to reconcile the majority of womankind to the tranquil dreaminess of obscurity.

The next thing to be done was dining—and most wretchedly done it was: but we found something to laugh at, nevertheless; for when the wine brought to us was found too bad to drink, and we ordered better, no less than four bottles were presented to us in succession, each one increasing in price, but being precisely of the same quality. When we charged the black-eyed daughter of the house with the fact, she said with perfect good-humour, but nowise denying it, that she was very sorry they had no better. When the bill was brought, the same damsel civilly hoped that we should not think ten sous (half-a-franc) too much to pay for having opened so many bottles. Now, as three of them were firmly corked, and carefully sealed besides, we paid our ten sous without any complaining.

The looking at a fête at St. Cloud made part of the business of the day; but in order to get there, we were obliged to mount into one of those indescribable vehicles by which the gay *bourgeoisie* of Paris are conveyed from palace to palace, and from *guinguette* to *guinguette*. We had dismissed our comfortable *citadine*, being assured that we should have no difficulty in finding another. In this, however, we were disappointed, the proportion of company appearing greatly to exceed that of the carriages which were to convey them, and we considered ourselves fortunate in securing places in an equipage which we should have scorned indignantly when we quitted Paris in the morning.

The whimsical gaiety of the crowd, all hurrying one way, was very amusing;

all anxious to reach St. Cloud before the promised half-hour's display of water-works were over; all testifying, by look, gesture, voice, and words, that light effervescence of animal spirits so essentially characteristic of the country, and all forming a moving panorama so gay and so bright as almost to make one giddy by looking at it.

Some among the capricious variety of vehicles were drawn by five or six horses. These were in truth nothing but gaily-painted waggons, hung on rude springs, with a flat awning over them. In several I counted twenty persons; but there were some few among them in which one or perhaps two seats were still vacant—and then the rapturous glee of the party was excited to the utmost by the efforts of the driver, as gay as themselves, to obtain customers to fill the vacancies.

Every individual overtaken on the road was invited by the most clamorous outcries to occupy the vacant seats. "St. Cloud! St. Cloud! St. Cloud!" shouted by the driver and re-echoed by all his company, rang in the startled ears of all they passed; and if a traveller soberly journeying in the contrary direction was met, the invitation was uttered with tenfold vehemence, accompanied by shouts of laughter; which, far from offending the party who provoked it, was invariably answered with equal frolic and fun. But when upon one occasion a carriage posting almost at full gallop towards Versailles was encountered, the ecstasy of mirth with which it was greeted exceeds description. "St. Cloud! St. Cloud! St. Cloud!—Tournez donc, messieurs—tournez à St. Cloud!" The shouts and vociferations were enough to frighten all the horses in the world excepting French ones; and they must be so thoroughly broken to the endurance of din, that there is little danger of their starting at it. I could have almost fancied that upon this occasion they took part in it; for they shook their ropes and their tassels, snorted and tossed, very much as if they enjoyed the fun.

After all, we, and many hundred others, arrived too late for the show, the supply of water failing even before the promised half-hour had elapsed. The gardens, however, were extremely full, and all the world looked as gay and as well-pleased as if nothing had gone wrong.

I wonder if these people ever grow old,—that is, old as we do, sitting in the chimney-corner, and dreaming no more of fêtes than of playing at blind-man's-buff. I have certainly seen here, as elsewhere, men, and women too, grey-headed, and wrinkled enough to be as solemn as the most venerable judge upon the bench; but I never saw any that did not seem ready to hop, skip, jump, waltz, and make love.

# LETTER XXI.

History of the Vicomte de B——. His opinions.—State of France.—Expediency.

I have had a curious conversation this morning with an old gentleman whom I believed to be a thorough legitimate, but who turns out, as you will see, something else—I hardly know what to call it—*doctrinaire* I suppose it must be, yet it is not quite that either.

But before I give you his opinions, let me present himself. M. le Vicomte de B—— is a person that I am very sure you would be happy to know anywhere. His residence is not in Paris, but at a château that he describes as the most profound retirement imaginable; yet it is not more than thirty leagues from Paris. He is a widower, and his only child is a daughter, who has been some years married.

The history of this gentleman, given as he gave it himself, was deeply interesting. It was told with much feeling, some wit, and no prolixity. Were I, however, to attempt to repeat it to you in the same manner, it would become long and tedious, and in every way as unlike as possible to what it was as it came fresh from the living fountain.

In brief, then, I will tell you that he was the younger son of an old and noble house, and, for seven years, page to Louis Seize. He must have been strikingly handsome; and young as he was at the time of the first revolution, he seems already to have found the court a very agreeable residence. He had held a commission in the army about two years, when his father, and his only brother, his elder by ten years, were obliged to leave the country, to save their lives.

The family was not a wealthy one, and great sacrifices were necessary to enable them to live in England. What remained became eventually the property of our friend, both father and brother having died in exile. With this remnant of fortune he married, not very prudently; and having lost his wife and disposed of his daughter in marriage, he is now living in his large dilapidated château, with one female servant, and an old man as major-domo, valet, and cook, who served with him in La Vendée, and who, by his description, must be a perfect Corporal Trim.

I would give a good deal to be able to accept the invitation I have received to pay him a visit at his castle. I think I should find just such a *ménage* as that which Scott so beautifully describes in one of his prefaces. But the wish is vain, such an excursion being quite impossible; so I must do without the castle, and content myself with the long morning visits that its agreeable owner is so kind as to make us.

I have seen him frequently, and listened with great interest to his little history; but it was only this morning that the conversation took a speculative turn. I was quite persuaded, but certainly from my own preconceived notions only, and not from anything I have heard him say, that M. de B—— was a devoted legitimate. An old noble—page to Louis Seize—a royalist soldier in La Vendée,—how could I think otherwise? Yet he talked to me as ... you shall hear.

Our conversation began by his asking me if I was conscious of much material change in Paris since I last visited it.

I replied, that I certainly saw some, but perhaps suspected more.

"I dare say you do," said he; "it is what your nation is very apt to do: but take my advice,—believe what you see, and nothing else."

"But what one can see in the course of a month or two is so little, and I hear so much."

"That is true; but do you not find that what you hear from one person is often contradicted by another?"

"Constantly," I replied.

"Then what can you do at last but judge by what you see?"

"Why, it appears to me that the better plan would be to listen to all parties, and let my balancing belief incline to the testimony that has most weight."

"Then be careful that this weight be not false. There are some who will tell you that the national feeling which for so many centuries has kept France together as a powerful and predominating people is loosened, melted, and gone;—that though there are Frenchmen left, there is no longer a French people."

"To any who told me so," I replied, "I would say, that the division they complained of, arose not so much from any change in the French character, as from the false position in which many were unhappily placed at the present moment. Men's hearts are divided because they are diversely drawn aside from a common centre."

"And you would say truly," said he; "but others will tell you, that regenerated France will soon dictate laws to the whole earth; that her flag will become the flag of all people—her government their government; and that their tottering monarchies will soon crumble into dust, to become part and parcel of her glorious republic."

"And to these I should say, that they appeared to be in a very heavy slumber, and that the sooner they could wake out of it and shake off their feverish dreams, the better it would be for them."

"But what would your inference be as to the state of the country from such reports as these?"

"I should think that, as usual, truth lay between. I should neither believe that France was so united as to constitute a single-minded giant, nor so divided as to have become a mass of unconnected atoms, or a race of pigmies."

"You know," he continued, "that the fashionable phrase for describing our condition at present is, that we are in *a state of transition*,—from butterflies to grubs, or from grubs to butterflies, I know not which; but to me it seems that the transition is over,—and it is high time that it should be so. The country has known neither rest nor peace for nearly half a century; and powerful as she has been and still is, she must at last fall a prey to whoever may think it worth their while to despoil her, unless she stops short while it is yet time, and strengthens herself by a little seasonable repose."

"But how is this repose to be obtained?" said I. "Some of you wish to have one king, some another, and some to have no king at all. This is not a condition in which a country is very likely to find repose."

"Not if each faction be of equal power, or sufficiently so to persevere in struggling for the mastery. Our only hope lies in the belief that there is no such equality. Let him who has seized the helm keep it: if he be an able helmsman, he will keep us in smooth water;—and it is no longer time for us to ask how he got his commission; let us be thankful that he happens to be of the same lineage as those to whose charge we have for so many ages committed the safety of our bark."

I believe my countenance expressed my astonishment; for the old gentleman smiled and said,

"Do I frighten you with my revolutionary principles?"

"Indeed, you surprise me a little," I replied: "I should have thought that the rights of a legitimate monarch would have been in your opinion indefeasible."

"Where is the law, my good lady, that may control necessity?... I speak not of my own feelings, or of those of the few who were born like myself in another era. Very terrible convulsions have passed over France, and perhaps threaten the rest of Europe. I have for many years stood apart and watched the storm; and I am quite sure, and find much comfort in the assurance, that the crimes and passions of men cannot change the nature of things. They may produce much misery, they may disturb and confuse the peaceful current of events; but man still remains as he was, and will seek his safety and his good, where he has ever found them—under the shelter of power."

"There, indeed, I quite agree with you. But surely the more lawful and right the power is, the more likely it must be to remain tranquil and undisputed in its influence."

"France has no longer the choice," said he, interrupting me abruptly. "I speak but as a looker-on; my political race is ended; I have more than once sworn allegiance to the elder branch of the house of Bourbon, and certainly nothing would tempt me to hold office or take oath under any other. But do you think it would be the duty of a Frenchman who has three grandsons native to the soil of France,—do you really think it the duty of such a one to invoke civil war upon the land of his fathers, and remembering only his king, to forget his country? I will not tell you, that if I could wake to-morrow morning and find a fifth Henry peacefully seated on the throne of his fathers, I might not rejoice; particularly if I were sure that he would be as likely to keep the naughty boys of Paris in order as I think his cousin Philippe is. Were there profit in wishing, I would wish for France a government so strong as should effectually prevent her from destroying herself; and that government should have at its head a king whose right to reign had come to him, not by force of arms, but by the will of God in lawful succession. But when we mortals have a wish, we may be thankful if the half of it be granted;—and, in truth, I think that I have the first and better half of mine to rejoice in. There is a stout and sturdy strength in the government of King Philippe, which gives good hope that France may recover under its protection from her sins and her sorrows, and again become the glory of her children."

So saying, M. de B—— rose to leave me, and putting out his hand in the English fashion, added, "I am afraid you do not like me so well as you did.... I am no longer a true and loyal knight in your estimation ... but something, perhaps, very like a rebel and a traitor?... Is it not so?"

I hardly knew how to answer him. He certainly had lost a good deal of that poetical elevation of character with which I had invested him; yet there was a mixture of honesty and honour in his frankness that I could not help esteeming. I thanked him very sincerely for the openness with which he had spoken, but confessed that I had not quite made up my mind to think that expediency was the right rule for human actions. It certainly was not the noblest, and therefore I was willing to believe that it was not the best.

"I must go," said he, looking at his watch, "for it is my hour of dining, or I think I could dispute with you a little upon your word *expediency*. Whatever is really expedient for us to do—that is, whatever is best for us in the situation in which we are actually placed, is really right. Adieu!—I shall present myself again ere long; and if you admit me, I shall be thankful."

So saying, he departed,—leaving us all, I believe, a little less in alt about him than before, but certainly with no inclination to shut our doors against him.

## LETTER XXII.

Père Lachaise.—Mourning in public.—Defacing the Tomb of Abelard and Eloïsa.—Baron Munchausen.—Russian Monument.—Statue of Manuel.

Often as I have visited the enclosure of Père Lachaise, it was with feelings of renewed curiosity and interest that I yesterday accompanied thither those of my party who had not yet seen it. I was well pleased to wander once more through the cypress alleys, now grown into fine gloomy funereal shades, and once more to feel that wavering sort of emotion which I always experience there;—one moment being tempted to smile at the fantastic manner in which affection has been manifested,—and the next, moved to tears by some touch of tenderness, that makes itself felt even amidst the vast collection of childish superstitions with which the place abounds.

This mournful garden is altogether a very solemn and impressive spectacle. What a world of mortality does one take in at one glance! It will set one thinking a little, however fresh from the busy idleness of Paris,—of Paris, that antidote to all serious thought, that especial paradise for the worshippers of Sans Souci.

A profusion of spring flowers are at this season hourly shedding their blossoms over every little cherished enclosure. There is beauty, freshness, fragrance on the surface.... It is a fearful contrast!

I do not remember any spot, either in church or churchyard, where the unequal dignity of the memorials raised above the dust which lies so very equally beneath them all is shown in a manner to strike the heart so forcibly as it does at Père Lachaise. Here, a shovelful of weeds have hardly room to grow; and there rises a costly pile, shadowing its lowly neighbour. On this side the narrow path, sorrow is wrapped round and hid from notice by the very poverty that renders it more bitter; while, on the other, wealth, rank, and pride heap decorations over the worthless clay, striving vainly to conceal its nothingness. It is an epitome of the world they have left: remove the marble and disturb the turf, human nature will be found to wear the same aspect under both.

Many groups in deep mourning were wandering among the tombs; so many indeed, that when we turned aside from one, with the reverence one always feels disposed to pay to sorrow, we were sure to encounter another. This manner of lamenting in public seems so strange to us! How would it be for a shy English mother, who sobs inwardly and hides the aching sorrow in her heart's core,—how would she bear to bargain at the public gate for a pretty garland, then enter amidst an idle throng, with the toy hanging on her finger, and, before the eyes of all who choose to look, suspend it over the grave of her lost child? An Englishwoman surely must lose her reason either before or after such an act;—if it were not the effect of madness, it would be the cause of it. Yet such is the effect of habit, or rather of the different tone of manners and of mind here, that one may daily and hourly see parents, most devoted to their children during their lives, and most heart-broken when divided from them by death, perform with streaming eyes these public lamentations.

It is nevertheless impossible, let the manner of it differ from our own as much as it may, to look at the freshly-trimmed flowers, the garlands, and all the pretty tokens of tender care which meet the eye in every part of this widespread mass of mortal nothingness, without feeling that real love and real sorrow have been at work.

One small enclosure attracted my attention as at once the most *bizarre* and the most touching of all. It held the little grassy tomb of a young child, planted round with choice flowers; and at its head rose a semicircular recess, containing, together with a crucifix and other religious emblems, several common playthings, which had doubtless been the latest joy of the lost darling. His age was stated to have been three years, and he was mourned as the first and only child after twelve years of marriage.

Below this melancholy statement was inscribed—

"Passans! priez pour sa malheureuse mère!"

Might we not say, that

Thought and affliction, passion, death itself,

They turn to favour and to prettiness?

It would, I believe, be more just, as well as more generous, instead of accusing the whole nation of being the victims of affectation instead of sorrow under every affliction that death can cause, to believe that they feel quite as sincerely as ourselves; though they have certainly a very different way of showing it.

I wish they, whoever they are, who had the command of such matters, would have let the curious tomb of Abelard and Eloïsa remain in decent tranquillity in its original position. Nothing can assimilate worse than do its Gothic form and decorations with every object around it. The paltry plaster tablet too, that has been stuck upon it for the purpose of recording the history of the tomb rather than of those who lie buried in it, is in villanously bad taste; and we can only hope that the elements will complete the work they have begun, and then this barbarous defacing will crumble away before our grandchildren shall know anything about it.

The thickly-planted trees and shrubs have grown so rapidly, as in many places to make it difficult to pass through them; and the ground appears to be extremely crowded nearly over its whole extent. A few neighbouring acres have been lately added to it; but their bleak, naked, and unornamented surface forbids the eye as yet to recognise this space as part of the enclosure. One pale solitary tomb is placed within it, at the very verge of the dark cypress line that marks the original boundary; and it looks like a sheeted ghost hovering about between night and morning.

One very noble monument has been added since I last visited the garden: it is dedicated to the memory of a noble Russian lady, whose long unspellable name I forget. It is of white or greyish marble, and of magnificent proportions, —lofty and elegant, yet massive and entirely simple. Altogether, it appeared to me to be as perfect in taste as any specimen of monumental architecture that I have ever seen, though it had not the last best grace of sculpture to adorn it. There is no effigy—no statue—scarcely an ornament of any kind, but it seems constructed with a view to unite equally the appearance of imposing majesty and enduring strength. This splendid mausoleum stands towards the top of the garden, and forms a predominating and very beautiful object from various parts of it.

Among the hundreds of names which one reads in passing,—I hardly know why, for they certainly convey but small interest to the mind,—we met with that of the *Baron Munchausen*. It was a small and unpretending-looking stone, but bore a host of blazing titles, by which it appears that this Baron, whom I, and all my generation, I believe, have ever looked upon as an imaginary personage, was in fact something or other very important to somebody or other who was very powerful. Why his noble name has been made such use of among us, I cannot imagine.

In the course of our wanderings we came upon this singular inscription:—

"Ci-gît Caroline,"—(I think the name is Caroline,)—"fille de Mademoiselle Mars."

Is it not wonderful what a difference twenty-one miles of salt-water can make in the ways and manners of people?

There are not many statues in the cemetery, and none of sufficient merit to add much to its embellishment; but there is one recently placed there, and standing loftily predominant above every surrounding object, which is strongly indicative of the period of its erection, and of the temper of the people to whom it seems to address itself. This is a colossal figure of Manuel. The countenance is vulgar, and the expression of the features violent and exaggerated: it might stand as the portrait of a bold factious rebel for ever.

## LETTER XXIII.

Remarkable People.—Distinguished People.—Metaphysical Lady.

Last night we passed our *soirée* at the house of a lady who had been introduced to me with this recommendation:—"You will be certain of meeting at Madame de V——'s many REMARKABLE PEOPLE."

This is, I think, exactly the sort of introduction which would in any city give the most piquant interest to a new acquaintance; but it does so particularly at Paris; for this attractive capital draws its collection of remarkable people from a greater variety of nations, classes, and creeds, than any other.

Nevertheless, this term "remarkable people" must not be taken too confidently to mean individuals so distinguished that all men would desire to gaze upon them; the phrase varying in its value and its meaning according to the feelings, faculties, and station of the speaker.

Everybody has got his or her own "remarkable people" to introduce to you; and I have begun to find out, among the houses that are open to me, what species of "remarkable people" I am likely to meet at each.

When Madame A—— whispers to me as I enter her drawing-room—"Ah! vous voilà! c'est bon; j'aurais été bien fâchée si vous m'aviez manquée; il y a ici, ce soir, une personne bien remarquable, qu'il faut absolument vous présenter,"—I am quite sure that I shall see some one who has been a marshal, or a duke, or a general, or a physician, or an actor, or an artist, to Napoleon.

But if it were Madame B—— who said the same thing, I should be equally certain that it must be a comfortable-looking doctrinaire, who was, had been, or was about to be in place, and who had made his voice heard on the winning side.

Madame C——, on the contrary, would not deign to bestow such an epithet on any one whose views and occupations were so earthward. It could only be some philosopher, pale with the labour of reconciling paradoxes or discovering a new element.

My charming, quiet, graceful, gentle Madame D—— could use it only when speaking of an ex-chancellor, or chamberlain, or friend, or faithful servant of the exiled dynasty.

As for the tall dark-browed Madame E——, with her thin lips and sinister smile, though she professes to hold a *salon* where talent of every party is welcome, she never cares much, I am very sure, for any remarkableness that is not connected with the great and immortal mischief of some revolution. She is not quite old enough to have had anything to do with the first; but I have no doubt that she was very busy during the last, and I am positive that she will never know peace by night or day till another can be got up. If her hopes fail on this point, she will die of atrophy; for nothing affords her nourishment but what is mixed up with rebellion against constituted authority.

I know that she dislikes me; and I suspect I owe the honour of being admitted to appear in her presence solely to her determination that I should hear everything that she thinks it would be disagreeable for me to listen to. I believe she fancies that I do not like to meet Americans; but she is as much mistaken in this as in most other of her speculations.

I really never saw or heard of any fanaticism equal to that, with which this lady worships destruction. That whatever is, is wrong, is the rule by which her judgment is guided in all things. It is enough for her that a law on any point is established, to render the thing legalised detestable; and were the republic about which she raves, and of which she knows as much as her lap-dog, to be established throughout France to-morrow, I am quite persuaded that we should have her embroidering a regal robe for the most legitimate king she could find, before next Monday.

Madame F——'s *remarkables* are almost all of them foreigners of the philosophic revolutionary class; any gentry that are not particularly well off at home, and who would rather prefer being remarkable and remarked a few hundred miles from their own country than in it.

Madame G——'s are chiefly musical personages. "Croyez-moi, madame," she says, "il n'y a que lui pour toucher le piano.... Vous n'avez pas encore entendu Mademoiselle Z——.... Quelle voix superbe!... Elle fera, j'en suis sûre, une fortune immense à Londres."

Madame H——'s acquaintance are not so "remarkable" for anything peculiar in each or any of them, as for being in all things exactly opposed to each other. She likes to have her parties described as "Les soirées antithestiques de Madame H——," and has a peculiar sort of pleasure in seeing people sitting side by side on her hearth-rug, who would be very likely to salute each other with a pistol-shot were they to meet elsewhere. It is rather a singular device for arranging a sociable party; but her*soirées* are very delightful *soirées*, for all that.

Madame J——'s friends are not "remarkable;" they are "distinguished." It is quite extraordinary what a number of distinguished individuals I have met at her house.

But I must not go through the whole alphabet, lest I should tire you. So let me return to the point from whence I set out, and take you with me to Madame de V——'s *soirée*. A large party is almost always a sort of lottery, and your good or bad fortune depends on the accidental vicinity of pleasant or unpleasant neighbours.

I cannot consider myself to have gained a prize last night; and Fortune, if she means to make things even, must place me to-night next the most agreeable person in Paris. I really think that should the same evil chance that beset me yesterday pursue me for a week, I should leave the country to escape from it. I will describe to you the manner of my torment as well as I can, but must fail, I think, to give you an adequate idea of it.

A lady I had never seen before walked across the room to me last night soon after I entered it, and making prisoner of Madame de V—— in the way, was presented to me in due form. I was placed on a sofa by an old gentleman with whom we have formed a great friendship, and for whose conversation I have a particular liking: he had just seated himself beside me, when my new acquaintance dislodged him by saying, as she attempted to squeeze herself in between us, "Pardon, monsieur; ne vous dérangez pas! ... mais si madame voulait bien me permettre" ... and before she could finish her speech, my old acquaintance was far away and my new one close beside me.

She began the conversation by some very obliging assurances of her wish to make my acquaintance. "I want to discuss with you," said she. I bowed, but trembled inwardly, for I do not like discussions, especially with "remarkable" ladies. "Yes," she continued, "I want to discuss with you many topics of vital interest to us all—topics on which I believe we now think differently, but on which I feel quite sure that we should agree, would you but listen to me."

I smiled and bowed, and muttered something civil, and looked as much pleased as I possibly could,—and recollected, too, how large Paris was, and how easy it would be to turn my back upon conviction, if I found that I could not face it agreeably. But, to say truth, there was something in the eye and manner of my new friend that rather alarmed me. She is rather pretty, nevertheless; but her bright eyes are never still for an instant, and she is one of those who aid the power of speech by that of touch, to which she has incessant recourse. Had she been a man, she would have seized all her friends by the button: but as it is, she can only lay her fingers with emphasis upon your arm, or grasp a handful of your sleeve, when she sees reason to fear that your attention wanders.

"You are a legitimatist! ... quel dommage! Ah! you smile. But did you know the incalculable injury done to the intellect by putting chains upon it!... My studies, observe, are confined almost wholly to one subject,—the philosophy of the human mind. Metaphysics have been the great object of my life from a very early age." (I should think she was now about seven or eight-and-twenty.) "Yet sometimes I have the weakness to turn aside from this noble pursuit to look upon the troubled current of human affairs that is rolling past me. I do not pretend to enter deeply into politics—I have no time for it; but I see enough to make me shrink from despotism and legitimacy. Believe me, it cramps the mind; and be assured that a constant succession of political changes keeps the faculties of a nation on the *qui vive*, and, abstractedly considered as a mental operation, must be incalculably more beneficial than the half-dormant state which takes place after any long continuance in one position, let it be what it may."

She uttered all this with such wonderful rapidity, that it would have been quite impossible for me to have made any observation upon it as she went along, if I had been ever so much inclined to do so. But I soon found that this was not expected of me.

"'Twas hers to speak, and mine to hear;"

and I made up my mind to listen as patiently as I could till I should find a convenient opportunity for changing my place.

At different times, and in different climes, I have heretofore listened to a good deal of nonsense, certainly; but I assure you I never did nor ever can expect again to hear such a profusion of wild absurdity as this lady uttered. Yet I am told that she has in many circles the reputation of being a woman of genius. It would be but a vain attempt did I endeavour to go on remembering and translating all she said; but some of her speeches really deserve recording.

After she had run her tilt against authority, she broke off, exclaiming—

"Mais, après tout,—what does it signify?... When you have once devoted yourself to the study of the soul, all these little distinctions do appear so trifling!... I have given myself wholly to the study of the soul; and my life passes in a series of experiments, which, if I do not wear myself out here," putting her hand to her forehead, "will, I think, eventually lead me to something important."

As she paused for a moment, I thought I ought to say something, and therefore asked her of what nature were the experiments of which she spoke. To which she replied—

"Principally in comparative anatomy. None but an experimentalist could ever imagine what extraordinary results arise from this best and surest mode of investigation. A mouse, for instance.... Ah, madame! would you believe it possible that the formation of a mouse could throw light upon the theory of the noblest feeling that warms the heart of man—even upon valour? It is true, I assure you: such are the triumphs of science. By watching the pulsations of that *chétif* animal," she continued, eagerly laying hold of my wrist, "we have obtained an immense insight into the most interesting phenomena of the passion of fear."

At this moment my old gentleman came back to me, but evidently without any expectation of being able to resume his seat. It was only, I believe, to see how I got on with my metaphysical neighbour. There was an infinite deal of humour in the glance he gave me as he said, "Eh bien, Madame Trollope, est-ce que Madame —— vous a donné l'ambition de la suivre dans ses sublimes études?"

"I fear it would prove beyond my strength," I replied. Upon which Madame —— started off anew in praise of *her* science—"the only science worthy the name; the science...."

Here my old friend stole off again, covered by an approaching tray of ices; and I soon after did the same; for I had been busily engaged all day, and I was weary,—so weary that I dreaded dropping to sleep at the very instant that Madame —— was exerting herself to awaken me to a higher state of intelligence.

I have not, however, told you one tenth part of the marvellous absurdities she poured forth; yet I suspect I have told you enough. I have never before met anything so pre-eminently ridiculous as this: but upon my saying so to my old friend as I passed him near the door, he assured me that he knew another lady, whose mania was education, and whose doctrines and manner of explaining them were decidedly more absurd than Madame ——'s philosophy of the soul.

"Be not alarmed, however; I shall not bestow her upon you, for I intend most carefully to keep out of her way. Do you know of any English ladies thus devoted to the study of the soul?"... I am sincerely happy to say that I do not.

## LETTER XXIV.

Expedition to the Luxembourg.—No admittance for Females.—Portraits of "Henri."—Republican Costume.—Quai Voltaire.—Mural Inscriptions.—Anecdote of Marshal Lobau.—Arrest.

Ever since the trials at the Luxembourg commenced, we have intended to make an excursion thither, in order to look at the encampment in the garden, at the military array around the palace, and, in short, to see all that is visible for female eyes in the general aspect of the place, so interesting at the present moment from the important business going on there.

I have done all that could be done to obtain admission to the Chamber during their sittings, and have not been without friends who very kindly interested themselves to render my efforts successful—but in vain; no ladies have been permitted to enter. Whether the feminine regrets have been lessened or increased by the daily accounts that are published of the outrageous conduct of the prisoners, I will not venture to say. *C'est égal*; get in we cannot, whether we wish it or not. It is said, indeed, that in one of the tribunes set apart for the public, a small white hand has been seen to caress some jet-black curls upon the head of a boy; and it was said, too, that the boy called himself George S——d: but I have heard of no other instance of any one not furnished with that important symbol of prerogative, *une barbe au menton*, who has ventured within the proscribed limits.

Our humble-minded project of looking at the walls which enclose the blustering rebels and their patient judges has been at length happily accomplished, and not without affording us considerable amusement.

In addition to our usual party, we had the pleasure of being accompanied by two agreeable Frenchmen, who promised to explain whatever signs and symbols might meet our eyes but mock our comprehension. As the morning was delightful, we agreed to walk to the place of our destination, and repose ourselves as much as the tossings of a *fiacre* would permit on the way home.

That our route lay through the Tuileries Gardens was one reason for this arrangement; and, as usual, we indulged ourselves for a delightful half-hour by sitting under the trees.

Whenever six or eight persons wish to converse together—not in *tête-à-tête*, but in a general confabulation, I would recommend exactly the place we occupied for the purpose, with the chairs of the party drawn together, not spread into a circle, but collected in a group, so that every one can hear, and every one can be heard.

Our conversation was upon the subject of various prints which we had seen exposed upon the Boulevards as we passed; and though our two Frenchmen were excellent friends, it was very evident that they did not hold the same opinions in politics;—so we had some very pleasant sparring.

We have been constantly in the habit of remarking a variety of portraits of a pretty, elegant-looking youth, sometimes totally without letters—and yet they were not proofs, excepting of an antique loyalty,—sometimes with the single word "Henri!"—sometimes with a sprig of the pretty weed we call "Forget-me-not,"—and sometimes with the name of "Le Duc de Bordeaux." As we passed one of the cases this morning which stand out before a large shop on the Boulevards, I remarked a new one: it was a pretty lithographic print, and being very like an original miniature which had been kindly shown me during a visit I paid in the Faubourg St. Germain, I stopped to buy it, and writing my name on the envelope, ordered it to be sent home.

M. P——, the gentleman who was walking beside me when I stopped, confirmed my opinion that it was a likeness, by his personal knowledge of the original; and it was not difficult to perceive, though he spoke but little on the subject, that an affectionate feeling for "THE CAUSE" and its young hero was at his heart.

M. de L——, the other gentleman who had joined our party, was walking behind us, and came up as I was making my purchase. He smiled. "I see what you are about," said he: "if you and P—— continue to walk together, I am sure you will plot some terrible treason before you get to the Luxembourg."

When we were seated in the Tuileries Gardens, M. de L—— renewed his attack upon me for what he called my seditious conduct in having encouraged the vender of a prohibited article, and declared that he thought he should but do his duty if he left M. P—— and myself in safe custody among the other rebellious characters at the Luxembourg.

"My sedition," replied M. P——, "is but speculative. The best among us now can only sigh that things are not quite as they should be, and be thankful that they are not quite as bad as they might be."

"I rejoice to find that you allow so much, mon cher," replied his friend. "Yes, I think it might be worse; par exemple, if such gentry as those yonder were to have their way with us."

He looked towards three youths who were stalking up the walk before us with the air of being deeply intent on some business of dire import. They looked like walking caricatures—and in truth they were nothing else.

They were republicans. Similar figures are constantly seen strutting upon the Boulevards, or sauntering, like those before us, in the Tuileries, or hovering in sinister groups about the Bois de Boulogne, each one believing himself to bear the brow of a Brutus and the heart of a Cato. But see them where or when you will, they take good care to be unmistakable; there is not a child of ten years old in Paris who cannot tell a republican when he sees him. In several print-shops I have seen a key to their mystical toilet which may enable the ignorant to read them right. A hat, whose crown if raised for a few inches more would be conical, is highest in importance, as in place; and the shade of Cromwell may perhaps glory in seeing how many desperate wrongheads still mimic his beaver. Then come the long and matted locks, that hang in heavy ominous dirtiness beneath it. The throat is bare, at least from linen; but a plentiful and very disgusting profusion of hair supplies its place. The waistcoat, like the hat, bears an immortal name—"Gilet à la Robespierre" being its awful designation; and the extent of its wide-spreading lapels is held to be a criterion of the expansive principles of the wearer. *Au reste*, a general air of grim and savage blackguardism is all that is necessary to make up the outward man of a republican of Paris in 1835.

But, oh! the grimaces by which I have seen human face distorted by persons wearing this masquerading attire! Some roll their eyes and knit their brows as if they would bully the whole universe; others fix their dark glances on the ground in fearful meditation; while other some there be who, while gloomily leaning against a statue or a tree, throw such terrific meaning into their looks as might naturally be interpreted into the language of the witches in Macbeth—

"We must, we will—we must, we will

Have much more blood,—and become worse,

And become worse" ... &c. &c.

The three young men who had just passed us were exactly of this stamp. Our legitimate friend looked after them and laughed heartily.

"C'est à nous autres, mon cher," said de L——, "to enjoy that sight. You and yours would have but small reason to laugh at such as these, if it were not the business of us and ours to take care that they should do you no harm. You may thank the eighty thousand National Guards of Paris for the pleasure of quizzing with such a complacent feeling of security these very ferocious-looking persons."

"For that I thank them heartily," replied M. P——; "only I think the business would have been quite as well done if those who performed it had the right to do so."

"Bah! Have you not tried, and found you could make nothing of it?"

"I think not, my friend," replied the legitimatist: "we were doing very well, and exerting ourselves to keep the unruly spirits in order, when you stepped in, and promised all the naughty boys in Paris a holiday if they would but make you master. They did make you master—they have had their holiday, and now...."

"And now ..." said I, "what will come next?"

Both the gentlemen answered me at once.

"Riots," said the legitimatist.

"Good order," said the doctrinaire.

We proceeded in our walk, and having crossed the Pont Royal, kept along the Quai Voltaire, to avoid the Rue du Bac; as we all agreed that, notwithstanding Madame de Staël spoke so lovingly of it at a distance, it was far from agreeable when near.

Were it not for a sort of English horror of standing before shop-windows, the walking along that Quai Voltaire might occupy an entire morning. From the first wide-spread display of "remarkable people" for five sous apiece—and there are heads among them which even in their rude lithography would repay some study—from this five-sous gallery of fame to the entrance of the Rue de Seine, it is an almost uninterrupted show;—books, old and new—rich, rare, and worthless; engravings that may be classed likewise,—*articles d'occasion* of all sorts,—but, far above all the rest, the most glorious museums of old carving and gilding, of monstrous chairs, stupendous candlesticks, grotesque timepieces, and ornaments without a name, that can be found in the world. It is here that the wealthy fancier of the massive splendour of Louis Quinze comes with a full purse, and it is hence that beyond all hope he departs with a light one. The present royal family of France, it is said, profess a taste for this princely but ponderous style of decoration; and royal carriages are often seen to stop at the door of *magasins* so heterogeneous in their contents as to admit all titles excepting only that of "*magasin de nouveautés*," but having at the first glance very greatly the air of a pawnbroker's shop.

During this lounge along the Quai Voltaire, I saw for the first time some marvellously uncomely portraits, with the names of each inscribed below, and a running title for all, classing them *en masse* as "*Les Prévenus d'Avril.*" If these be faithful portraits, the originals are to be greatly pitied; for they seem by nature predestined to the evil work they have been about. Every one of them looks

"Worthy to be a rebel, for to that

The multiplying villanies of nature

Do swarm upon him."

It should seem that the materials for rebellion were in Shakspeare's days much of the same kind as they are in ours. If these be portraits, the originals need have no fear of the caricaturist before their eyes—their "villanies of nature" could hardly be exaggerated; and I should think that H. B. himself would try his pencil upon them in vain.

On the subject which the examination of these *prévenus d'Avril* naturally led to, our two French friends seemed to be almost entirely of the same opinion; the legitimatist confessing that "any king was better than none," and the doctrinaire declaring that he would rather the country should have gone without the last revolution, glorious and immortal as it was, than that it should be exposed to another, especially such a one as MM. les Prévenus were about to prepare for them.

Being arrived at *le quartier Latin*, we amused ourselves by speculating upon the propensity manifested by very young men, who were still subjected to restraint, for the overthrow and destruction of everything that denotes authority or threatens discipline. Thus the walls in this neighbourhood abounded with inscriptions to that effect; "*A bas Philippe!*"—"*Les Pairs sont des assassins!*"—"*Vive la République!*" and the like. Pears of every size and form, with scratches signifying eyes, nose, and mouth, were to be seen in all directions: which being interpreted, denotes the contempt of the juvenile students for the reigning monarch. A more troublesome evidence of this distaste for authority was displayed a few days ago by four or five hundred of these disorderly young men, who assembling themselves together, followed with hootings and shoutings M. Royer Collard, a professor lately appointed by the government to the medical school, from the college to his home in the Rue de Provence.

Upon all such occasions, this government, or any other, would do well to follow the hint given them by an admirable manœuvre of General Lobau's, the commander-in-chief of the National Guard. I believe the anecdote is very generally known; but, in the hope that you may not have heard it, I will indulge myself by telling you the story, which amused me infinitely; and it is better that I should run the risk of your hearing it twice, than of your not hearing it at all.

A party of *les jeunes gens de Paris*, who were exerting themselves to get up a little republican *émeute*, had assembled in considerable numbers in the Place Vendôme. The drums beat—the commandant was summoned and appeared. The young malcontents closed their ranks, handled their pocket-knives and walking-sticks, and prepared to stand firm. The general was seen to dismiss an aide-de-camp, and a few anxious moments followed, when something looking fearfully like a military engine appeared advancing from the Rue de la Paix. Was it cannon?... A crowd of high-capped engineers surrounded it, as with military order and address it wheeled about and approached the spot where the rioters had formed their thickest phalanx. The word of command was given, and in an instant the whole host were drenched to their skins with water.

Many who saw this memorable rout, in which the laughing *pompiers* followed with their leather pipes the scampering heroes, declare that no military manœuvre ever produced so rapid an evacuation of troops. There is something in the tone and temper of this proceeding of the National Guard which appears to me strikingly indicative of the easy, quiet, contemptuous spirit in which these powerful guardians of the existing government contemplate its republican enemies.

Having reached the Luxembourg and obtained admission to the gardens, we again rested ourselves, that we might look about at our ease upon a scene that was not only quite novel, but certainly very singular to those who were accustomed to the ordinary aspect of the place.

In the midst of lilacs and roses an encampment of small white tents showed their warlike fronts. Arms, drums, and all sorts of military accoutrements were visible among them; while loitering troops, some smoking, some reading, some sleeping, completed the unwonted appearance of the scene.

It would have been impossible, I believe, in all France to have fixed ourselves on a spot where our two French friends would have found so many incitements to unity of opinion and feeling as this. Our conversation, therefore, was not only very amicable, but ran some risk of being dull from the mere want of contradiction; for to a hearty conscientious condemnation of the proceedings which led to this trial of the *prévenus d'Avril* there was an unanimous sentence passed *nem. con.* throughout the whole party.

M. de L—— gave us some anecdotes of one or two of the persons best known among the prisoners; but upon being questioned respecting the others, he burst out indignantly in the words of Corneille—

——"Le reste ne vaut pas l'honneur d'être nommé:

Un tas d'hommes perdus de dettes et de crimes,

Que pressent de nos loix les ordres légitimes,

Et qui désespérant de les plus éviter,

Si tout n'est renversé, ne sauraient subsister."

"Ben trovato!" exclaimed P——; "you could not have described them better—but...."

This "but" would very probably have led to observations that might have put our *belle harmonie* out of tune, or at least have produced the renewal of our peaceable sparring, had not a little bustle among the trees at a short distance behind us cut short our session.

It seems that ever since the trials began, the chief duty of the gendarmes—(I beg pardon, I should say, of *la Garde de Paris*)—has been to prevent any assembling together of the people in knots for conversation and gossipings in the courts and gardens of the Luxembourg. No sooner are two or three persons observed standing together, than a policeman approaches, and with a tone of command pronounces, "Circulez, messieurs!—circulez, s'il vous plaît." The reason for this precaution is, that nightly at the Porte St. Martin a few score of *jeunes gens* assemble to make a very idle and unmeaning noise, the echo of which regularly runs from street to street till the reiterated report amounts to the announcement of an *émeute*. We are all now so used to these harmless little *émeutes* at the Porte St. Martin, that we mind them no more than General Lobau himself: nevertheless, it is deemed proper, trumpery as the cause may be, to prevent anything like a gathering together of the mob in the vicinity of the Luxembourg, lest the same hundred-tongued lady who constantly magnifies the hootings of a few idle mechanics into an *émeute* should spread a report throughout France that the Luxembourg was besieged by the people. The noise which had disturbed us was occasioned by the gathering together of about a dozen persons; but a policeman was in the midst of the group, and we heard rumours of an *arrestation*. In less than five minutes, however, everything was quiet again: but we marked two figures so picturesque in their republicanism, that we resumed our seats while a sketch was made from them, and amused ourselves the while in fancying what the ominous words could be that were so cautiously exchanged between them. M. de L—— said that there could be no doubt that they ran thus:

"Ce soir, à la Porte St. Martin!"
Answer.--"J'y serai."

## LETTER XXV.

Chapelle Expiatoire.—Devotees seen there.—Tri-coloured flag out of place there.—Flower Market of the Madeleine.—Petites Maîtresses.

Of all the edifices finished in Paris since my last visit, there is not one which altogether pleases me better than the little "Chapelle Expiatoire" erected in memory of Louis the Sixteenth, and his beautiful but ill-starred queen.

This monument was planned and in part executed by Louis the Eighteenth, and finished by Charles the Tenth. It stands upon the spot where many butchered victims of the tyrant mob were thrown in 1793. The story of the royal bodies having been destroyed by quicklime is said to have been fabricated and circulated for the purpose of preventing any search after them, which might, it was thought, have produced a dangerous reaction of feeling among the whim-governed populace.

These bodies, and several others, which were placed in coffins, and inscribed with the names of the murdered occupants, lay buried together for many years after the revolution in a large *chantier*, or wood-yard, at no great distance from the place of execution.

That this spot had been excavated for the purpose of receiving these sad relics, is a fact well known, and it was never lost sight of from the terrible period at which the ground was so employed; but the unseemly vault continued undisturbed till after the restoration, when the bodies of the royal victims were sought and found. Their bones were then conveyed to the long-hallowed shrine of St. Denis; but the spot where the mangled remains were first thrown was consecrated, and is now become the site of this beautiful little Chapelle Expiatoire.

The enclosure in which this building stands is of considerable extent, reaching from the Rue de l'Arcade to the Rue d'Anjou. This space is lined with closely-planted rows of cypress-trees on every side, which are protected by a massive railing, neatly painted. The building itself and all its accompaniments are in excellent taste; simple, graceful, and solemn.

The interior is a small Greek cross, each extremity of which is finished by a semicircle surmounted by a semi-dome. The space beneath the central dome is occupied by chairs and benches covered with crimson velvet, for the use of the faithful—in every sense—who come to attend the mass which is daily performed there.

As long as the daughter of the murdered monarch continued to reside in Paris, no morning ever passed without her coming to offer up her prayers at this expiatory shrine.

One of the four curved extremities is occupied by the altar; that opposite to it, by the entrance; and those on either side, by two well-composed and impressive groups in white marble—that to the right of the altar representing Marie Antoinette bending beside a cross supported by an angel,—and that to the left, the felon-murdered monarch whose wretched and most unmerited destiny she shared. On the pedestal of the king's statue is inscribed his will; on that of the queen, her farewell letter to the Princess Elizabeth.

Nothing can exceed the chaste delicacy of the few ornaments admitted into the chapel. They consist only, I think, of golden candlesticks, placed in niches in the white marble walls. The effect of the whole is beautiful and impressive.

I often go there; yet I can hardly understand what the charm can be in the little building itself, or in the quiet mass performed there without music, which can so attract me. It is at no great distance from our apartments in the Rue de Provence, and a walk thither just occupies the time before breakfast. I once went there on a Sunday morning with some of my family; but then it was full —indeed so crowded, that it was impossible to see across the building, or feel the beauty of its elegant simplicity. The pale figures of the royal dead, the foully murdered, were no longer the principal objects; and though I have no doubt that all present were right loyal spirits, with whose feelings I am well enough disposed to sympathise, yet I could not read each saddened brow, and attach a romance to it, as I never fail to do during my week-day visits.

There are two ladies, for example, whom I constantly see there, ever in the same place, and ever in the same attitude. The elder of these I feel perfectly sure must have passed her youth near Marie Antoinette, for it is at the foot of her statue that she kneels—or I might almost say that she prostrates herself, for she throws her arms forward on a cushion that is placed before her, and suffers her aged head to fall upon them, in a manner that speaks more sorrow than I can describe. The young girl who always accompanies and kneels beside her may, I think, be her granddaughter. They have each of them "*Gentlewoman born*" written on every feature, in characters not to be mistaken. The old lady is very pale, and the young one looks as if she were not passing a youth of gaiety and enjoyment.

There is a grey-headed old man, too, who is equally constant in his attendance at this melancholy chapel. He might sit as a model for a portrait of *le bon vieux temps*; but he has a stern though sad expression of countenance, which seems to be exactly a masculine modification of what is passing at the heart and in the memory of the old lady at the opposite side of the chapel. These are figures which send the thoughts back for fifty years; and seen in the act of assisting at a mass for the souls of Louis Seize and his queen, produce a powerful effect on the imagination.

I have ventured to describe this melancholy spot, and what I have seen there, the more particularly because, easy as it is of access, you might go to Paris a dozen times without seeing it, as in fact hundreds of English travellers do. One reason for this is, that it is not opened to the public gaze as a show, but can only be entered during the hour of prayer, which is inconveniently early in the day.

As this sad and sacred edifice cannot justly be considered as a public building, the elevation of the tri-coloured flag upon it every fête-day might, I think, have been spared.

Another, and a very different novelty, is the new flower-market, that is now kept under the walls and columns of the majestic church of La Madeleine. This beautiful collection of flowers appears to me to produce from its situation a very singular effect: the relative attributes of art and nature are reversed;—for here, art seems sublime, vast, and enduring; while nature is small, fragile, and perishing.

It has sometimes happened to me, after looking at a work of art which raised my admiration to enthusiasm, that I have next sought some marvellous combination of mountain and valley, rock and river, forest and cataract, and felt as I gazed on them something like shame at remembering how nearly I had suffered the work of man to produce an equal ecstasy. But here, when I raised my eyes from the little flimsy crowd of many-coloured blossoms to the simple, solemn pomp of that long arcade, with its spotless purity of tint and its enduring majesty of graceful strength, I felt half inclined to scorn myself and those around me for being so very much occupied by the roses, pinks, and mignonette spread out before it.

Laying aside, however, all philosophical reflections on its locality, this new flower-market is a delightful acquisition to the Parisian *petite maîtresse*. It was a long expedition to visit the *marché aux fleurs* on the distant quay near Notre Dame; and though its beauty and its fragrance might well repay an hour or two stolen from the pillow, the sweet decorations it offered to the boudoir must have been oftener selected by the *maître d'hôtel* or the *femme de chambre* than by the fair lady herself. But now, three times in the week we may have the pleasure of seeing numbers of graceful females in that piquant species of dishabille, which, uniting an equal portion of careful coquetry and saucy indifference, gives to the morning attire of a pretty, elegant, Frenchwoman, an air so indescribably attractive.

Followed by a neat *soubrette*, such figures may now be often seen in the flower-market of the Madeleine before the brightness of the morning has faded either from their eyes, or the blossoms they so love to gaze upon. The most ordinary linen gown, made in the form of a wrapper—the hair *en papillote*—the plain straw-bonnet drawn forward over the eyes, and the vast shawl enveloping the whole figure, might suffice to make many an *élégante* pace up and down the fragrant alley incognita, did not the observant eye remark that a veil of rich lace secured the simple bonnet under the chin—that the shawl was of cashmere—and that the little hand, when ungloved to enjoy the touch of a myrtle or an orange blossom, was as white as either.

## LETTER XXVI.

Delicacy in France and in England.—Causes of the difference between them.

There is nothing perhaps which marks the national variety of manners between the French and the English more distinctly than the different estimate they form of what is delicate or indelicate, modest or immodest, decent or indecent: nor does it appear to me that all the intimacy of intercourse which for the last twenty years has subsisted between the two nations has greatly lessened this difference.

Nevertheless, I believe that it is more superficial than many suppose it to be; and that it arises rather from contingent circumstances, than from any original and native difference in the capability of refinement in the two nations.

Among the most obvious of these varieties of manner, is the astounding freedom with which many things are alluded to here in good society, the slightest reference to which is in our country banished from even the most homely class. It seems that the opinion of Martine is by no means peculiar to herself, and that it is pretty generally thought that

"Quand on se fait entendre, on parle toujours bien."

In other ways, too, it is impossible not to allow that there exists in France a very perceptible want of refinement as compared to England. No Englishman, I believe, has ever returned from a visit to Paris without adding his testimony to this fact; and notwithstanding the Gallomania so prevalent amongst us, all acknowledge that, however striking may be the elegance and grace of the higher classes, there is still a national want of that uniform delicacy so highly valued by all ranks, above the very lowest, with us. Sights are seen and inconveniences endured with philosophy, which would go nigh to rob us of our wits in July, and lead us to hang ourselves in November.

To a fact so well known, and so little agreeable in the detail of its examination, it would be worse than useless to draw your attention, were it not that there is something curious in tracing the manner in which different circumstances, seemingly unconnected, do in reality hang together and form a whole.

The time certainly has been, when it was the fashion in England, as it is now in France, to call things, as some one coarsely expresses it, *by their right names*; very grave proof of which might be found even in sermons—and from thence downwards through treatises, essays, poems, romances, and plays.

Were we indeed to form our ideas of the tone of conversation in England a century ago from the familiar colloquy found in the comedies then written and acted, we must acknowledge that we were at that time at a greater distance from the refinement we now boast, than our French neighbours are at present.

I do not here refer to licentiousness of morals, or the coarse avowal of it; but to a species of indelicacy which might perhaps have been quite compatible with virtue, as the absence of it is unhappily no security against vice.

The remedy of this has proceeded, if I mistake not, from causes much more connected with the luxurious wealth of England, than with the severity of her virtue. You will say, perhaps, that I have started off to an immense distance from the point whence I set out; but I think not—for both in France and England I find abundant reason to believe that I am right in tracing this remarkable difference between the two countries, less to natural disposition or character, than to the accidental facilities for improvement possessed by the one people, and not by the other.

It would be very easy to ascertain, by reference to the various literary records I have named, that the improvement in English delicacy has been gradual, and in very just proportion to the increase of her wealth, and the fastidious keeping out of sight of everything that can in any way annoy the senses.

When we cease to hear, see, and smell things which are disagreeable, it is natural that we should cease to speak of them; and it is, I believe, quite certain that the English take more pains than any other people in the world that the senses—those conductors of sensation from the body to the soul—shall convey to the spirit as little disagreeable intelligence of what befalls the case in which it dwells, as possible. The whole continent of Europe, with the exception of some portion of Holland perhaps, (which shows a brotherly affinity to us in many things,) might be cited for its inferiority to England in this respect. I remember being much amused last year, when landing at Calais, at the answer made by an old traveller to a novice who was making his first voyage.

"What a dreadful smell!" said the uninitiated stranger, enveloping his nose in his pocket-handkerchief.

"It is the smell of the continent, sir," replied the man of experience. And so it was.

There are parts of this subject which it is quite impossible to dwell upon, and which unhappily require no pen to point them out to notice. These, if it were possible, I would willingly leave more in the dark than I find them. But there are other circumstances, all arising from the comparative poverty of the people, which tend to produce, with a most obvious dependency of thing on thing, that deficiency of refinement of which I am speaking.

Let any one examine the interior construction of a Paris dwelling of the middle class, and compare it to a house prepared for occupants of the same rank in London. It so happens that everything appertaining to decoration is to be had *à bon marché* at Paris, and we therefore find every article of the ornamental kind almost in profusion. Mirrors, silk hangings, or-molu in all forms; china vases, alabaster lamps, and timepieces, in which the onward step that never returns is marked with a grace and prettiness that conceals the solemnity of its pace,—all these are in abundance; and the tenth part of what would be considered necessary to dress up a common lodging in Paris, would set the London fine lady in this respect upon an enviable elevation above her neighbours.

But having admired their number and elegant arrangement, pass on and enter the ordinary bed-rooms—nay, enter the kitchens too, or you will not be able to judge how great the difference is between the two residences.

In London, up to the second floor, and often to the third, water is forced, which furnishes an almost unlimited supply of that luxurious article, to be obtained with no greater trouble to the servants than would be required to draw it from a tea-urn. In one kitchen of every house, generally in two, and often in three, the same accommodation is found; and when, in opposition to this, it is remembered that very nearly every family in Paris receives this precious gift of nature doled out by two buckets at a time, laboriously brought to them by porters, clambering in *sabots*, often up the same stairs which lead to their drawing-rooms, it can hardly be supposed that the use of it is as liberal and unrestrained as with us.

Against this may be placed fairly enough the cheapness and facility of the access to the public baths. But though personal ablutions may thus be very satisfactorily performed by those who do not rigorously require that every personal comfort should be found at home, yet still the want of water, or any restraint upon the freedom with which it is used, is a vital impediment to that perfection of neatness, in every part of the establishment, which we consider as so necessary to our comfort.

Much as I admire the Church of the Madeleine, I conceive that the city of Paris would have been infinitely more benefited, had the sums expended upon it been used for the purpose of constructing pipes for the conveyance of water to private dwellings, than by all the splendour received from the beauty of this imposing structure.

But great and manifold as are the evils entailed by the scarcity of water in the bed-rooms and kitchens of Paris, there is another deficiency greater still, and infinitely worse in its effects. The want of drains and sewers is the great defect of all the cities in France; and a tremendous defect it is. That people who from their first breath of life have been obliged to accustom their senses and submit without a struggle to the sufferings this evil entails upon them,—that people so circumstanced should have less refinement in their thoughts and words than ourselves, I hold to be natural and inevitable. Thus, you see, I have come round like a preacher to his text, and have explained, as I think, very satisfactorily, what I mean by saying that the indelicacy which so often offends us in France does not arise from any natural coarseness of mind, but is the unavoidable result of circumstances, which may, and doubtless will change, as the wealth of the country and its familiarity with the manners of England increases.

This withdrawing from the perception of the senses everything that can annoy them,—this lulling of the spirit by the absence of whatever might awaken it to a sensation of pain,—is probably the last point to which the ingenuity of man can reach in its efforts to embellish existence.

The search after pleasure and amusement certainly betokens less refinement than this sedulous care to avoid annoyance; and it may be, that as we have gone farthest of all modern nations in this tender care of ourselves, so may we be the first to fall from our delicate elevation into that receptacle of things past and gone which has engulfed old Greece and Rome. Is it thus that the Reform Bill, and all the other horrible Bills in its train, are to be interpreted?

As to that other species of refinement which belongs altogether to the intellect, and which, if less obvious to a passing glance, is more deep and permanent in its dye than anything which relates to manners only, it is less easy either to think or to speak with confidence. France and England both have so long a list of mighty names that may be quoted on either side to prove their claim to rank high as literary contributors to refinement, that the struggle as to which ranks highest can only be fairly settled by both parties agreeing that each country has a fair right to prefer what they have produced themselves. But, alas! at the present moment, neither can have great cause to boast. What is good, is overpowered and stifled by what is bad. The uncontrolled press of both countries has thrown so much abominable trash upon literature during the last few years, that at present it might be difficult to say whether general reading would be most dangerous to the young and the pure in England or in France.

That the Hugo school has brought more nonsense with its mischief, is, I think, clear: but it is not impossible that this may act as an antidote to its own poison. It is a sort of humbug assumption of talent which will pass out of fashion as quickly as Morrison's pills. We have nothing quite so silly as this; but much I fear that, as it concerns our welfare as a nation, we have what is more deeply dangerous.

As to what is moral and what is not so, plain as at first sight the question seems to be, there is much that is puzzling in it. In looking over a volume of "Adèle et Théodore" the other day,—a work written expressly "*sur l'éducation*," and by an author that we must presume meant honestly and spoke sincerely,—I found this passage:—

"Je ne connais que trois romans véritablement moraux;—Clarisse, le plus beau de tous; Grandison, et Pamela. Ma fille les lira en Anglais lorsqu'elle aura dix-huit ans."

The venerable Grandison, though by no means *sans tache*, I will let pass: but that any mother should talk of letting her daughter of "dix-huit ans" read the others, is a mystery difficult to comprehend, especially in a country where the young girls are reared, fostered, and sheltered from every species of harm, with the most incessant and sedulous watchfulness. I presume that Madame de Genlis conceived that, as the object and moral purpose of these works were good, the revolting coarseness with which some of their most powerful passages are written could not lead to evil. But this is a bold and dangerous judgment to pass when the question relates to the studies of a young girl.

I think we may see symptoms of the feeling which would produce such a judgment, in the tone of biting satire with which Molière attacks those who wished to banish what might "faire insulte à la pudeur des femmes." Spoken as he makes Philaminte speak it, we cannot fail to laugh at the notion: yet ridicule on the same subject would hardly be accepted, even from Sheridan, as jesting matter with us.

"Mais le plus beau projet de notre académie,

Une entreprise noble, et dont je suis ravie,

Un dessein plein de gloire, et qui sera vanté

Chez tous les beaux-esprits de la postérité,

C'est le retranchement de ces syllabes sales

Qui dans les plus beaux mots produisent des scandales;

Ces jouets éternels des sots de tous les temps,

Ces fades lieux communs de nos méchans plaisans;

Ces sources d'un amas d'équivoques infâmes

Dont on vient faire insulte à la pudeur des femmes."

Such an academy might be a very comical institution, certainly; but the duties it would have to perform would not suffer a professor's place to become a sinecure in France.

## LETTER XXVII.

Objections to quoting the names of private individuals.—Impossibility of avoiding Politics.—*Parceque* and *Quoique*.—Soirée Antithestique.

It would be a pleasure to me to give you the names of many persons with whom I have become acquainted in Paris, and I should like to describe exactly the *salons* in which I met them; but a whole host of proprieties forbid this. Where individuals are so well known to fame as to render the echoing of their names a matter of ordinary recurrence, I can of course feel no scruple in repeating the echo—one reverberation more can do no harm: but I will never be the first to name any one, either for praise or for blame, beyond the sanctuary of their own circle.

I must therefore restrict myself to the giving you the best general idea I can of the tone and style of what I have seen and heard; and if I avail myself of the conversations I have listened to, it shall be in such a manner as to avoid the slightest approach to personal allusion.

This necessary restraint, however, is not submitted to without regret: it must rob much of what I would wish to repeat of the value of authority; and when I consider how greatly at variance my impressions are on many points to some which have been publicly proclaimed by others, I feel that I deserve some praise for suppressing names which would stamp my statements with a value that neither my unsupported assertions, nor those of any other traveller, can be supposed to bear. Those who best know what I lose by this will give me credit for it; and I shall be sufficiently rewarded for my forbearance if it afford them a proof that I am not unworthy the flattering kindness I have received.

We all declare ourselves sick of politics, and a woman's letters, at least, ought if possible to be free from this wearily pervading subject: but the describing a human being, and omitting to mention the heart and the brain, would not leave the analysis more defective, than painting the Parisians at this moment without permitting their politics to appear in the picture.

The very air they breathe is impregnated with politics. Were all words expressive of party distinctions to be banished from their language—were the curse of Babel to fall upon them, and no man be able to discourse with his neighbour,—still political feeling would find itself an organ whereby to express its workings. One man would wear a pointed hat, another a flat one; one woman would be girt with a tri-coloured sash, and another with a white one. Some exquisites would be closely buttoned to the chin, while the lapels of others would open wide in all the expansive freedom of republican unrestraint. One set would be seen adorning Napoleon's pillar with trophies; another, prostrate before the altar of the elder Bourbon's monumental chapel; a third, marshalling themselves under the bloody banner of Robespierre to the tune of "Dansons la Carmagnole;" whilst a fourth, by far the most numerous, would be brushing their national uniforms, attending to their prosperous shops, and giving a nod of good-fellowship every time his majesty the king passes by.

Some friends of mine entered a shop the other day to order some article of furniture. While they remained there, a royal carriage passed, and one of the party said—

"It is the queen, I believe?"

"Yes, sir," replied the *ébéniste*, "it is the lady that it pleases us to call the queen. We may certainly call her so if we like it, for we made her ourselves; and if we find it does not answer, we shall make another.—May I send you home this table, sir?..."

When politics are thus lightly mixed up with all things, how can the subject be wholly avoided without destroying the power of describing anything as we find it?

Such being the case, I cannot promise that all allusion to the subject shall be banished from my letters; but it shall be made as little predominant as possible. Could I indeed succeed in transferring the light tone in which these weighty matters are generally discussed to the account I wish to give you of them, I need not much fear that I should weary you.

Whether it be essentially in the nature of the people, or only a transitory feature of the times, I know not; but nothing strikes me so forcibly as the airy, gay indifference with which subjects are discussed on which hang the destinies of the world. The most acute—nay, often the most profound remarks are uttered in a tone of badinage; and the probabilities of future events, vital to the interests of France, and indeed of Europe, are calculated with as idle an air, and with infinitely more *sang froid*, than the chances at a game of *rouge et noir*.

Yet, behind this I suspect that there is a good deal of sturdy determination in all parties, and it will be long ere France can be considered as one whole and united people. Were the country divided into two, instead of into three factions, it is probable that the question of which was to prevail would be soon brought to an issue; but as it is, they stand much like the uncles and nieces in the Critic, each keeping the other two in check.

Meanwhile this temporary division of strength is unquestionably very favourable to the present government; in addition to which, they derive much security from the averseness which all feel, excepting the naughty boys and hungry desperadoes, to the disturbance of their present tranquillity. It is evident that those who do not belong to the triumphant majority are disposed for the most part to wait a more favourable opportunity of hostilely and openly declaring themselves; and it is probable that they will wait long. They know well, and are daily reminded of it, that all the power and all the strength that possession can give are vested in the existing dynasty; and though much deeply-rooted feeling exists that is inimical to it, yet so many of all parties are firmly united to prevent farther anarchy and revolution, that the throne of Louis-Philippe perhaps rests on as solid a foundation as that of any monarch in Europe: the fear of renewed tumult acts like the key-stone of an arch, keeping firm, sound, and in good condition, what would certainly fall to pieces without it.

In addition to this wholesome fear of pulling their own dwellings about their ears, there is also another fear that aids greatly in producing the same result. Many of the riotous youths who so essentially assisted in creating the confusion which ended in uncrowning one king and crowning another, are, as far as I can understand, quite as well disposed to make a row now as they were then: but they know that if they do, they will most incontestably be whipped for it; and therefore, though they pout a little in private, they are, generally speaking, very orderly in public. Every one, not personally interested in the possible result of another uproar, must rejoice at this improvement in discipline. The boys of France must now submit to give way before her men; and as long as this lasts, something like peace and prosperity may be hoped for.

Yet it cannot be denied, I think, that among these prudent men—these doctrinaires who now hold the high places, there are many who, "with high thoughts, such as Lycurgus loved," still dream of a commonwealth; or that there are others who have not yet weaned their waking thoughts from meditations on faith, right, and loyalty. But nevertheless, all unite in thinking that they had better "let things be," than risk making them worse.

Nothing is more common than to hear a conversation end by a cordial and unanimous avowal of this prudent and sagacious sentiment, which began by an examination of general principles, and the frank acknowledgment of opinions which would certainly lead to a very different conclusion.

It is amusing enough to remark how these advocates for expediency contrive each of them to find reasons why things had better remain as they are, while all these reasons are strongly tinted by their various opinions.

"Charles Dix," says a legitimate in principle, but a *juste-milieu* man in practice,—"Charles Dix has abdicated the throne, which otherwise must unquestionably be his by indefeasible right. His heir-apparent has followed the example. The country was in no state to be governed by a child; and what then was left for us, but to take a king from the same race which so for many ages has possessed the throne of France. *Louis-Philippe est roi,* PARCEQU'*il est*

Bourbon."

"Pardonnez-moi," replies another, who, if he could manage it without disturbing the tranquillity about him, would take care to have it understood that nothing more legitimate than an elective monarchy could be ever permitted in France,—"Pardonnez-moi, mon ami; *Louis-Philippe est roi,* QUOIQU'*il est Bourbon.*"

These two parties of the *Parceques* and the *Quoiques,* in fact, form the great bulwarks of King Philippe's throne; for they both consist of experienced, practical, substantial citizens, who having felt the horrors of anarchy, willingly keep their particular opinions in abeyance rather than hazard a recurrence of it. They, in truth, form between them the genuine *juste-milieu* on which the present government is balanced.

That there is more of the practical wisdom of expediency than of the dignity of unbending principle in this party, can hardly be denied. They are "wiser in their generation than the children of light;" but it is difficult, "seeing what we have seen, seeing what we see," to express any heavy sentence of reprobation upon a line of conduct which ensures, for the time at least, the lives and prosperity of millions. They tell me that my friend the Vicomte has sapped my legitimate principles; but I deny the charge, though I cannot deliberately wish that confusion should take the place of order, or that the desolation of a civil war should come to deface the aspect of prosperity that it is so delightful to contemplate.

This discrepancy between what is right and what is convenient—this wavering of principle and of action, is the inevitable consequence of repeated political convulsions. When the times become out of joint, the human mind can with difficulty remain firm and steadfast. The inconceivable variety of wild and ever-changing speculations which have long overborne the voice of established belief and received authority in this country, has brought the principles of the people into a state greatly resembling that of a wheel radiated with every colour of the rainbow, but which by rapid movement is left apparently without any colour at all.

Our last *soirée* was at the house of a lady who takes much interest in showing me "le Paris d'aujourd'hui," as she calls it. "Chère dame!" she exclaimed as I entered, "I have collected *une société délicieuse* for you this evening."

She had met me in the ante-room, and, taking my arm within hers, led me into the *salon.* It was already filled with company, the majority of which were gentlemen. Having found room for us on a sofa, and seated herself next to me, she said—

"I will present whomsoever you choose to know; but before I bring anybody up, I must explain who they all are."

I expressed my gratitude, and she began:—"That tall gentleman is a great republican, and one of the most respectable that we have left of the *clique*. The party is very nearly worn out among the *gens comme il faut*. His father, however, is of the same party, and still more violent, I believe, than himself. Heaven knows what they would be at!... But they are both deputies, and if they died to-morrow, would have, either father or son, a very considerable mob to follow them to Père Lachaise; not to mention the absolute necessity which I am sure there would be to have troops out: c'est toujours quelque chose, n'est-ce pas? I know that you hate them all—and, to say truth, so do I too;—mais, chère amie! qu'est-ce que cela fait? I thought you would like to see them: they really begin to get very scarce in *salons*."

I assured her that she was quite right, and that nothing in the whole Jardin des Plantes could amuse me better.

"Ah ça!" she rejoined, laughing; "voilà ce que c'est d'être raisonnable. Mais regardez ce beau garçon leaning against the chimneypiece. He is one of *les fidèles sans tache*. Is he not handsome? I have him at all my parties; and even the ministers' ladies declare that he is perfectly charming."

"And that little odd-looking man in black," said I, "who is he?... What a contrast!"

"N'est-ce pas? Do they not group well together? That is just the sort of thing I like—it amuses everybody: besides, I assure you, he is a very remarkable person,—in short, it is M——, the celebrated atheist. He writes for the ——. But the Institute won't have him: however, he is excessively talked of—and that is everything.... Then I have two peers, both of them highly distinguished. There is M. de ——, who, you know, is King Philippe's right hand; and the gentleman sitting down just behind him is the dear old Duc de ——, who lived ages in exile with Louis Dix-huit.... That person almost at your elbow, talking to the lady in blue, is the Comte de P——, a most exemplary Catholic, who always followed Charles Dix in all religious processions. He was half distracted, poor man! at the last revolution; but they say he is going to dine with King Philippe next week: I long to ask him if it is true, but I am afraid, for fear he should be obliged to answer 'Yes;'—that would be so embarrassing!... Oh, by the way, that is a peer that you are looking at now;—he has refused to sit on the trial.... Now, have I not done *l'impossible* for you?"

I thanked her gratefully, and as I knew I could not please her better than by showing the interest I took in her menagerie, I inquired the name of a lady who was talking with a good deal of vehemence at the opposite side of the room.

"Oh! that's a person that I always call my '*dame de l'Empire.*' Her husband was one of Napoleon's creations; and Josephine used to amuse herself without ceasing by making her talk—her language and accent are *impayables*!"

"And that pretty woman in the corner?"

"Ah! ... she is charming!... It is Madame V——, daughter of the celebrated Vicomte de ——, so devoted, you know, to the royal cause. But she is lately married to one of the present ministers—quite a love-match; which is an innovation, by the way, more hard to pardon in France than the introduction of a new dynasty. Mais c'est égal—they are all very good friends again.... Now, tell me whom I shall introduce to you?"

I selected the heroine of the love-match; who was not only one of the prettiest creatures I ever saw, but so lively, intelligent, and agreeable, that I have seldom passed a pleasanter hour than that which followed the introduction. The whole of this heterogeneous party seemed to mix together with the greatest harmony; the only cold glance I saw given being from the gentleman designated as "King Philippe's right hand," towards the tall republican deputy of whose funeral my friend had predicted such honours. The *dame de l'Empire* was indulging in a lively flirtation with one of the peers *sans tache*; and I saw the fingers of the exemplary Catholic, who was going to dine with King Philippe, in the *tabatière* of the celebrated atheist. I then remembered that this was one of the *soirées antithestiques* so much in fashion.

## LETTER XXVIII.

New Publications.—M. de Lamartine's "Souvenirs, Impressions, Pensées, et Paysages."—Tocqueville and Beaumont.—New American regulation.—M. Scribe.—Madame Tastu.—Reception of different Writers in society.

Though among the new publications sent to me for perusal I have found much to fatigue and disgust me, as must indeed be inevitable for any one accustomed for some scores of years to nourish the heart and head with the literature of the "*bon vieux temps*"—which means, in modern phrase, everything musty, rusty, rococo, and forgotten,—I have yet found some volumes which have delighted me greatly.

M. de Lamartine's "Souvenirs, Impressions, Pensées, et Paysages" in the East, is a work which appears to me to stand solitary and alone in the world of letters. There is certainly nothing like it, and very little that can equal it, in my estimation, either as a collection of written landscapes or as a memorial of poetical feeling, just sentiment, and refined taste.

His descriptions may perhaps have been, in some rare instances, equalled in mere graphic power by others; but who has painted anything which can excite an interest so profound, or an elevation of the fancy so lofty and so delightful?

Alas! that the scenes he paints should be so utterly beyond one's reach! How little, how paltry, how full of the vulgar interests of this "working-day world," do all the other countries of the earth appear after reading this book, when compared to Judea! But there are few who could visit it as Lamartine has done,—there are very few capable of feeling as he felt—and none, I think, of describing as he describes. His words live and glow upon the paper; he pours forth sunshine and orient light upon us,—we hear the gale whispering among the palm-trees, see Jordan's rapid stream rushing between its flowery banks, and feel that the scene to which he has transported us is holy ground.

The exalted tone of his religious feelings, and the poetic fervour with which he expresses them, might almost lead one to believe that he was inspired by the sacred air he breathed. It seems as if he had found the harps which were hung up of old upon the trees, and tuned them anew to sing of the land of David; he has "beheld the beauty of the Lord, and inquired in his temple," and the result is exactly what it should be.

The manner in which this most poetic of travellers, while standing on the ruins of Tyre, speaks of the desolation and despair that appear settling upon the earth in these latter days, is impressive beyond anything I know of modern date.

Had France produced no other redeeming volumes than these, there is enough within them to overpower and extinguish the national literary disgrace with which it has been reproached so loudly; and it is a comfort to remember that this work is as sure to live, as the literary labours of the diabolic school are to perish. It is perhaps good for us to read trash occasionally, that we may learn to value at their worth such thoughts as we find here; and while there are any left on earth who can so think, so feel, and so write, our case is not utterly hopeless.

Great, indeed, is the debt that we owe to an author like this, who, seizing upon the imagination with power unlimited, leads it only into scenes that purify and exalt the spirit. It is a tremendous power, that of taking us how and where he will, which is possessed by such an author as this. When it is used for evil, it resembles fearfully the action of a fiend, tempting, dragging, beckoning, cajoling to destruction: but when it is for good, it is like an angel's hand leading us to heaven.

I intended to have spoken to you of many other works which have pleased me;

but I really at this moment experience the strangest sort of embarrassment imaginable in referring to them. Many agreeable new books are lying about before me; but while my head is so full of Lamartine and the Holy Land, everything seems to produce on me the effect of platitude and littleness.

I must, however, conquer this so far as to tell you that you ought to read both Tocqueville and Beaumont on the United States. By the way, I am assured that the Americans declare themselves determined to change their line of conduct altogether respecting the national manner of receiving European sketches of themselves. This new law is to embrace three clauses. The first will enforce the total exclusion, from henceforth and for evermore, of all European strangers from their American homes; the second will recommend that all citizens shall abstain from reading anything, in any language written, or about to be written, concerning them and their affairs; and the third, in case the other two should fail, seems to take the form of a vow, protesting that they never will storm, rave, scold, or care about anything that anybody can say of them more. If this passes during the presidentship of General Jackson, it will immortalize his reign more than paying off the national debt.

Having thus, somehow or other, slipped from the Holy Land to the United States of America, I feel sufficiently subdued in spirit to speak of lesser things than Lamartine's "Pilgrimage."

On one point, indeed, a sense of justice urges me, when on the subject of modern productions, to warn you against the error of supposing that all the new theatrical pieces, which come forth here as rapidly and as brilliantly as the blossoms of the gum cistus, and which fade almost as soon, are of the nature and tendency of those I have mentioned as belonging to the Victor Hugo school. On the contrary, I have seen many, and read more, of these little comedies and vaudevilles, which are not only free from every imputation of mischief, but absolutely perfect in their kind.

The person whose name is celebrated far above all others for this species of composition, is M. Scribe; and were it not that his extraordinary facility enables him to pour forth these pretty trifles in such abundance as already to have assured him a very large fortune, which offers an excellent excuse in these *positif* times for him, I should say that he would have done better had he written less.

He has shown on several occasions, as in "L'Ambitieux," "Bertrand et Raton," &c. that he can succeed in that most difficult of tasks, good legitimate comedy, as well as in the lighter labour of striking off a sparkling vaudeville. It is certain, indeed, that, spite of all we say, and say in some respects so justly, respecting the corrupted taste of France at the present era, there never was a time when her stage could boast a greater affluence of delightful little pieces than at present.

I really am afraid to enter more at large upon this theme, from a literal *embarras de richesses*. If I begin to name these pretty, lively trifles, I shall run into a list much too long for your patience: for though Scribe is still the favourite as well as the most fertile source of these delightful novelties, there are one or two others who follow him at some little distance, and who amongst them produce such a sum total of new pieces in the year as would make an English manager tremble to think of;—but here the chief cost of bringing them out is drawn, not from the theatrical treasury, but from the ever-fresh wit and spirit of the performers.

Such an author as Scribe is a national museum of invention—a never-failing source of new enjoyment to his lively countrymen, and he has probably tasted the pleasures of a bright and lasting reputation as fully as any author living. We are already indebted to him for many charming importations; and, thanks to the Yates talent, we begin to be not unworthy of receiving such. If we cannot have Shakspeare, Racine, and Molière got up for us quite "in the grand style of former years," these bright, light, biting, playful, graceful little pieces are by far the best substitutes for them, while we wait with all the patience we can for a new growth of players, who shall give honour due to the next tragedy Miss Mitford may bestow upon us.

Another proof that it is not necessary to be vicious in order to be in vogue at Paris, and that purity is no impediment to success, is the popularity of Madame Tastu's poetry. She writes as a woman ought to write—with grace, feeling, delicacy, and piety.

Her literary efforts, however, are not confined to the "flowery path of poesy;" though it is impossible not to perceive that she lingers in it with delight, and that when she leaves it, she does so from no truant inclination to wander elsewhere, but from some better impulse. Her work entitled "Education Maternelle" would prove a most valuable acquisition to English mothers desirous themselves of giving early lessons in French to their children. The pronunciation and accentuation are marked in a manner greatly to facilitate the task, especially to a foreigner; whose greatest difficulty, when attempting to teach the language without the aid of a native master, is exactly what these initiatory lessons are so well calculated to obviate.

It is no small source of consolation and of hope, at a period when a sort of universal epidemic frenzy appears to have seized upon the minds of men, leading them to advocate as good that which all experience shows to be evil, and to give specimens of dirty delirium that might be collected in an hospital, by way of exalted works of imagination,—it is full of hope and consolation to find that, however rumour may clamour forth tidings of these sad ravings whenever they appear, fame still rests only with such as really deserve it.

Let a first-rate collector of literary lions at Paris make it known that M. de Lamartine would appear at her *soirée,* and the permission to enter there would be sought so eagerly, that before eleven o'clock there would not be standing-room in her apartments, though they might be as spacious as any the "belle ville" can show. But let it be announced that the authors of any of the obscene masques and mummings which have disgraced the theatres of France would present themselves, and depend upon it they would find space sufficient to enact the part of Triboulet at the moment when he exclaims in soliloquy,

"Que je suis grand ici!"

## LETTER XXIX.

Sunday in Paris.—Family Groups.—Popular Enjoyment.—Polytechnic Students.—Their resemblance to the figure of Napoleon.—Enduring attachment to the Emperor.—Conservative spirit of the English Schools.—Sunday in the Gardens of the Tuileries.—Religion of the Educated.—Popular Opinion.

Sunday is a delightful day in Paris—more so than in any place I ever visited, excepting Francfort. The enjoyment is so universal, and yet so domestic; were I to form my idea of the national character from the scenes passing before my eyes on that day, instead of from books and newspapers, I should say that the most remarkable features in it, were conjugal and parental affection.

It is rare to see either a man or a woman, of an age to be wedded and parents, without their being accompanied by their partner and their offspring. The cup of light wine is drunk between them; the scene that is sought for amusement by the one is also enjoyed by the other; and whether it be little or whether it be much that can be expended on this day of jubilee, the man and wife share it equally.

I have entered many churches during the hours of the morning masses, in many different parts of the town, and, as I have before stated, I have uniformly found them extremely crowded; and though I have never remarked any instances of that sort of penitential devotion so constantly seen in the churches of Belgium when the painfully extended arms remind one of the Hindoo solemnities, the appearance of earnest and devout attention to what is going on is universal.

It is not till after the grand mass is over that the population pours itself out over every part of the town, not so much to seek as to meet amusement. And they are sure to find it; for not ten steps can be taken in any direction without encountering something that shall furnish food for enjoyment of some kind or other.

There is no sight in the world that I love better than a numerous populace during their hours of idleness and glee. When they assemble themselves together for purposes of legislation, I confess I do not greatly love or admire them; but when they are enjoying themselves, particularly when women and children share in the enjoyment, they furnish a delightful spectacle—and nowhere can it be seen to greater advantage than in Paris. The nature of the people—the nature of the climate—the very form and arrangement of the city, are all especially favourable to the display of it. It is in the open air, under the blue vault of heaven, before the eyes of thousands, that they love to bask and disport themselves. The bright, clear atmosphere seems made on purpose for them; and whoever laid out the boulevards, the quays, the gardens of Paris, surely remembered, as they did so, how necessary space was for the assembling together of her social citizens.

The young men of the Polytechnic School make a prominent feature in a Paris Sunday; for it is only on the *jours de fête* that they are permitted to range at liberty through the town: but all occasions of this kind cause the streets and public walks to swarm with young Napoleons.

It is quite extraordinary to see how the result of a strong principle or sentiment may show itself externally on a large body of individuals, making those alike, whom nature has made as dissimilar as possible. There is not one of these Polytechnic lads, the eldest of whom could hardly have seen the light of day before Napoleon had left the soil of France for ever,—there is hardly one of them who does not more or less remind one of the well-known figure and air of the Emperor. Be they tall, be they short, be they fat, be they thin, it is the same,—there is some approach (evidently the result of having studied their worshipped model closely in paintings, engravings, bronzes, marbles, and Sèvres china,) to that look and bearing which, till the most popular tyrant that ever lived had made it as well known as sunshine to the eyes of France, was as little resembling to the ordinary appearance and carriage of her citizens as possible.

The tailor can certainly do much towards making the exterior of one individual look like the exterior of another; but he cannot do all that we see in the mien of a Polytechnic scholar that serves to recall the extraordinary man whose name, after years of exile and of death, is decidedly the most stirring that can be pronounced in France. Busy, important, and most full of human interest has been the period since his downfall; yet his memory is as fresh among them as if he had marched into the Tuileries triumphant from one of his hundred victories but yesterday.

O, if the sovereign people could but understand as well as read!... And O that some Christian spirit could be found who would interpret to them, in such accents as they would listen to, the life and adventures of Napoleon the Great! What a deal of wisdom they might gain by it! Where could be found a lesson so striking as this to a people who are weary of being governed, and desire, one and all, to govern themselves? With precisely the same weariness, with precisely the same desire, did this active, intelligent, and powerful people throw off, some forty years ago, the yoke of their laws and the authority of their king. Then were they free as the sand of the desert—not one individual atom of the mighty mass but might have risen in the hurricane of that tempest as high as the unbridled wind of his ambition could carry him; and what followed? Why, they grew sick to death of the giddy whirl, where each man knocked aside his neighbour, and there was none to say "Forbear!" Then did they cling, like sinking souls in the act of drowning, to the first bold man who dared to replace the yoke upon their necks; they clung to him through years of war that mowed down their ranks as a scythe mows down the ripe corn, and yet they murmured not. For years they suffered their young sons to be torn from their sides while they still hung to them with all the first fondness of youth, and yet they murmured not;—for years they lived uncheered by the wealth that commerce brings, uncheered by any richer return of labour than the scanty morsel that sustained their life of toil, and yet they murmured not: for they had once more a prince upon the throne—they had once more laws, firmly administered, which kept them from the dreaded horrors of anarchy; and they clung to their tyrant prince, and his strict and stern enactments, with a devotion of gratitude and affection which speaks plainly enough their lasting thankfulness to the courage which was put forth in their hour of need to relieve them from the dreadful burden of self-government.

This gratitude and affection endures still—nothing will ever efface it; for his military tyranny is passed away, and the benefits which his colossal power enabled him to bestow upon them remain, and must remain as long as France endures. The only means by which another sovereign may rival Napoleon in popularity, is by rivalling him in power. Were some of the feverish blood which still keeps France in agitation to be drawn from her cities to reinforce her military array, and were a hundred thousand of the sons of France marched off to restore to Italy her natural position in Europe, power, glory, and popularity would sustain the throne, and tranquillity be restored to the people. Without some such discipline, poor young France may very probably die of a plethora. If she has not this, she must have a government as absolute as that of Russia to keep her from mischief: and that she will have one or the other before long, I have not the least doubt in the world; for there are many very clever personages at and near the seat of power who will not be slow to see or to do what is needful.

Meanwhile this fine body of young men are, as I understand, receiving an education calculated to make them most efficient officers, whenever they are called upon to serve. Unfortunately for the reputation of the Polytechnic School, their names were brought more forward than was creditable to those who had the charge of them, during the riots of 1830. But the government which the men of France accepted from the hands of the boys really appears to be wiser and better than they had any right to expect from authority so strangely constituted. The new government very properly uses the strength given it, for the purpose of preventing the repetition of the excesses to which it owes its origin; and these fine lads are now said to be in a state of very respectable discipline, and to furnish no contemptible bulwark to the throne.

It is otherwise, however, as I hear, with most of the bodies of young men collected together in Paris for the purpose of education. The silly cant of republicanism has got among them; and till this is mended, continued little riotous outbreakings of a naughty-boy spirit must be expected.

One of the happiest circumstances in the situation of poor struggling England at present is, that her boys are not republican. On the contrary, the rising spirit among us is decidedly conservative. All our great schools are tory to the heart's core. The young English have been roused, awakened, startled at the peril which threatens the land of their fathers! The *penny king* who has invaded us has produced on them the effect usual on all invasions; and rather than see him and his popish court succeed in conquering England, they would rush from their forms and their cloisters to repel him, shouting, "Alone we'll do it, BOYS!"—and they would do it, too, even if they had no fathers to help them.

But I have forgotten my Sunday holiday, while talking about the gayest and happiest of those it brings forth to decorate the town. Many a proud and happy mother may on these occasions be seen leaning on the arm of a son that she is very conscious looks like an emperor; and many a pretty creature, whom her familiarity, as well as her features, proclaims to be a sister, shows in her laughing eyes that the day which gives her smart young brother freedom is indeed a *jour de fête* for her.

You will be weary of the Tuileries Gardens; but I cannot keep out of them, particularly when talking of a Paris Sunday, of whose prettiest groups they are the rendezvous: the whole day's history may be read in them. As soon as the gates are open, figures both male and female, in dishabille more convenient than elegant, may be seen walking across them in every direction towards the *sortie* which leads towards the quay, and thence onwards to *Les Bains Vigier*. Next come the after-breakfast groups: and these are beautiful. Elegant young mothers in half-toilet accompany their *bonnes,* and the pretty creatures committed to their care, to watch for an hour the happy gambols which the presence of the "chère maman" renders seven times more gay than ordinary.

I have watched such, repeatedly, with extreme amusement; often attempting to read, but never able to pursue the occupation for three-quarters of a minute together, till they at last abandon it altogether, and sit with the useless volume upon their knee, complacently answering all the baby questions that may be proposed to them, while watching with the smiling satisfaction of well-pleased maternity every attitude, every movement, and every grimace of the darling miniatures in which they see themselves, and perhaps one dearer still.

From about ten till one o'clock the gardens swarm with children and their attendants: and pretty enough they are, and amusing too, with their fanciful dresses and their baby wilfulness. Then comes the hour of early dinners: the nurses and the children retreat; and were it possible that any hour of the day could find a public walk in Paris unoccupied, it would be this.

The next change shows the gradual influx of best bonnets,—pink, white, green, blue. Feathers float onwards, and fresh flowers are seen around: gay barouches rush down the Rues Castiglione and Rivoli; cabs swing round every corner, all to deposit their gay freight within the gardens. By degrees, double, treble rows of chairs are occupied on either side of every walk, while the whole space between is one vast moving mass of pleasant idleness.

This lasts till five; and then, as the elegant crowd withdraws, another, less graceful perhaps, but more animated, takes its place. Caps succeed to bonnets; and unchecked laughter, loud with youth and glee, replaces the whispered gallantry, the silent smile, and all the well-bred ways of giving and receiving thoughts with as little disturbance to the circumambient air as possible.

From this hour to nightfall the multitude goes on increasing; and did one not know that every theatre, every guinguette, every boulevard, every café in Paris were at the same time crammed almost to suffocation, one might be tempted to believe that the whole population had assembled there to recreate themselves before the windows of the king.

Among the higher ranks the Sunday evening at Paris is precisely the same as that of any other day. There are the same number of *soirées* going on, and no more; the same number of dinner-parties, just as much card-playing, just as much dancing, just as much music, and just as much going to the opera; but the other theatres are generally left to the *endimanchés*.

You must not, however, imagine that no religious exercises are attended to among the rich and noble because I have said nothing especially about them on this point. On the contrary, I have great reason to believe that it is not alone the attractive eloquence of the popular preachers which draws such multitudes of wealthy and high-born females into the fashionable churches of Paris; but that they go to pray as well as to listen. Nevertheless, as to the general state of religion amongst the educated classes in Paris, it is quite as difficult to obtain information as it is to learn with anything like tolerable accuracy the average state of their politics. It is not that there is the least reserve or apparent hanging back when either subject is discussed; on the contrary, all seem kindly eager to answer every question, and impart to you all the information it is possible to wish for: but the variety of statements is inconceivable; and as I have repeatedly listened to very strong and positive assertions respecting the opinions of the majority, from those in whose sincerity I have perfect confidence, but which have been flatly contradicted by others equally deserving of credit, I am led to suppose that in effect the public mind is still wavering on both subjects. There is, in fact, but one point upon which I truly and entirely believe that an overwhelming majority exists,—and this is in the aversion felt for any farther trial of a republican form of government.

The party who advocate the cause of democracy do indeed make the most noise—it is ever their wont to do so. Neither the Chamber of Deputies nor the Chamber of Peers can assemble nightly at a given spot to scream "Vive le Roi!" nor are the quiet citizens, who most earnestly wish to support the existing government, at all more likely to leave their busy shops for this purpose than the members of the two Chambers are to quit their *hôtels*;—so that any attempt to judge the political feelings of the people by the outcries heard in the streets must of necessity lead to error. Yet it is of such judgments, both at home and abroad, that we hear the most.

As to the real private feelings on the subject of religion which exist among the educated portion of the people, it is still more difficult to form an opinion, for on this subject the strongest indications are often declared to prove nothing. If churches filled to overflowing be proof of national piety, then are the people pious: and farther than this, no looker-on such as myself should, I think, attempt to go.

## LETTER XXX.

Madame Récamier.—Her Morning Parties.—Gérard's Picture of Corinne.—Miniature of Madame de Staël.—M. de Châteaubriand.—Conversation on the degree in which the French Language is understood by Foreigners.—The necessity of speaking French.

Of all the ladies with whom I have become acquainted in Paris, the one who appears to me to be the most perfect specimen of an elegant Frenchwoman is Madame Récamier,—the same Madame Récamier that, I will not say how many years ago, I remember to have seen in London, the admired of all eyes: and, wonderful to say, she is so still. Formerly I knew her only from seeing her in public, where she was pointed out to me as the most beautiful woman in Europe; but now that I have the pleasure of her acquaintance, I can well understand, though you who know her only by the reputation of her early beauty may not, how and why it is that fascinations generally so evanescent are with her so lasting. She is, in truth, the very model of all grace. In person, manner, movement, dress, voice, and language, she seems universally allowed to be quite perfect; and I really cannot imagine a better mode of giving a last finish to a young lady's study of the graces, than by affording her an opportunity of observing every movement and gesture of Madame Récamier.

She is certainly a monopolist of talents and attractions which would suffice, if divided in ordinary proportions, to furnish forth a host of charming women. I never met with a Frenchman who did not allow, that though his countrywomen were charming from *agrémens* which seem peculiarly their own, they have fewer faultless beauties among them than may be found in England; but yet, as they say, "Quand une Française se mêle d'être jolie, elle est furieusement jolie." This *mot* is as true in point of fact as piquant in expression;—a beautiful Frenchwoman is, perhaps, the most beautiful woman in the world.

The perfect loveliness of Madame Récamier has made her "a thing to wonder at:" and now that she has passed the age when beauty is at its height, she is perhaps to be wondered at still more; for I really doubt if she ever excited more admiration than she does at present. She is followed, sought, looked at, listened to, and, moreover, beloved and esteemed, by a very large circle of the first society in Paris, among whom are numbered some of the most illustrious literary names in France.

That her circle, as well as herself, is delightful, is so generally acknowledged, that by adding my voice to the universal judgment, I perhaps show as much vanity, as gratitude for the privilege of being admitted within it: but no one, I believe, so favoured could, when speaking of the society of Paris, omit so striking a feature of it as the *salon* of Madame Récamier. She contrives to make even the still-life around her partake of the charm for which she is herself so remarkable, and there is a fine and finished elegance in everything about her that is irresistibly attractive: I have often entered drawing-rooms almost capable of containing her whole suite of apartments, and found them infinitely less striking in their magnificence than her beautiful little *salon* in the Abbaye-aux-Bois.

The rich draperies of white silk, the delicate blue tint that mixes with them throughout the apartment,—the mirrors, the flowers,—all together give an air to the room that makes it accord marvellously well with its fair inhabitant. One might fancy that Madame Récamier herself was for ever *vouée au blanc*, for no drapery falls around her that is not of snowy whiteness—and indeed the mixture of almost any colour would seem like profanation to the exquisite delicacy of her appearance.

Madame Récamier admits morning visits from a limited number of persons, whose names are given to the servant attending in the ante-room, every day from four till six. It was here I had the pleasure of being introduced to M. de Châteaubriand, and had afterwards the gratification of repeatedly meeting him; a gratification that I shall assuredly never forget, and for which I would have willingly sacrificed one-half of the fine things which reward the trouble of a journey to Paris.

The circle thus received is never a large one, and the conversation is always general. The first day that I and my daughters were there, we found, I think, but two ladies, and about half a dozen gentlemen, of whom M. de Châteaubriand was one. A magnificent picture by Gérard, boldly and sublimely conceived, and executed in his very best manner, occupies one side of the elegant little *salon*. The subject is Corinne, in a moment of poetical excitement, a lyre in her hand, and a laurel crown upon her head. Were it not for the modern costume of those around her, the figure must be mistaken for that of Sappho: and never was that impassioned being, the martyred saint of youthful lovers, portrayed with more sublimity, more high poetic feeling, or more exquisite feminine grace.

The contemplation of this *chef-d'œuvre* naturally led the conversation to Madame de Staël. Her intimacy with Madame Récamier is as well known as the biting reply of the former to an unfortunate man, who having contrived to place himself between them, exclaimed,—"Me voilà entre l'esprit et la beauté!"

To which bright sally he received for answer—"Sans posséder ni l'un ni l'autre."

My knowledge of this intimacy induced me to take advantage of the occasion, and I ventured to ask Madame Récamier if Madame de Staël had in truth intended to draw her own character in that of Corinne.

"Assuredly ..." was the reply. "The soul of Madame de Staël is fully developed in her portrait of that of Corinne." Then turning to the picture, she added, "Those eyes are the eyes of Madame de Staël."

She put a miniature into my hand, representing her friend in all the bloom of youth, at an age indeed when she could not have been known to Madame Récamier. The eyes had certainly the same dark beauty, the same inspired expression, as those given to Corinne by Gérard. But the artist had too much taste or too little courage to venture upon any farther resemblance; the thick lips and short fat chin of the real sibyl being changed into all that is loveliest in female beauty on the canvass.

The apparent age of the face represented in the miniature points out its date with tolerable certainty; and it gives no very favourable idea of the taste of the period; for the shock head of crisped Brutus curls is placed on arms and bust as free from drapery, though better clothed in plumpness, than those of the Medicean Venus.

As we looked first at one picture, then at the other, and conversed on both, I was struck with the fine forehead and eyes, delightful voice, and peculiarly graceful turn of expression, of a gentleman who sat opposite to me, and who joined in this conversation.

I remarked to Madame Récamier that few romances had ever had the honour of being illustrated by such a picture as this of Gérard, and that, from many circumstances, her pleasure in possessing it must be very great.

"It is indeed," she replied: "nor is it my only treasure of the kind—I am so fortunate as to possess Girodet's original drawing from Atala, the engraving from which you must often have seen. Let me show you the original."

We followed her to the dining-room, where this very interesting drawing is placed. "You do not know M. de Châteaubriand?" said she.

I replied that I had not that pleasure.

"It is he who was sitting opposite to you in the *salon*."

I begged that she would introduce him to me; and upon our returning to the drawing-room she did so. The conversation was resumed, and most agreeably —every one bore a part in it. Lamartine, Casimir Delavigne, Dumas, Victor Hugo, and some others, passed under a light but clever and acute review. Our Byron, Scott, &c. followed; and it was evident that they had been read and understood. I asked M. de Châteaubriand if he had known Lord Byron: he replied, "Non;" adding, "Je l'avais précédé dans la vie, et malheureusement il m'a précédé au tombeau."

The degree in which any country is capable of fully appreciating the literature of another was canvassed, and M. de Châteaubriand declared himself decidedly of opinion that such appreciation was always and necessarily very imperfect. Much that he said on the subject appeared incontrovertibly true, especially as respecting the slight and delicate shadows of expression of which the subtile grace so constantly seems to escape at the first attempt to convert it into another idiom. Nevertheless, I suspect that the majority of English readers —I mean the English readers of French—are more *au fait* of the original literature of France than M. de Châteaubriand supposes.

The habit, so widely extended amongst us, of reading this language almost from infancy, gives us a greater familiarity with their idiom than he is aware of. He doubted if we could relish Molière, and named Lafontaine as one beyond the reach of extra-Gallican criticism or enjoyment.

I cannot agree to this, though I am not surprised that such an idea should exist. Every English person that comes to Paris is absolutely obliged to speak French, almost whether they can or can not. If they shrink from doing so, they can have no hope of either speaking or being spoken to at all. This is alone sufficient to account very satisfactorily, I think, for any doubt which may prevail as to the national proficiency in the language. No Frenchman that is at all in the habit of meeting the English in society but must have his ears and his memory full of false concords, false tenses, and false accents; and can we wonder that he should set it down as a certain fact, that they who thus speak cannot be said to understand the language they so mangle? Yet, plausible as the inference is, I doubt if it be altogether just. Which of the most accomplished Hellenists of either country would be found capable of sustaining a familiar conversation in Greek? The case is precisely the same; for I have known very many whose power of tasting the beauty of French writing amounted to the most critical acuteness, who would have probably been unintelligible had they attempted to converse in the language for five minutes together; whereas many others, who have perhaps had a French valet or waiting-maid, may possess a passably good accent and great facility of imitative expression in conversation, who yet would be puzzled how to construe with critical accuracy the easiest passage in Rousseau.

A very considerable proportion of the educated French read English, and often appear to enter very ably into the spirit of our authors; but there is not one in fifty of these who will pronounce a single word of the language in conversation. Though they endure with a polite gravity, perfectly imperturbable, the very drollest blunders of which language is capable, they cannot endure to run the risk of making blunders in return. Everything connected with the externals of good society is held as sacred by the members of it; and if they shrink from offending *la bienséance* by laughing at the mistakes of others, they avoid, with at least an equal degree of caution, the unpardonable offence of committing any themselves.

I do not believe that it would be possible for a French person to enter into conversation merely for the pleasure of conversing, and not from the pressure of absolute necessity, unless he were certain, or at least believed himself to be so, that he should express himself with propriety and elegance. The idea of uttering the brightest or the noblest thought that ever entered a human head, in an idiom ridiculously broken, would, I am sure, be accompanied with a feeling of repugnance sufficient to tame the most animated and silence the most loquacious Frenchman in existence.

It therefore falls wholly upon the English, in this happy period of constant and intimate intercourse between the nations, to submit to the surrender of their vanity, to gratify their love for conversation; blundering on in conscious defiance of grammar and accent, rather than lose the exceeding pleasure of listening in return to the polished phrase, the graceful period, the epigrammatic turn, which make so essential a part of genuine high-bred French conversation.

But the doubts expressed by M. de Châteaubriand as to the possibility of the last and best grace of French writing being fully appreciated by foreigners, was not confined wholly to the English,—the Germans appeared to share it with us; and one who has been recently proclaimed as the first of living German critics was quoted as having confounded in his style, names found among the immortals of the French Pantheon, with those of such as live and die; *Monsieur* Fontaine, and *Monsieur*Bruyère, being expressions actually extant in his writings.

More than once, during subsequent visits to Madame Récamier, I led her to speak of her lost and illustrious friend. I have never been more interested than while listening to all which this charming woman said of Madame de Staël: every word she uttered seemed a mixture of pain and pleasure, of enthusiasm and regret. It is melancholy to think how utterly impossible it is that she should ever find another to replace her. She seems to feel this, and to have surrounded herself by everything that can contribute to keep the recollection of what is for ever gone, fresh in her memory. The original of the posthumous portrait of Madame de Staël by Gérard, made so familiar to all the world by engravings—nay, even by Sèvres vases and tea-cups, hangs in her bed-room. The miniature I have mentioned is always near her; and the inspired figure of her Corinne, in which it is evident that Madame Récamier traces a resemblance to her friend beyond that of features only, appears to be an object almost of veneration as well as love.

It is delightful to approach thus to a being that I have always been accustomed to contemplate as something in the clouds. Admirable and amiable as my charming new acquaintance is in a hundred ways, her past intimacy and ever-enduring affection for Madame de Staël have given her a still higher interest in my eyes.

## LETTER XXXI.

Exhibition of Sèvres China at the Louvre.—Gobelins and Beauvais Tapestry.—Legitimatist Father and Doctrinaire Son.—Copies from the Medicean Gallery.

We are just returned from an exhibition at the Louvre; and a very splendid exhibition it is—though, alas! but a poor consolation for the hidden treasures of the picture-gallery. Several magnificent rooms are now open for the display of works in tapestry and Sèvres porcelain; and however much we might have preferred seeing something else there, it is impossible to deny that these rooms contain many objects as wonderful perhaps in their way as any that the higher branches of art ever produced.

The copy of Titian's portrait of his mistress, on porcelain, and still more perhaps that of Raphaël's "Virgin and St. John watching the sleep of the infant Jesus," (the *Parce somnum rumpere,*) are, I think, the most remarkable; both being of the same size as the originals, and performed with a perfection of colouring that is almost inconceivable.

That the fragile clay of which porcelain is fabricated should so lend itself to the skill of the workman,—or rather, that the workman's skill should so triumph over the million chances which exist against bringing unbroken out of the fire a smooth and level *plaque* of such extent,—is indeed most wonderful. Still more so is the skill which has enabled the artist to prophesy, as he painted with his greys and his greens, that the tints which flowed from his pencil of one colour, should assume, from the nicely-regulated action of an element the most difficult to govern, hues and shades so exquisitely imitative of his great original.

But having acknowledged this, I have nothing more to say in praise of a *tour de force* which, in my opinion, can only be attempted by the sacrifice of common sense. The *chefs-d'œuvre* of a Titian or a Raphaël are treasures of which we may lawfully covet an imitation; but why should it be attempted in a manner the most difficult, the most laborious, the most likely to fail, and the most liable to destruction when completed?—not to mention that, after all, there is in the most perfect copy on porcelain a something—I am mistress of no words to define it—which does not satisfy the mind.

As far as regards my own feelings indeed, I could go farther, and say that the effect produced is to a certain degree positively disagreeable,—not quite unlike that occasioned by examining needlework performed without fingers, or watch-papers exquisitely cut out by feet instead of hands. The admiration demanded is less for the thing itself, than for the very defective means employed to produce it. Were there indeed none other, the inventor would deserve a statue, and the artist, like Trisotin, should take the air "*en carrosse doré:*" but as it is, I would rather see a good copy on canvass than on china.

Far different, however, is the effect produced by this beautiful and ingenious branch of art when displayed in the embellishment of cups and plates, vases and tea-trays. I never saw anything more gracefully appropriate to the last high finish of domestic elegance than all the articles of this description exhibited this year at the Louvre. It is impossible to admire or to praise them too much; or to deny that, wonderfully as similar manufactories have improved in England within the last thirty years, we have still nothing equal to the finer specimens of the Sèvres porcelain.

These rooms were, like every other place in Paris where human beings know that they shall meet each other, extremely full of company; and I have certainly never seen such ecstasy of admiration produced by any objects exhibited to the public eye, as was elicited by some of the articles displayed on this occasion: they are indeed most beautiful; the form, the material, the workmanship, all perfect.

The Sèvres manufactory must, I think, have some individuals attached to it who have made the theory of colour an especial study. It is worth while to walk round the vast table, or rather platform, raised in the middle of the apartment, for the purpose of examining the different sets, with a view only to observe the effect produced on the eye by the arrangement of colours in each.

The finest specimens, after the wonderful copies from pictures which I have already mentioned, are small breakfast-sets—for a *tête-à-tête*, I believe,— enclosed in large cases lined either with white satin or white velvet. These cases are all open for inspection, but with a stout brass bar around, to protect them from the peril of too near an approach. The lid is so formed as exactly to receive the tray; while the articles to be placed upon it, when in use, are arranged each in its own delicate recess, with such an attention to composition and general effect as to show all and everything to the greatest possible advantage.

Some of these exquisite specimens are decorated with flowers, some with landscapes, and others with figures, or miniatures of heads, either superlative in beauty or distinguished by fame. These beautiful decorations, admirable as they all are in design and execution, struck me less than the perfect taste with which the reigning colour which pervades each set, either as background, lining, or border, is made to harmonize with the ornaments upon it.

It is a positive pleasure, independent of the amusement which may be derived from a closer examination, to cast the eye over the general effect produced by the consummate taste and skill thus displayed. Those curious affinities and antipathies among colours, which I have seen made the subject of many pretty experimental lectures, must, I am sure, have been studied and acted upon by the *colour-master* of each department; and the result is to my feelings productive of a pleasure, from the contemplation of the effect produced, as distinct from the examination of the design, or of any other circumstance connected with the art, as the gratification produced by the smell of an orange-blossom or a rose: it is a pleasure which has no connexion with the intellect, but arises solely from its agreeable effect on the sense.

The eye seems to be unconsciously soothed and gratified, and lingers upon the rich, the soft, or the brilliant hues, with a satisfaction that positively amounts to enjoyment.

Whoever may be occupied by the "delightful task" of fitting up a sumptuous drawing-room, will do well to take a tour round a room filled with sets of Sèvres porcelain. The important question of "What colours shall we mix?" would receive an answer there, with the delightful certainty that no solecism in taste could possibly be committed by obeying it.

The Gobelins and Beauvais work for chairs, screens, cushions, and various other articles, makes a great display this year. It is very beautiful, both in design and execution; and at the present moment, when the stately magnificence of the age of Louis Quinze is so much in vogue—in compliment, it is said, to the taste of the Duc d'Orléans,—this costly manufacture is likely again to flourish.

Never can a large and lofty chamber present an appearance of more princely magnificence than when thus decorated; and the manner in which this elaborate style of ancient embellishment is now adopted to modern use, is equally ingenious and elegant.

Some political economists talk of the national advantage of decreasing labour by machinery, while others advocate every fashion which demands the work of hands. I will not attempt to decide on which side wisdom lies; but, in our present imperfect condition, everything that brings an innocent and profitable occupation to women appears to me desirable.

The needles of France are assuredly the most skilful in the world; and set to work as they are upon designs that rival those of the Vatican in elegance, they produce a perfection of embroidery that sets all competition at defiance.

In pursuing my way along the rail which encloses the specimens exhibited—a progress which was necessarily very slow from the pressure of the crowd,—I followed close behind a tall, elegant, aristocratic-looking gentleman, who was accompanied by his son—decidedly his son,—the boy "fathered himself;" I never saw a stronger likeness. Their conversation, which I overheard by no act of impertinent listening, but because I could not possibly avoid it, amused me much. I am seldom thrown into such close contact with strangers without making a fancy-sketch of who and what they are; but upon this occasion I was thrown out,—it was like reading a novel, the *dénouement* of which is so well concealed as to evade guessing. The boy and his father were not of one mind; their observations were made in the spirit of different parties: the father, I suspect, was a royalist,—the son, I am sure, was a young doctrinaire. The crowd hung long upon the spot where a magnificent collection of embroidery for the seats and backs of a set of chairs was displayed. "They are for the Duke of Orleans," said the father.

"Yes, yes," said the boy; "they are fit for him—they are princely."

"They are fit for a king!" said the father with a sigh.

The lad paused for a moment, and then said, *avec intention*, as the stage directions express it, "Mais lui aussi, il est fils de St. Louis; n'est-ce pas?" The father answered not, and the crowd moved on.

All I could make of this was, that the boy's instructor, whether male or female, was a faithful disciple of the "P<small>ARCEQU</small>'*il est Bourbon*" school; and whatever leaven of wavering faith may be mixed up with this doctrine, it forms perhaps the best defence to be found for attachment to the reigning dynasty amongst those who are too young to enter fully into the expediency part of the question.

In the last of the suite of rooms opened for this exhibition, are displayed splendid pieces of tapestry from subjects taken from Rubens' Medicean Gallery.

That the achievement of these enormous combinations of stitches must have been a labour of extreme difficulty, there can be no doubt; but notwithstanding my admiration for French needles, I am tempted to add, in the words of our uncompromising moralist, "Would it had been impossible!"

## LETTER XXXII.

Eglise Apostolique Française.—Its doctrine.—L'Abbé Auzou.—His Sermon on "les Plaisirs Populaires."

Among the multitude of friendly injunctions to see this, and to hear that, which have produced me so much agreeable occupation, I have more than once been very earnestly recommended to visit the "Eglise Apostolique Française" on the Boulevard St. Denis, for the purpose of hearing l'Abbé Auzou, and still more, that I might have an opportunity of observing the peculiarities of this mode of worship, or rather of doctrine; for, in fact, the ceremonies at the altar differ but little, as far as I can perceive, from those of the Church of Rome, excepting that the evident poverty of the establishment precludes the splendour which usually attends the performance of its offices. I have no very satisfactory data by which to judge of the degree of estimation in which this new sect is held: by some I have heard them spoken of as apostles, and by others as a Paria caste unworthy of any notice.

Before hearing M. L'Abbé Auzou, or attending the service at his church, I wished to read some of the publications which explain their tenets, and accordingly called at the little bureau behind their chapel on the Boulevard St. Denis, where we were told these publications could be found. Having purchased several pamphlets containing catechism, hymns, sermons, and so forth, we entered into conversation with the young man who presided in this obscure and dark closet, dignified by the name of "Secrétariat de l'Eglise Apostolique Française."

He told us that he was assistant minister of the chapel, and we found him extremely conversible and communicative.

The chief differences between this new church and those which have preceded it in the reform of the Roman Catholic religion, appears to consist in the preservation of the external forms of worship, which other reformers have rejected, and also of several dogmas, purely doctrinal, and wholly unconnected with those principles of church power and church discipline, the abuse of which was the immediate cause of all protestant reform.

They acknowledge the real presence. I find in the *Catéchisme* these questions and answers:

"Jésus-Christ est-il sous le pain, ou bien sous le vin?—Il est sous les deux espèces à la fois.

"Et quand l'hostie est partagée?—Jésus-Christ est tout entier en chaque partie.

"Que faut-il faire pendant le jour où l'on a communié?—Assister aux offices, et ensuite se réjouir de son bonheur avec ses parens et ses amis."

Their clergy are permitted to marry. They deny that any power of absolution rests with the priest, allowing him only that of intercession by prayer for the forgiveness of the penitent. Auricular confession is not enjoined, but recommended as useful to children. They profess entire toleration to every variety of Christian belief; but as the "Eglise Française" refuses to acknowledge dependance upon any *secte étrangère*,—by which phrase I conceive the Church of Rome to be meant,—they also declare, "d'après l'Evangile, que la religion ne doit jamais intervenir dans les gouvernemens temporels."

They recognise the seven sacraments, only modifying that of penitence, as above mentioned. They deny the eternity of punishment, but I find no mention of purgatory. They do not enjoin fasting. I find in the *Catéchisme* the following explanation of their doctrine on this head, which appears to be extremely reasonable.

"L'Eglise Française n'impose donc pas le jeûne et l'abstinence?—Non; l'Eglise Apostolique Française s'en rapporte pour le jeûne aux fidèles eux-mêmes, et ne reconnaît en aucune façon le précepte de l'abstinence; mais, plus prudente dans ses principes, elle substitue à un jeûne de quelques jours une sobriété continuelle, et remplace une abstinence périodique par une tempérance de chaque jour, de chaque année, de toute la vie."

In all this there appears little in doctrine, excepting the admission of the divine presence in the elements of the eucharist, that differs greatly from most other reformed churches: nevertheless, the ceremonies are entirely similar to those of the Roman Catholic religion.

But whatever there may be either of good or of evil in this mixture, its effect must, I think, prove absolutely nugatory on society, from the entire absence of any church government or discipline whatever. That this is in fact the case, is thus plainly stated in the preface to their published Catechism:—

"L'Eglise Apostolique Française ne reconnaît aucune hiérarchie; elle repousse en conséquence l'autorité de tout pouvoir spirituel étranger, et de tout autre pouvoir qui en dépend ou qui s'y soumet. Elle ne reconnaît d'autre autorité spirituelle que celle qu'exercerait la réunion de ses fidèles; réunion qui, suivant les principes des apôtres, constitue seule ce que de leur temps on appelait Eglise.

"Elle n'est point salariée par l'état. L'administration de ses secours spirituels est gratuite. Elle n'a de tarif, ni pour les baptêmes, ni pour les mariages, ni enfin pour les inhumations. Elle vit de peu, et s'en remet à la générosité, ou plutôt à la volonté, des fidèles.

"Ne reconnaissant pas d'hiérarchie, elle ne reconnaît pas non plus de division de territoire, soit en arrondissement, soit en paroisse: elle accueille donc tous les Chrétiens qui se présentent à elle pour mander à ses prêtres l'accomplissement des fonctions de ministres de Jésus-Christ."

The *décousu* principles of the day can hardly be carried farther than this. A rope of sand is the only fitting emblem for a congregation so constituted; and, like a rope of sand, it must of necessity fall asunder, for there is no principle of union to prevent it.

After I had finished my studies on the subject, I heard a sermon preached in the church,—not, however, by M. l'Abbé Auzou, who was ill, but by the same person with whom we had conversed at the *Secrétariat*. His sermon was a strong exposition of the abuses practised by the clergy of the Church of Rome, —a theme certainly more fertile than new.

In reading some of the most celebrated discourses of the Abbé Auzou, I was the most struck with one entitled—"Discours sur les Plaisirs Populaires, les Bals, et les Spectacles." The text is from St. Matthew,—"Come unto me all ye that labour and are heavy laden, and I will give you rest ... for my yoke is easy, and my burden is light."

In this singular discourse, among some things that are reasonable, and more that are plausible, it is impossible to avoid seeing a spirit of lawless uncontrol, which seems to breathe more of revolution than of piety.

I am no advocate for a Judaical observance of the Sabbath, nor am I ignorant of the fearful abuses which have arisen from man's daring to arrogate to himself a power vested in God alone,—the power of forgiving the sins of man. The undue authority assumed by the sovereign pontiff of Rome is likewise sufficiently evident, as are many other abuses justly reprobated in the sermons of the Abbé Auzou. Nevertheless, education, observation, and I might say experience, have taught me that religion requires and demands that care, protection, and government which are so absolutely essential to the well-being of every community of human beings who would unite together for one general object. To talk of a self-governing church, is just as absurd as to talk of a self-governing ship, or a self-governing family.

It should seem, by the reprobation expressed against the severity of the Roman Catholic clergy in these sermons, as well as from anecdotes which I have occasionally heard in society, that the Church of Rome and the Church of Calvin are alike hostile to every kind of dissipation, and that at the present moment they have many points of discipline in common—at least as respects the injunctions laid upon their congregations respecting their private conduct.

M. l'Abbé Auzou says, in speaking of revolutionary reforms,—

"Rien n'est changé dans le sacerdoce; et l'on peut dire aussi des prêtres toujours romains, qu'ils n'ont rien oublié, qu'ils n'ont rien appris. Cependant, sous le règne de Napoléon leur orgueil a fléchi devant le grand intérêt de leur réinstallation.... Aussi, au retour de leur roi légitime, cet orgueil comprimé s'est-il relevé dans toute sa hauteur. Rome a placé son trône à côté de celui d'un roi, un peu philosophe, a-t-on dit, mais perclus et impotent. Et enfin, lorsque son successeur, d'abord accueilli par le peuple, est tombé entre les mains des prêtres, ceux-ci, profitant de son âge et de sa faiblesse, ont exploité les erreurs d'une jeunesse fougueuse, qui cependant lui avaient valu le surnom de Chevalier Français. Alors nous avons vu ce roi sacrifier sa popularité à leurs exigeances; appeler toute la nation à l'expiation de ses fautes personnelles, à son repentir, à sa pénitence; et la forcer à renier, pour ainsi dire, trente ans de gloire et de liberté.... Un roi que le remords poursuit, dévore, et qui ne reconnaît d'autre recours que dans le prêtre qui l'a soumis à sa loi par la menace et la terreur de l'enfer; ce roi, sous le coup d'une absolution conditionnelle et toujours suspendue, abdique, sans le savoir, en faveur de son confesseur....

"Roi! tu languis dans l'exil, et tes fautes sont punies jusque dans les dernières générations!

"Les prêtres, les prêtres romains se sont cependant soumis à un nouveau prince, à qui la souveraineté nationale a remis le sceptre; ils prient enfin pour lui ... et l'on sait avec quelle sincérité.

"Mais, peuple, comme leur joug s'appesantit sur toi!... Dans leur fureur mal-déguisée ils le disent.... La maison du Seigneur est déserte, et tu te rues avec fureur vers les plaisirs, les fêtes, les bals et les spectacles! Anathême donc contre les plaisirs, les fêtes et les bals! Anathême contre les spectacles!

"Ne sont-ce point là, mes frères, les paroles qui tombent chaque jour menaçantes de la chaire de l'Eglise Romaine?...

"Combien notre langage sera différent! Le Dieu des Juifs est bien notre Dieu; mais sa colère a été désarmée par le sacrifice que son fils lui a offert pour notre rédemption.

"Pourquoi ce sang répandu sur la croix pour nos péchés si la satisfaction de nos besoins physiques, si nos fonctions intellectuelles, si l'entrainement des passions qui constituent notre être peuvent à chaque instant nous faire tomber dans le péché et nous précipiter dans l'abîme?

"Aussi nous vous disons dans notre chaire apostolique,—Exécutez les commandemens de Dieu, adorez et glorifiez notre Père qui est aux cieux, pratiquez la morale de l'Evangile, aimez votre prochain comme vous-mêmes, et vous aurez accompli la loi de Jésus-Christ ... et nous ajoutons,—Vous êtes membre de la société pour laquelle vous avez été créés, et cette société vous impose des devoirs; en échange elle vous procure des jouissances et des plaisirs: remplissez vos devoirs et livrez-vous ensuite sans crainte aux jouissances et aux plaisirs qu'elle vous présente. Votre participation à ces mêmes plaisirs, à ces mêmes jouissances, est encore une partie de vos devoirs, et vous aurez accompli encore une fois la loi de Jésus-Christ."

This doctrine may assuredly entitle the Eglise Apostolique Française to the appellation of a New Church.

M. l'Abbé Auzou goes on yet farther in the same strain:—

"Anathême!... Arme vieille, rouillée, émoussée, et que vous cherchez en vain à retremper dans le fiel de la colère et de la vengeance!... Anathême aux plaisirs! Et quoi! parceque Dieu a dit à notre premier père, Vous mangerez votre pain à la sueur de votre visage, l'homme serait condamné à rester toujours courbé sous le joug du travail? N'aura-t-il à espérer aucun adoucissement à ses peines?...

"Non, sans doute ... vous dira le clergé romain, puisque Dieu a consacré le septième jour au repos?

"Et quel est ce repos?

"Sera-ce celui, qu'en vous servant du bras du séculier, vous avez tenté de lui imposer par une ordonnance préscrivant de fermer tous les établissemens qui décorent notre cité, nos cafés, nos restaurans, pour ne tolérer que l'ouverture des officines du pharmacien?—ordonnance dont une caricature spirituelle a fait si prompte justice."

The following picture of a fanatical Sunday takes me back at once to America. There, however, its worst effect was to steep the senses in the unnecessary oblivion of a few more hours of sleep; but in Paris I should really expect that such restraint, were it indeed possible to impose it, would literally drive the sensitive and mobile population to madness.

"Et quel est donc ce repos?

"Sera-ce l'immobilité des corps; l'abandon de toutes nos facultés; l'oisiveté; l'ennui, compagnon inséparable de l'oisiveté; la prière; la méditation,—la méditation plus pénible pour la plupart des hommes que le travail des mains; et, enfin, vos sermons intolérans, et, qui pis est peut-être, si ennuyeux?

"Ah! imposer à l'homme un pareil repos ne serait que suspendre son travail pour lui faire porter, comme à St. Simon de Cyrène, la croix de Jésus-Christ jusqu'au sommet escarpé du Calvaire."

The Abbé then proceeds to promulgate his bull for the permission of all sorts of Parisian delights; nay, he takes a very pretty and picturesque ramble into the country, where "les jeunes garçons et les jeunes filles s'y livrent à des danses rustiques"—and, in short, gives so animated a picture of the pleasures which ought to await the Sabbath both in town and country, that it is almost impossible to read it without feeling a wish that every human being who through the six days of needful labour has been "weary worn with care" should pass the seventh amid the bright and cheering scenes he describes. But he effectually checks this feeling of sympathy with his views by what follows. He describes habitual drunkenness with the disgust it merits; but strangely qualifies this, by adding to his condemnation of the "homme dégradé qui, oubliant chaque jour sa dignité dans les excès d'une hideuse ivrognerie, *n'attend pas le jour que Dieu a consacré au repos*, à la distraction, aux plaisirs, pour se livrer à son ignoble passion," these dangerous words:—

"Mais condamnerons-nous sans retour notre frère pour un jour d'intempérance passagère, et blamerons-nous celui qui, cherchant dans le vin, ce présent du Ciel, un moment d'oubli des misères humaines, n'a point su s'arrêter à cette douce ivresse, oublieuse des maux et créatrice d'heureuses illusions?"

Is not this using the spur where the rein is most wanting? I am persuaded that it is not the intention of the Abbé Auzou to advocate any species of immorality; but all the world, and particularly the French world perhaps, is so well disposed to amuse itself *coûte qui coûte*, that I confess I doubt the wisdom of enforcing the necessity of so doing from the pulpit.

The unwise, unauthorised, and most unchristian severity of the Calvinistic and Romish priesthood may, I think, lawfully and righteously be commented upon and reprobated both in the pulpit and out of it; but this reprobation should not clothe itself in license, or in any language that can be interpreted as such. There are many, I should think, in every Christian land, both clergy and laity, but neither popish nor Calvinistic, who would shrink both from the sentiment and expression of the following passage:—

"Rappelons-nous que le patriarche Noé, lui qui planta la vigne et exprima le jus de son fruit, en abusa une fois, et que Dieu ne lui en fit point le reproche: Dieu punit, au contraire, le fils qui n'avait point caché cette faiblesse d'un père."

There is some worldly wisdom, however, in the exclamation he addresses to his intolerant brethren.

"Et vous, prêtres aveugles et impolitiques, laissez le peuple se livrer à ses plaisirs innocens; faites en sorte qu'il se contente de sa position; qu'il ne compare pas cette position pénible, douloureuse, avec l'oisiveté dans laquelle vous vivez vous-mêmes, et que vous ne devez qu'à la nouvelle dîme qui s'exprime de son front."

He then proceeds to say, that it is not the poor only who are subjected to this severity, but the rich also ... "que le prêtre de la secte romaine veut arrêter, troubler dans ses plaisirs, dans ses délassemens."... "Un repas par lequel on célèbre l'union de deux jeunes cœurs, l'union de deux familles, et dans lequel règnent la joie, *et peut-être aussi un peu plus que de la gaîté*, est l'objet de la censure inexorable de ces prêtres rigides.... Ils oublient que celui qu'ils disent être leur maître a consacré ces réunions par sa présence, et que le vin ayant manqué par le trop grand usage qu'on en avait fait, il n'en a pas moins changé l'eau en vin. Ils sont tous disposés à répondre comme ce Janséniste à qui l'on rappelait cet intéressant épisode de la vie de Jésus,—'Ce n'est pas ce qu'il a fait de mieux.'—Impie! ... tu blasphêmes contre ton maître!...

"Ah! mes frères, admirons, nous, dans la sincérité de notre cœur, cet exemple de bienveillance et de *sociabilité pratique*, et bénissons la bonté de Jésus."

Then follows an earnest defence, or rather eulogy, of dancing. But though I greatly approve the exercise for young people, and believe it to be as innocent as it is natural, I would not, were I called upon to preach a sermon, address my hearers after this manner:—

"Quant aux bals, je ne chercherai point à les excuser, à les défendre, par *des exemples puisés dans l'écriture sainte*. Je ne vous représenterai point David dansant devant l'arche.... Je ne vous le donnerai pas non plus pour modèle, à vous, jeunes gens de notre France *si polie, si élégante*, car sans doute *il dansait mal*; puisque, suivant la Bible, Michal sa femme, voyant le roi David qui sautait et dansait, se moqua de lui et le méprisa dans son cœur." There is about as much piety as good taste in this.

I have already given you such long extracts, that I must omit all he says,—and it is much in favour of this amusement. Such forbearance is the more necessary, as I must give you a passage or two more on other subjects. Among the general reasons which he brings forward to prove that fêtes and festivals are beneficial to the people, he very justly remarks that the occupation they afford to industry is not the least important, observing that the popish church takes no heed of such things; and then adds, addressing the manufacturers,—

"Et lorsque le besoin se fera sentir et pour vous et vos enfans, allez à l'Archevêché! ... à l'Archevêché! ... un jour la colère du peuple a éclaté,—

"Je n'ai fait que passer, il n'était déjà plus."...

The date which this sermon bears on its title-page is 1834; but the event to which this line from Racine alludes was the destruction of the archiepiscopal palace, which took place, if I mistake not, in 1831. If the "*il n'était déjà plus*" alludes to the palace, it is correct enough, for destruction could not have done its work better: but if it be meant to describe the fate of Monseigneur l'Archevêque de Paris, the preacher is not a prophet; for, in truth, the sacrilegious rout "n'a fait que passer," and Monseigneur has only risen higher from the blow. Public orators of all kinds should be very cautious, in these moveable times, how they venture to judge from to-day what may be tomorrow. The only oracular sentence that can be uttered at present with the least chance of success from the developement of the future is, "Who can say what may happen next?" All who have sufficient prudence to restrict their prescience to this acute form of prophecy, may have the pleasure, let come what may, of turning to their neighbours triumphantly with the question—"Did I not tell you that something was going to happen?"—but it is dangerous to be one atom more precise. Even before this letter can reach you, my friend, M. l'Abbé's interpretation of "il n'était déjà plus" may be more correct than mine. I say this, however, only to save my credit with you in case of the worst; for my private opinion is, that Monseigneur was never in a more prosperous condition in his life, and that, "as no one can say what will happen next," I should not be at all astonished if a cardinal's hat were speedily to reward him for all he has done and suffered.

I certainly intended to have given you a few specimens of the Abbé Auzou's manner of advocating theatrical exhibitions; but I fear they would lead me into too great length of citation. He is sometimes really eloquent upon the subject: nevertheless, his opinions on it, however reasonable, would have been delivered with better effect from the easy-chair of his library than from the pulpit of his church. It is not that what would be good when heard from the one could become evil when listened to from the other: but the preacher's pulpit is intended for other uses; and though the visits to a well-regulated theatre may be as lawful as eating, and as innocent too, we go to the house of God in the hope of hearing tidings more important than his minister's assurance that they are so.

## LETTER XXXIII.

Establishment for Insane Patients at Vanves.—Description of the arrangements.—Englishman.—His religious madness.

You will think perhaps that I have chosen oddly the object which has induced me to make an excursion out of town, and obliged me to give up nearly an entire day at Paris, when I tell you that it was to visit an institution for the reception of the insane. There are, however, few things which interest me more than an establishment of this nature; especially when, as in the present instance, my manner of introduction to it is such as to give me the hope of hearing the phenomena of these awful maladies discussed by those well acquainted with them. The establishment of MM. Voisin and Fabret, at Vanves, was mentioned to me as one in which many improvements in the mode of treating alienation of mind have been suggested and tried with excellent effect; and having the opportunity of visiting it in company with a lady who was well acquainted with the gentlemen presiding over it, I determined to take advantage of it. My friend, too, knew how to direct my attention to what was most interesting, from having had a relation placed there, whom for many months she had been in the constant habit of visiting.

Her introduction obtained for me the most attentive reception, and the fullest explanation of their admirable system, which appears to me to combine, and on a very large and noble scale, everything likely to assuage the sufferings, soothe the spirits, and contribute to the health of the patients.

Vanves is situated at the distance of one league from Paris, in a beautiful part of the country; and the establishment itself, from almost every part of the high ground on which it is placed, commands views so varied and extensive, as not only to render the principal mansion a charming residence, but really to make the walks and drives within the enclosure of the extensive premises delightful.

The grounds are exceedingly well laid out, with careful attention to the principal object for which they are arranged, but without neglecting any of the beauty of which the spot is so capable. They have shade and flowers, distant views and sheltered seats, with pleasant walks, and even drives and rides, in all directions. The enclosure contains about sixty acres, to every part of which the patients who are well enough to walk about can be admitted with perfect safety.

In this park are situated two or three distinct lodges, which are found occasionally to be of the greatest utility, in cases where the most profound quiet is necessary, and yet where too strict confinement would be injurious. Indeed, it appears to me that the object principally kept in view throughout all the arrangements, is the power of keeping patients out of sight and hearing of each other till they are sufficiently advanced towards recovery to make it a real pleasure and advantage to associate together.

As soon as they reach this favourable stage of their convalescence, they mix with the family in very handsome rooms, where books, music, and a billiard-table assist them to pass the hours without *ennui*. Every patient has a separate sleeping-apartment, in none of which are the precautions necessary for their safety permitted to be visible. What would wear the appearance of iron bars in every other place of the kind that I have seen, are here made to look like very neat *jalousies*. Not a bolt or a bar is perceptible, nor any object whatever that might shock the spirit, if at any time a gleam of recovered intellect should return to visit it.

This cautious keeping out of sight of the sufferers everything that might awaken them to a sense of their own condition, or that of the other patients, appears to me to be the most peculiar feature of the discipline, and is evidently one of the objects most sedulously kept in view. Next to this I should place the system of inducing the male patients to exercise their limbs, and amuse their spirits, by working in the garden, at any undertaking, however *bizarre* and profitless, which can induce them to keep mind and body healthily employed. I know not if this has been systematically resorted to elsewhere; but the good sense of it is certainly very obvious, and the effect, as I was told, is found to be very generally beneficial; though it occasionally happens that some among them have fancied their dignity compromised by using a spade or a hoe,—and then some of the family join with them in the labour, to prove that it is merely a matter of amusement: in short, everything likely to cheer or soothe the spirits seems brought into use among them.

The ground close adjoining to the house is divided into many small well-enclosed gardens; the women's apartments opening to some, the men's to others of them. In several of these gardens I observed neat little tables, such as are used in the *restaurans* of Paris, with a clean cloth, and all necessary appointments, placed pleasantly and commodiously in the shade, at each of which was seated one person, who was served with a separate dinner, and with every appearance of comfort. Had I not known their condition, I should in many instances have thought the spectacle a very pleasing one.

M. Voisin walked through all parts of the establishment with us, and there appeared to exist a perfectly good understanding between him and his patients. Among many regulations, which all appeared excellent, he told me that the friends of his inmates were permitted at all times, and under all circumstances, to visit them without any restraint whatever: an arrangement which can only be productive of confidence and advantage to all parties; as it is perfectly inconceivable that any one who had felt obliged to place an unhappy friend or relative under restraint should wish to interfere with the discipline necessary for his ultimate advantage; whereas a contrary system is likely to give occasion to constant doubts and fears on one hand, and to the possibility of ill treatment or unnecessary restraint on the other. In one of the courts appropriated to the use of such male patients as were sufficiently convalescent to permit their associating together, and amusing themselves with the different games in which they are permitted to share, we saw a young Englishman, now rapidly recovering, but who had scrawled over the walls of his own sleeping-apartment, poor fellow! with a pencil, a vast quantity of writing, almost wholly on religious subjects; proving but too plainly that he was one of the many victims of fanaticism. Every thought seemed pregnant with suffering, and sometimes bursts of agony were scrawled in trembling characters, that spoke the very extremity of terror. "Who is there can endure fire and flame for ever, for ever, and for ever?" "Death is before us—Hell follows it!" "The bottomless pit—groans—tortures—anguish—for ever!"... Such sentences as these were still legible, though much had been obliterated.

Who can wonder that a mind thus occupied should lose that fine balance with which nature has arranged our faculties, making one keep watch and ward over the other?... This poor fellow lost his wits under the process of conversion: Judgment being entirely overthrown, Imagination had vaulted into its seat, pregnant with visions black as night, dark—oh! far darker than the tomb! "palled in the dunnest smoke of hell," and armed with every image for the eternity of torture that the ingenuity of man could devise. Who can wonder at his madness? And how many crimes are there recorded in the Newgate Calendar which equal in atrocity that of so distorting a mind, that sought to raise its humble hopes towards heaven!

I felt particularly interested for this poor lunatic, both as my countryman, and the victim of by far the most fearful tyranny that man can exercise on man. Against all other injury it is not difficult to believe that a steadfast spirit can arm itself and say with Hamlet,

"I do not set my life at a pin's fee."

But against this, it were a vain boast to add,

"And for my soul, what can it do to that,

Being a thing immortal as itself?"

For, alas! it is that very immortality which gives hope, comfort, and strength under every other persecution that paralyses the sufferer under this, and arms with such horrid strength the blasphemous wretch who teaches him to turn in terror from his God.

M. Voisin told me that this unfortunate young man had been for some time daily becoming more calm and tranquil, and that he entertained not any doubt of his ultimate recovery.

Excepting this my poor countryman, the only patient I saw whose situation it was particularly painful to contemplate was a young girl who had only arrived the preceding day. There was in her eyes a restless, anxious, agitated manner of looking about on all things, and gathering a distinct idea from none—a vague uncertainty as to where she was, not felt with sufficient strength to amount to wonder, but enough to rob her of all the feeling of repose which belongs to home. Poor girl! perhaps some faltering, unfixable thought brought at intervals the figure of her mother to her; for as I looked at her pale face, its vacant expression received more than once a sad but passing gleam of melancholy meaning. She coughed frequently; but the cough seemed affected,

—or rather, it appeared to be an effort not so much required by her lungs, as by the need of some change, some relief—she knew not what, nor where nor how to seek it. She appeared very desirous of shaking off the attendance of a woman who was waiting upon her, and her whole manner indicated a sort of fretful unrest that it made one wretched to contemplate. But here again I was comforted by the assurance that there were no symptoms which forbade hope of recovery.

I remember being told, when visiting the lunatic asylum near New York, that the most frequent causes of insanity were ascertained to be religion and drunkenness. Near Paris I find that love, high play, and politics are considered as the principal causes of this calamity; and certainly nothing can be more accordant with what observation would teach one to expect than both these statements. At New York the physician told me that madness arising from excessive drinking admitted, in the great majority of cases, of a perfect cure; but that religious aberration of intellect was much more enduring.

At Paris I have heard the same; for here also it occasionally happens, though not often, that the reason becomes disturbed by repeated and frequent intoxication: but where either politics or love has taken such hold of the mind as to disturb the reasoning power, the recovery is less certain and more slow.

Dr. Voisin told me that he uniformly found the first symptoms of insanity appear in the wavering, indifferent, and altered state of the affections towards relations and friends;—apathy, coldness, and, in some cases, dislike, and even violent antipathy, being sure to appear, wherever previous attachment had been the most remarkable. They sometimes, but not very often, take capricious fits of fondness for strangers; but never with any show of reason, and never for any length of time. The most certain symptom of an approach towards recovery is when the heart appears to be re-awakened to its natural feelings and old attachments.

There was one old lady that I watched eating her dinner of vegetables and fruit at a little table in one of the gardens, who had adorned her bonnet with innumerable scraps of trumpery, and set it on her head with the most studied and coquettish air imaginable: she fed herself with the grace or grimace of a young beauty, eating grapes of a guinea a pound, from a plate of crystal, with a golden fork. I am sure she was enjoying all the happiness of feeling herself beautiful, elegant, and admired: and when I looked at the wrinkled ruin of her once handsome face, I could hardly think her madness a misfortune; for though I did not obtain any pitiful story concerning her, or any history of the cause which brought her there, I felt sure that it must in some way or other be connected with some feeling of deeply-mortified vanity: and if I am right in my conjecture, what has the world left for her equal in consolation to the wild fancies which now shed such simpering complacency over her countenance? And might we not exclaim for her in all kindness—

"Let but the cheat endure!—She asks not aught beside?"

What was passing in this poor old head, it was easy enough to guess—wild as it was, and wide from the truth. But there was another, which, though I studied it as long as I could possibly contrive to do so, wholly baffled me; and yet I would have given much to know what thoughts were flitting through that young brain.

She was a young girl, extremely pretty, with coal-black hair and eyes, and seated, quite apart from all, upon a pleasant shady bench in one of the gardens. Her face was like a fair landscape, over which passes cloud and sunshine in rapid succession: for one moment she smiled, and the next seemed preparing to weep; but before a tear could fall, her fine teeth were again displayed in an unmeaning smile. O, what could be the fleeting visions formed that worked her fancy thus? Could it be memory? Or was the fitful emotion caused by the galloping vagaries of an imagination which outstripped the power of reason to follow it? Or was it none of this, but a mere meaningless movement of the muscles, that worked in idle mockery of the intellect that used to govern them?

I have sometimes thought it very strange that people should feel such deep delight in watching on the stage the representation of the utmost extremity of human woe that the mind of man can contrive to place before them; and I have wondered more, much more, at the gathering together of thousands and tens of thousands, whenever the law has doomed that some wretched soul should be separated by the hand of man from the body in which it has sinned: but I doubt if my own intense interest in watching poor human nature when deprived of reason is not stranger still. I can in no way account for it; but so it is. I can never withdraw myself from the contemplation of a maniac without reluctance; and yet I am always conscious of painful feelings as long as it lasts, and perfectly sure that I shall be followed by more painful feelings still when it is over.

It is certain, however, that the comfort, the tenderness, the care, so evident in every part of the establishment at Vanves, render the contemplation of insanity there less painful than I ever found it elsewhere; and when I saw the air of healthy physical enjoyment (at least) with which a large number of the patients prepared to take their pastime, during their hours of exercise, each according to his taste or whim, amid the ample space and well-chosen accessories prepared for them, I could not but wish that every retreat fitted up for the reception of this unfortunate portion of the human race could be arranged on the same plan and governed by the same principles.

# LETTER XXXIV.

Riot at the Porte St. Martin.—Prevented by a shower of Rain.—The Mob in fine weather.—How to stop Emeutes.—Army of Italy.—Théâtre Français.—Mademoiselle Mars in Henriette.—Disappearance of Comedy.

Though Paris is really as quiet at present as any great city can possibly be, still we continue to be told regularly every morning, "qu'il y avait une émeute hier soir à la Porte St. Martin." But I do assure you that these are very harmless little pastimes; and though it seldom happens that the mysterious hour of revolution-hatching passes by without some arrest taking place, the parties are always liberated the next morning; it having appeared clearly at every examination that the juvenile aggressors, who are seldom above twenty years of age, are as harmless as a set of croaking bull-frogs on the banks of the Wabash. The continually repeated mention, however, of these nightly meetings, induced two gentlemen of our party to go to this often-named Porte St. Martin a few nights ago, in hopes of witnessing the humours of one of these small riotings. But on arriving at the spot they found it perfectly tranquil—everything wore the proper stillness of an orderly and well-protected night. A few military were, however, hovering near the spot; and of these they made inquiry as to the cause of a repose so unlike what was usually supposed to be the state of this celebrated quarter of the town.

"Mais ne voyez-vous pas que l'eau tombe, messieurs?" said the national guard stationed there: "c'est bien assez pour refroidir le feu de nos républicains. S'il fait beau demain soir, messieurs, nous aurons encore notre petit spectacle."

Determined to know whether there was any truth in these histories or not, and half suspecting that the whole thing, as well as the assurance of the civil *militaire* to boot, was neither more nor less than a hoax, they last night, the weather being remarkably fine, again attempted the adventure, and with very different success.

On this occasion, there was, by their description, as pretty a little riot as heart could wish. The numbers assembled were stated to be above four hundred: military, both horse and foot, were among them; pointed hats were as plenty as blackberries in September, and "banners waved without a blast" on the tottering shoulders of little ragamuffins who had been hired for two sous apiece to carry them.

On this memorable evening, which has really made a figure this morning in some of the republican journals, a considerable number of the most noisy portion of the mob were arrested; but, on the whole, the military appear to have dealt very gently with them; and our friends heard many a crazy burst of artisan eloquence, which might have easily enough been construed into treason, answered with no rougher repartee than a laughing "Vive le Roi!"

At one point, however, there was a vehement struggle before a young hero, equipped cap-à-pie à la Robespierre, could be secured; and while two of the civic guard were employed in taking him, a little fellow of about ten years old, who had a banner as heavy as himself on his shoulder, and who was probably squire of the body to the prisoner, stood on tiptoe before him at the distance of a few feet, roaring "Vive la République!" as loud as he could bawl.

Another fellow, apparently of the very lowest class, was engaged, during the whole time that the tumult lasted, in haranguing a party that he had collected round him. His arms were bare to the shoulders, and his gesticulation exceedingly violent.

"Nous avons des droits!" he exclaimed with great vehemence.... "Nous avons des droits!... Qui est-ce qui veut les nier?... Nous ne démandons que la charte.... Qu'ils nous donnent la charte!"...

The uproar lasted about three hours, after which the crowd quietly dispersed; and it is to be hoped that they may all employ themselves honestly in their respective callings, till the next fine evening shall again bring them together in the double capacity of actors and spectators at the "petit spectacle."

The constant repetition of this idle riot seems now to give little disturbance to any one; and were it not that the fines and imprisonments so constantly, and sometimes not very leniently inflicted, evidently show that they are thought worth some attention, (though, in fact, this system appears to produce no effect whatever towards checking the daring demonstrations of disaffection manifested by the rabble and their newspaper supporters,) one might deem this indifference the result of such sober confidence of strength in the government, as left them no anxiety whatever as to anything which this troublesome faction could achieve.

Such, I believe, is in fact the feeling of King Philippe's government: nevertheless, it would certainly conduce greatly to the well-being of the people of Paris, if such methods were resorted to as would effectually and at once put a stop to such disgraceful scenes.

"LIBERTY AND ORDER" is King Philippe's motto: he could only improve it by adding "Repose and Quiet;" for never can he reign by any other power than that given by the hope of repose and tranquillity. The harassed nation looks to him for these blessings; and if it be disappointed, the result must be terrible.

Louis-Philippe is neither Napoleon nor Charles the Tenth. He has neither the inalienable rights of the one, nor the overpowering glory of the other; but should he be happy enough to discover a way of securing to this fine but strife-worn and weary country the tranquil prosperity that it now appears beginning to enjoy, he may well be considered by the French people as greater than either.

Bold, fearless, wise, and strong must be the hand that at the present hour can so wield the sceptre of France; and I think it may reasonably be doubted if any one could so wield it, unless its first act were to wave off to a safe distance some of the reckless spirits who are ready to lay down their lives on the scaffold—or in a gutter—or over a pan of charcoal, rather than "live peaceably in that state of life unto which it has pleased God to call them."

If King Louis-Philippe would undertake a crusade to restore independence to Italy, he might convert every traitor into a hero. Let him address the army raised for the purpose in the same inspiring words that Napoleon used of yore. "Soldats!... Partons! Rétablir le capitole.... Réveiller le peuple romain engourdi par plusieurs siècles d'esclavage.... Tel sera le fruit de vos victoires. Vous rentrerez alors dans vos foyers, et vos concitoyens diront en vous montrant—Il était de l'armée d'Italie!" And then let him institute a new order, entitled "L'Ordre Impérial de la Redingote grise," or "L'Ordre indomptable des Bras croisés," and accord to every man the right of admission to it, with the honour to boot of having an eagle embroidered on the breast of his coat if he conducted himself gallantly and like a Frenchman in the field of battle, and we should soon find the Porte St. Martin as quiet as the Autocrat's dressing-room at St. Petersburg.

If such an expedient as this were resorted to, there would no longer be any need of that indecent species of safety-valve by which the noxious vapour generated by the ill-disposed part of the community is now permitted to escape. It may be very great, dignified, and high-minded for a king and his ministers to laugh at treasonable caricatures and seditious pleasantries of all sorts,—but I do greatly doubt the wisdom of it. Human respect is necessary for the maintenance and support of human authority; and that respect will be more profitably shown by a decent degree of general external deference, than by the most sublime kindlings of individual admiration that ever warmed the heart of a courtier. This "*avis au lecteur*" might be listened to with advantage, perhaps, in more countries than one.

Since I last gave you any theatrical news, we have been to see Mademoiselle Mars play the part of Henriette in Molière's exquisite comedy of "Les Femmes Savantes;" and I really think it the most surprising exhibition I ever witnessed. Having seen her in "Tartuffe" and "Charlotte Brown" from a box in the first circle, at some distance from the stage, I imagined that the distance had a good deal to do with the effect still produced by the grace of form, movement, and toilet of this extraordinary woman.

To ascertain, therefore, how much was delusion and how much was truth in the beauty I still saw or fancied, I resolved upon the desperate experiment of securing that seat in the balcony which is nearest to the stage. It was from this place that I saw her play Henriette; a character deriving no aid whatever from trick or stage effect of any kind; one, too, whose charm lies wholly in simple, unaffected youthfulness: there are no flashes of wit, no startling hits either of pathos or pleasantry—nothing but youth, gentleness, modesty, and tenderness —nothing but a young girl of sixteen, rather more quiet and retiring than usual. Yet this character, which seems of necessity to require youth and beauty in the performer, though little else, was personated by this miraculous old lady in a manner that not only enchanted me—being, as I am, *rococo*—but actually drew forth from the omnipotent *jeunes gens* in the *parterre* such clamorous rapture of applause as must, I think, have completely overset any actress less used to it than herself. Is not this marvellous?

How much it is to be regretted that the art of writing comedy has passed away! They have vaudevilles here—charming things in their way; and we have farces at home that certainly cannot be thought of without enjoying the gratification of a broad grin. But for comedy, where the intellect is called upon as well as the muscles, it is dead and gone. The "Hunchback" is perhaps the nearest approach to it, whose birth I remember in our country, and "Bertrand and Raton" here; but in both cases the pleasurable excitement is produced more by the plot than the characters—more by the business of the scene than by the wit and elegance of the dialogue, except perhaps in the pretty wilfulness of Julia in the second act of the "Hunchback." But even here I suspect it was more the playful grace of the enchanting actress who first appeared in the part, than anything in the words "set down for her," which so delighted us.

We do now and then get a new tragedy,—witness "Fazio" and "Rienzi;" but Comedy—genuine, easy, graceful, flowing, talking Comedy—is dead: I think she followed Sheridan to the grave and was buried with him! But never is one so conscious of the loss, or so inclined to mourn it, as after seeing a comedy of Molière's of the first order,—for his pieces should be divided into classes, like diamonds. What a burst of new enjoyment would rush over all England, or all France, if a thing like "The School for Scandal" or "Les Femmes Savantes" were to appear before them!

Fancy the delight of sitting to hear wit—wit that one did not know by rote, bright, sparkling, untasted as yet by any—new and fresh from the living fountain!—not coming to one in the shape of coin, already bearing the lawful stamp of ten thousand plaudits to prove it genuine, and to refuse to accept which would be treason; but as native gold, to which the touchstone of your own intellect must be applied to test its worth! Shall we ever experience this?

It is strange that the immense mass of material for comedy which the passing scenes of this singular epoch furnish should not be worked up by some one. Molière seems not to have suffered a single passing folly to escape him. Had he lived in these days, what delicious whigs, radicals, "penny-rint" kings, from our side of the water,—what tragic poets, republicans, and parvenus from his own, would he have cheered us withal!

Rousseau says, that when a theatre produces pieces which represent the real manners of the people, they must greatly assist those who are present at them to see and amend what is vicious or absurd in themselves, "comme on ôte devant un miroir les taches de son visage." The idea is excellent; and surely there never was a time when it would be so easy or so useful to put it in practice. Would the gods but send a Sheridan to England and a Molière to France, we might yet live to see some of our worst misfortunes turned to jest, and, like the man choking in a quinsey, laugh ourselves into health again.

## LETTER XXXV.

Soirée dansante.—Young Ladies.—Old Ladies.—Anecdote.—The Consolations of Chaperones.—Flirtations.—Discussion upon the variations between young Married Women in France and in England.—Making love by deputy.—Not likely to answer in England.

Last night we were at a ball,—or rather, I should say, a "*soirée dansante;*" for at this season, though people may dance from night to morning, there are no balls. But let it be called by what name it may, it could not have been more gay and agreeable were this the month of January instead of May.

There were several English gentlemen present, who, to the great amusement of some of the company, uniformly selected their partners from among the young ladies. This may appear very natural to you; but here it is thought the most unnatural proceeding possible.

To a novice in French society, there is certainly no circumstance so remarkable as the different position which the unmarried hold in the drawing-rooms of England and *les salons* of France. With us, the prettiest things to look at, and the partners first sought for the dance, are the young girls. Brilliant in the perfection of their youthful bloom, graceful and gay as young fawns in every movement of the most essentially juvenile of all exercises, and eclipsing the light elegance of their own toilet by loveliness that leaves no eyes to study its decoration,—it is they who, in spite of diamonds and of blonde, of wedded beauty or of titled grace, ever appear to be the principal actors in a ball-room. But "they manage these matters" quite otherwise "in France."

Unfortunately, it may sometimes happen among us, that a coquettish matron may be seen to lead the giddy waltz with more sprightliness than wisdom; but she always does it at the risk of being *mal notée* in some way or other, more or less gravely, by almost every person present;—nay, I would by no means encourage her to be very certain that her tonish partner himself would not be better pleased to whirl round the mazy circle with one of the slight, light, sylph-like creatures he sees flying past him, than with the most fashionable married woman in London.

But in Paris all this is totally reversed; and, what is strange enough, you will find in both countries that the reason assigned for the difference between them arises from national attention to good morals.

On entering a French ball-room, instead of seeing the youngest and loveliest part of the company occupying the most conspicuous places, surrounded by the gayest men, and dressed with the most studied and becoming elegance, you must look for the young things quite in the background, soberly and quietly attired, and almost wholly eclipsed behind the more fully-blown beauties of their married friends.

It is really marvellous, considering how very much prettier a girl is at eighteen than she can possibly be some dozen years afterwards, to see how completely fashion will nevertheless have its own way, making the worse positively appear the better beauty.

All that exceeding charm and fascination which is for ever and always attributed to an elegant Frenchwoman, belongs wholly, solely, and altogether to her after she becomes a wife. A young French girl, "*parfaitement bien élevée*," looks ... "*parfaitement bien élevée;*" but it must be confessed, also, that she looks at the same time as if her governess (and a sharp one) were looking over her shoulder. She will be dressed, of course, with the nicest precision and most exact propriety; her corsets will forbid a wrinkle to appear in her robe, and her *friseur* deny permission to any single hair that might wish to deviate from the station appointed for it by his stiff control. But if you would see that graceful perfection of the toilet, that unrivalled *agacerie* of costume which distinguishes a French woman from all others in the world, you must turn from mademoiselle to madame. The very sound of the voice, too, is different. It should seem as if the heart and soul of a French girl were asleep, or at least dozing, till the ceremony of marriage awakened them. As long as it is mademoiselle who speaks, there is something monotonous, dull, and uninteresting in the tone, or rather in the tune, of her voice; but when madame addresses you, all the charm that manner, cadence, accent can bestow, is sure to greet you.

In England, on the contrary, of all the charms peculiar to youthful loveliness, I know none so remarkable as the unconstrained, fresh, natural, sweet, and joyous sound of a young girl's voice. It is as delicious as the note of the lark, when rising in the first freshness of morning to meet the sun. It is not restrained, held in, and checked into tameness by any fear lest it should too early show its syren power.

Even in the dance itself, the very arena for the display of youthful gracefulness, the young French girl fails, when her well-taught steps are compared with the easy, careless, fascinating movements of the married woman.

In the simple kindness of manner too, which, if there were no other attraction, would ever suffice to render an unaffected, good-natured young girl charming, there must be here a cautious restraint. A *demoiselle Française* would be prevented by *bienséance* from showing it, were she the gentlest-hearted creature breathing.

A young Englishman of my acquaintance, who, though he had been a good deal in French society, was not initiated into the mysteries of female education, recounted to me the other day an adventure of his, which is german to the matter, though not having much to do with our last night's ball. This young man had for a long time been very kindly received in a French family, had repeatedly dined with them, and, in fact, considered himself as admitted to their house on the footing of an intimate friend.

The only child of this family was a daughter, rather pretty, but cold, silent, and repulsive in manner—almost awkward, and utterly uninteresting. Every attempt to draw her into conversation had ever proved abortive; and though often in her company, the Englishman hardly thought she could consider him as an acquaintance.

The young man returned to England; but, after some months, again revisited Paris. While standing one day in earnest contemplation of a picture at the Louvre, he was startled at being suddenly addressed by an extremely beautiful woman, who in the kindest and most friendly manner imaginable asked him a multitude of questions—made a thousand inquiries after his health—invited him earnestly to come and see her, and concluded by exclaiming—"Mais c'est un siècle depuis que je vous ai vu."

My friend stood gazing at her with equal admiration and surprise. He began to remember that he had seen her before, but when or where he knew not. She saw his embarrassment and smiled. "Vous m'avez oublié donc?" said she. "Je m'appelle Eglé de P——.... Mais je suis mariée...."

But to return to our ball.

As I saw the married women taken out to dance one after the another, till at last there was not a single dancing-looking man left, I felt myself getting positively angry; for, notwithstanding the assistance given by my ignorant countrymen, there were still at least half a dozen French girls unprovided with chevaliers.

They did not, however, look by many degrees so sadly disappointed as English girls would do did the same misfortune betide them. They, like the poor eels, were used to it; and the gentlemen, too, were cruelly used to the task of torture,—making their pretty little feet beat time upon the floor, while they watched the happy wedded in pairs—not wedded pairs—swim before their eyes in mazes which they would most gladly have threaded after them.

When at length all the married ladies, young and old, were duly provided for, several staid and very respectable-looking gentlemen emerged from corners and sofas, and presenting themselves to the young expectants, were accepted with quiet, grateful smiles, and permitted to lead them to the dance.

Old ladies like myself, whose fate attaches them to the walls of a ball-room, are accustomed to find their consolation and amusement from various sources. First, they enjoy such conversation as they can catch; or, if they will sit tolerably silent, they may often hear the prettiest airs of the season exceedingly well played. Then the whole arena of twinkling feet is open to their criticism and admiration. Another consolation, and frequently a very substantial one, is found in the supper;—nay, sometimes a passing ice will be caught to cheer the weary watcher. But there is another species of amusement, the general avowal of which might lead the younger part of the civilized world to wish that old ladies wore blinkers: I allude to the quiet contemplation of half a dozen sly flirtations that may be going on around them,—some so well managed! ... some so clumsily!

But upon all these occasions, in England, though well-behaved old ladies will always take especial care not so to see that their seeing shall be seen, they still look about them with no feeling of restraint—no consciousness that they would rather be anywhere else than spectators of what is going forward near them. They feel, at least I am sure I do, a very comfortable assurance that the fair one is engaged, not in marring, but in making her fortune. Here again I may quote the often-quoted, and say, "They manage all these matters differently at least, if not better, in France."

In England, if a woman is seen going through all the manœuvres of the flirting exercise, from the first animating reception of the "How d'ye do?" to the last soft consciousness which fixes the eyes immovably on the floor, while the head, gently inclined, seems willing to indulge the happy ear in receiving intoxicating draughts of *parfait amour,*—when this is seen in England, even should the lady be past eighteen, one feels assured that she is not married; but here, without scandal or the shadow of scandal be it spoken, one feels equally well assured that she is. She may be a widow—or she may flirt in the innocence of her heart, because it is the fashion; but she cannot do it, because she is a young lady intending to be married.

I was deeply engaged in these speculations last night, when an elderly lady—who for some reason or other, not very easy to divine, actually never waltzes—came across the room and placed herself by my side. Though she does not waltz, she is a very charming person; and as I had often conversed with her before, I now welcomed her approach with great pleasure.

"A quoi pensez-vous, Madame Trollope?" said she: "vous avez l'air de méditer."

I deliberated for a moment whether I should venture to tell her exactly what was passing in my mind; but as I deliberated, I looked at her, and there was that in her countenance which assured me I should have no severity to fear if I put her wholly in my confidence: I therefore replied very frankly,—

"I am meditating; and it is on the position which unmarried women hold in France."

"Unmarried women?... You will scarcely find any such in France," said she.

"Are not those young ladies who have just finished their quadrille unmarried?"

"Ah!... But you cannot call them unmarried women. *Elles sont des demoiselles.*"

"Well, then, my meditations were concerning them."

"Eh bien...."

"Eh bien.... It appears to me that the ball is not given—that the music does not play—that the gentlemen are not *empressé,* for them."

"No, certainly. It would be quite contrary to our ideas of what is right if it were so."

"With us it is so different!... It is always the young ladies who are, at least, the ostensible heroines of every ball-room."

"The ostensible heroines?"... She dwelt rather strongly upon the adjective, adding with a smile,—"Our ostensible, are our real heroines upon these occasions."

I explained. "The real heroines," said I, "will, I confess, in cases of ostentation and display, be sometimes the ladies who give balls in return."

"Well explained," said she, laughing: "I certainly thought you had another meaning. You think, then," she continued, "that our young married women are made of too much importance among us?"

"Oh no!" I replied eagerly: "it is, in my opinion, almost impossible to make them of too much importance; for I believe that it is entirely upon their influence that the tone of society depends."

"You are quite right. It is impossible for those who have lived as long as we have in the world to doubt it: but how can this be, if, upon the occasions which bring people together, they are to be overlooked, while young girls who have as yet no position fixed are brought forward instead?"

"But surely, being brought forward to dance in a waltz or quadrille, is not the sort of consequence which we either of us mean?"

"Perhaps not; but it is one of its necessary results. Our women marry young,— as soon, in fact, as their education is finished, and before they have been permitted to enter the world, or share in the pleasures of it. Their destiny, therefore, instead of being the brightest that any women enjoy, would be the most *triste*, were they forbidden to enter into the amusements so natural to their age and national character, because they were married."

"But may there not be danger in the custom which throws young females, thus early and irrevocably engaged, for the first time into the society, and, as it were, upon the attentions of men whom it has already become their duty not to consider as too amiable?"

"Oh no!... If a young woman be well-disposed, it is not a quadrille, or a waltz either, that will lead her astray. If it could, it would surely be the duty of all the legislators of the earth to forbid the exercise for ever."

"No, no, no!" said I earnestly; "I mean nothing of the kind, I assure you: on the contrary, I am so convinced, from the recollections of my own feelings, and my observations on those of others, that dancing is not a fictitious, but a real, natural source of enjoyment, the inclination for which is inherent in us, that, instead of wishing it to be forbidden, I would, had I the power, make it infinitely more general and of more frequent occurrence than it is: young people should never meet each other without the power of dancing if they wished it."

"And from this animating pleasure, for which you confess that there is a sort of *besoin* within us, you would exclude all the young women above seventeen —because they are married?... Poor things!... Instead of finding them so willing as they generally are to enter on the busy scenes of life, I think we should have great difficulty in getting their permission to *monter un ménage* for them. Marriage would be soon held in abhorrence if such were its laws."

"I would not have them such, I assure you," replied I, rather at a loss how to explain myself fully without saying something that might either be construed into coarseness of thinking and a cruel misdoubting of innocence, or else into a very uncivil attack upon the national manners: I was therefore silent.

My companion seemed to expect that I should proceed, but after a short interval resumed the conversation by saying,—"Then what arrangement would you propose, to reconcile the necessity of dancing with the propriety of keeping married women out of the danger which you seem to imagine might arise from it?"

"It would be too national were I to reply, that I think our mode of proceeding in this case is exactly what it ought to be."

"But such is your opinion?"

"To speak sincerely, I believe it is."

"Will you then have the kindness to explain to me the difference in this respect between France and England?"

"The only difference between us which I mean to advocate is, that with us the amusement which throws young people together under circumstances the most likely, perhaps, to elicit expressions of gallantry and admiration from the men, and a gracious reception of them from the women, is considered as befitting the single rather than the married part of the community."

"With us, indeed, it is exactly the reverse," replied she,—"at least as respects the young ladies. By addressing the idle, unmeaning gallantry inspired by the dance to a young girl, we should deem the cautious delicacy of restraint in which she is enshrined transgressed and broken in upon. A young girl should be given to her husband before her passions have been awakened or her imagination excited by the voice of gallantry."

"But when she is given to him, do you think this process more desirable than before?"

"Certainly it is not desirable; but it is infinitely less dangerous. When a girl is first married, her feelings, her thoughts, her imagination are wholly occupied by her husband. Her mode of education has ensured this; and afterwards, it is at the choice of her husband whether he will secure and retain her young heart for himself. If he does this, it is not a waltz or quadrille that will rob him of it. In no country have husbands so little reason to complain of their wives as in France; for in no country does the manner in which they live with them depend so wholly on themselves. With you, if your novels, and even the strange trials made public to all the world by your newspapers, may be trusted, the very reverse is the case. Previous attachments—early affection broken off before the marriage, to be renewed after it—these are the histories we hear and read; and most assuredly they do not tempt us to adopt your system as an amendment upon our own."

"The very notoriety of the cases to which you allude proves their rare occurrence," replied I. "Such sad histories would have but little interest for the public, either as tales or trials, if they did not relate circumstances marked and apart from ordinary life."

"Assuredly. But you will allow also that, however rare they may be in England, such records of scandal and of shame are rarer still in France?"

"Occurrences of the kind do not perhaps produce so much sensation here," said I.

"Because they are more common, you would say. Is not that your meaning?" and she smiled reproachfully.

"It certainly was not my meaning to say so," I replied; "and, in truth, it is neither a useful nor a gracious occupation to examine on which side the Channel the greater proportion of virtue may be found; though it is possible some good might be done on both, were the education in each country to be modified by the introduction of what is best in the other."

"I have no doubt of it," said she; "and as we go on exchanging fashions so amicably, who knows but we may live to see your young ladies shut up a little more, while their mothers and fathers look out for a suitable marriage for them, instead of inflicting the awkward task upon themselves? And in return, perhaps, our young wives may lay aside their little coquetries and become *mères respectables* somewhat earlier than they do now. But, in truth, they all come to it at last."

As she finished speaking these words, a new waltz sounded, and again a dozen couples, some ill, some well matched, swam past us. One of the pairs was composed of a very fine-looking young man, with blue-black *favoris* and *moustaches*, tall as a tower, and seeming, if air and expression may be trusted, very tolerably well pleased with himself. His *danseuse* might unquestionably have addressed her husband, who sat at no great distance from us, drawing up his gouty feet under his chair to let her pass, in these touching words:—

"Full thirty times hath Phœbus' cart gone round

Neptune's salt wash and Tellus' orbed ground,

And thirty dozen moons, with borrow'd sheen,

About the world have times twelve thirties been,

Since Love our hearts and Hymen did our hands

Unite commutual in most sacred bands."

My neighbour and I looked up and exchanged glances as they went by. We both laughed.

"At least you will allow," said she, "that this is one of the cases in which a married lady may indulge her passion for the dance without danger of consequences?"

"I am not quite sure of that," replied I. "If she be not found guilty of sin, she will scarcely obtain a verdict that shall acquit her of folly. But what can induce that magnificent personage, who looks down upon her as if engaged in measuring the distance between them—what could induce him to request the honour of enclosing her venerable waist in his arm?"

"Nothing more easily explained. That little fair girl sitting in yonder corner, with her hair so tightly drawn off her forehead, is her daughter—her only daughter, and will have a noble *dot*. Now you understand it?... And tell me, in case his speculation should not succeed, is it not better that this excellent lady, who waltzes so very like a duck, should receive all the eloquence with which he will seek to render himself amiable, upon her time-steeled heart, than that the delicate little girl herself should have to listen to it?"

"And you really would recommend us to adopt this mode of love-making by deputy, letting the mamma be the substitute, till the young lady has obtained a brevet to listen to the language of love in her own person? However excellent the scheme may be, dear lady, it is vain to hope that we shall ever be able to introduce it among us. The young ladies, I suspect, would exclaim, as you do here, when explaining why you cannot permit any English innovations among you, "Ce n'est pas dans nos mœurs."

I assure you, my friend, that I have not composed this conversation *à loisir* for your amusement, for I have set down as nearly as possible what was said to me, though I have not quite given it all to you; but my letter is already long enough.

# LETTER XXXVI.

Improvements of Paris.—Introduction of Carpets and Trottoirs.—Maisonnettes.—Not likely to answer in Paris.—The necessity of a Porter and Porter's Lodge.—Comparative Expenses of France and England.—Increasing Wealth of the Bourgeoisie.

Among the many recent improvements in Paris which evidently owe their origin to England, those which strike the eye first, are the almost universal introduction of carpets within doors, and the frequent blessing of a *trottoir* without. In a few years, unless all paving-stones should be torn up in search of more immortality, there can be no doubt that it will be almost as easy to walk in Paris as in London. It is true that the old streets are not quite wide enough to admit such enormous esplanades on each side as Regent and Oxford Streets; but all that is necessary to safety and comfort may be obtained with less expense of space; and to those who knew Paris a dozen years ago, when one had to hop from stone to stone in the fond hope of escaping wet shoes in the Dog-days—tormented too during the whole of this anxious process with the terror of being run over by carts, fiacres, concous, cabs, and wheelbarrows;—whoever remembers what it was to walk in Paris then, will bless with an humble and grateful spirit the dear little pavement which, with the exception of necessary intervals to admit of an approach to the portes-cochère of the various *hôtels,* and a few short intervals beside, which appear to have been passed over and forgotten, borders most of the principal streets of Paris now.

Another English innovation, infinitely more important in all ways, has been attempted, and has failed. This was the endeavour to introduce *maisonnettes*, or small houses calculated for the occupation of one family. A few such have been built in that new part of the town which stretches away in all directions behind the Madeleine; but they are not found to answer—and that for many reasons which I should have thought it very easy to foresee, and which I suspect it would be very difficult to obviate.

In order to come at all within reach of the generality of French incomes, they must be built on too small a scale to have any good rooms; and this is a luxury, and permits a species of display, to which many are accustomed who live in unfurnished apartments, for which they give perhaps fifteen hundred or two thousand francs a year. Another accommodation which habit has made it extremely difficult for French families to dispense with, and which can be enjoyed at an easy price only by sharing it with many, is a porter and a porter's lodge. Active as is the race of domestic servants in Paris, their number must, I think, be doubled in many families, were the arrangement of the porter's lodge to be changed for our system of having a servant summoned every time a parcel, a message, a letter, or a visit arrives at the house.

Nor does the taking charge of these by any means comprise the whole duty of this servant of many masters; neither am I at all competent to say exactly what does: but it seems to me that the answer I generally receive upon desiring that anything may be done is, "Oui, madame, le portier ou la portière fera cela;" and were we suddenly deprived of these factotums, I suspect that we should be immediately obliged to leave our apartments and take refuge in an hôtel, for I should be quite at a loss to know what or how many additional "helps" would be necessary to enable us to exist without them.

That the whole style and manner of domestic existence throughout all the middling classes of such a city as Paris should hang upon their porters' lodges, seems tracing great effects to little causes; but I have been so repeatedly told that the failure of the *maisonnettes* has in a great degree arisen from this, that I cannot doubt it.

I know not whether anything which prevents their so completely changing their mode of life as they must do if living in separate houses, is to be considered as an evil or not. The Parisians are a very agreeable, and apparently a very happy population; and who can say what effect the quiet, steady, orderly mode of each man having a small house of his own might produce? What is admirable as a component part of one character, is often incongruous and disagreeable when met in another; and I am by no means certain if the snug little mansion which might be procured for the same rent as a handsome apartment, would not tend to circumscribe and tame down the light spirits that now send *locataires* of threescore springing to their elegant *premier* by two stairs at a time. And the prettiest and best *chaussés* little feet in the world too, which now trip *sans souci* over the common stair, would they not lag painfully perhaps in passing through a low-browed hall, whose neatness or unneatness had become a private and individual concern? And might not many a bright fancy be damped while calculating how much it would cost to have a few statues and oleanders in it?—and the head set aching by meditating how to get "ce vilain escalier frotté" from top to bottom? Yet all these, and many other cares which they now escape, must fall upon them if they give up their apartments for *maisonnettes*.

The fact, I believe, is, that French fortunes, taken at the average at which they at present stand, could not suffice to procure the pretty elegance to which the middle classes are accustomed, unless it were done by the sacrifice of some portion of that costly fastidiousness which English people of the same rank seem to cling to as part of their prerogative.

Though I am by no means prepared to say that I should like to exchange my long-confirmed habit of living in a house of my own for the Parisian mode of inhabiting apartments, I cannot but allow that by this and sundry other arrangements a French income is made to contribute infinitely more to the enjoyment of its possessor than an English one.

Let any English person take the trouble of calculating, let their revenue be great or small, how much of it is expended in what immediately contributes to their personal comfort and luxury, and how much of it is devoted to the support of expenses which in point of fact add to neither, and the truth of this statement will become evident.

Rousseau says, that "cela se fait," and "cela ne se fait pas," are the words which regulate everything that goes on within the walls of Paris. That the same words have at least equal power in London, can hardly be denied; and, unfortunately for our individual independence, obedience to them costs infinitely more on our side of the water than it does on this. Hundreds are annually spent, out of very confined incomes, to support expenses which have nothing whatever to do with the personal enjoyment of those who so tax themselves; but it must be submitted to, because "cela se fait," or "cela ne se fait pas." In Paris, on the contrary, this imperative phrase has comparatively no influence on the expenditure of any revenue, because every one's object is not to make it appear that he is as rich as his neighbour, but to make his means, be they great or small, contribute as much as possible to the enjoyment and embellishment of his existence.

It is for this reason that a residence in Paris is found so favourable an expedient in cases of diminished or insufficient fortune. A family coming hither in the hope of obtaining the mere necessaries of life at a much cheaper rate than in England would be greatly disappointed: some articles are cheaper, but many are considerably dearer; and, in truth, I doubt if at the present moment anything that can be strictly denominated a necessary of life is to be found cheaper in Paris than in London.

It is not the necessaries, but the luxuries of life that are cheaper here. Wine, ornamental furniture, the keep of horses, the price of carriages, the entrance to theatres, wax-lights, fruit, books, the rent of handsome apartments, the wages of men-servants, are all greatly cheaper, and direct taxes greatly less. But even this is not the chief reason why a residence in Paris may be found economical to persons of any pretension to rank or style at home. The necessity for parade, so much the most costly of all the appendages to rank, may here be greatly dispensed with, and that without any degradation whatever. In short, the advantage of living in Paris as a matter of economy depends entirely upon the degree of luxury to be obtained. There are certainly many points of delicacy and refinement in the English manner of living which I should be very sorry to see given up as national peculiarities; but I think we should gain much in many ways could we learn to hang our consequence less upon the comparison of what others do. We shudder at the cruel madness of the tyrant who would force every form to reach one standard; but those are hardly less mad who insist that every one, to live *comme il faut,* must live, or appear to live, exactly as others do, though the means of doing so may vary among the silly set so prescribed to, from an income that may justify any extravagance to one that can honestly supply none.

This is a folly of incalculably rarer occurrence here than in England; and it certainly is no proof of the good sense of our "most thinking people," that for one private family brought to ruin by extravagance in France, there are fifty who suffer from this cause in England.

It is easy to perceive that our great wealth has been the cause of this. The general scale of expense has been set so high, that thousands who have lived in reference to that, rather than to their individual fortunes, have been ruined by the blunder; and I really know no remedy so likely to cure the evil as a residence in Paris; not, however, so much as a means of saving money, as of making a series of experiments which may teach them how to make the best and most enjoyable use of it.

I am persuaded, that if it were to become as much the fashion to imitate the French independence of mind in our style of living, as it now is to copy them in ragoûts, bonnets, moustaches, and or-molu, we should greatly increase our stock of real genuine enjoyment. If no English lady should ever again feel a pang at her heart because she saw more tall footmen in her neighbour's hall than in her own—if no sighs were breathed in secret in any club-house or at any sale, because Jack Somebody's stud was a cut above us—if no bills were run up at Gunter's, or at Howell and James's, because it was worse than death to be outdone,—we should unquestionably be a happier and a more respectable people than we are at present.

It is, I believe, pretty generally acknowledged by all parties, that the citizens of France have become a more money-getting generation since the last revolution than they ever were before it. The security and repose which the new dynasty seems to have brought with it, have already given them time and opportunity to multiply their capital; and the consequence is, that the shop-keeping propensities with which Napoleon used to reproach us have crossed the Channel, and are beginning to produce very considerable alterations here.

It is evident that the wealth of the *bourgeoisie* is rapidly increasing, and their consequence with it; so rapidly, indeed, that the republicans are taking fright at it,—they see before them a new enemy, and begin to talk of the abominations of an aristocratic *bourgeoisie.*

There is, in fact, no circumstance in the whole aspect of the country more striking or more favourable than this new and powerful impulse given to trade. It is the best ballast that the vessel of the state can have; and if they can but contrive that nothing shall happen to occasion its being thrown overboard, it may suffice to keep her steady, whatever winds may blow.

The wide-spreading effect of this increasing wealth among the *bourgeoisie* is visible in many ways, but in none more than in the rapid increase of handsome dwellings, which are springing up, as white and bright as new-born mushrooms, in the north-western division of Paris. This is quite a new world, and reminds me of the early days of Russell Square, and all the region about it. The Church of the Madeleine, instead of being, as I formerly remember it, nearly at the extremity of Paris, has now a new city behind it; and if things go on at the same rate at which they seem to be advancing at present, we shall see it, or at least our children will, occupying as central a position as St. Martin's-in-the-Fields. An excellent market, called Marché de la Madeleine, has already found its way to this new town; and I doubt not that churches, theatres, and restaurans innumerable will speedily follow.

The capital which is now going so merrily on, increasing with almost American rapidity, will soon ask to be invested; and when this happens, Paris will be seen running out of town with the same active pace that London has done before her; and twenty years hence the Bois de Boulogne may very likely be as thickly peopled as the Regent's Park is now.

This sudden accession of wealth has already become the cause of a great increase in the price of almost every article sold in Paris; and if this activity of commerce continue, it is more than probable, that the hitherto moderate fortunes of the Parisian *boursier* and merchant will grow into something resembling the colossal capitals of England, and we shall find that the same causes which have hitherto made England dear will in future prevent France from being cheap. It will then happen, that many deficiencies which are now perceptible, and which furnish the most remarkable points of difference between the two countries, will disappear; great wealth being in many instances all that is required to make a French family live very much like an English one. Whether they will not, when this time arrives, lose on the side of unostentatious enjoyment more than they will gain by increased splendour, may, I think, be very doubtful. For my own part, I am decidedly of opinion, that as soon as heavy ceremonious dinners shall systematically take place of the present easy, unexpensive style of visiting, Paris will be more than half spoiled, and the English may make up their minds to remain proudly and pompously at home, lest, instead of a light and lively contrast to their own ways, they may chance to find a heavy but successful rivalry.

# LETTER XXXVII.

Horrible Murder.—La Morgue.—Suicides.—Vanity.—Anecdote.—Influence of Modern Literature.—Different appearance of Poverty in France and England.

We have been made positively sick and miserable by the details of a murder, which seems to show that we live in a world where there are creatures ten thousand times more savage than any beast that ranges the forest,

"Be it ounce, or cat, or bear,

Pard, or boar with bristled hair."

This horror was perpetrated on the person of a wretched female, who appeared, by the mangled remains which were found in the river, to have been very young. But though thus much was discovered, it was many days ere, among the thousands who flocked to the Morgue to look at the severed head and mangled limbs, any one could be found to recognise the features. At length, however, the person with whom she had lodged came to see if she could trace any resemblance between her lost inmate and these wretched relics of a human being.

She so far succeeded as to convince herself of the identity; though her means of judging appeared to be so little satisfactory, that few placed any reliance upon her testimony. Nevertheless, she at length succeeded in having a man taken up, who had lived on intimate terms with the poor creature whose sudden disappearance had induced this woman to visit the Morgue when the description of this mangled body reached her. He immediately confessed the deed, in the spirit, though not in the words, of the poet:—

"Mourons: de tant d'horreurs qu'un trépas me délivre!

Est-ce un malheur si grand que de cesser de vivre?

Je ne crains pas le nom que je laisse après moi."

The peculiarly horrid manner in which the crime was committed, and the audacious style in which the criminal appears to brave justice, will, it is thought, prevent any *extenuating circumstances* being pleaded, as is usually done, for the purpose of commuting the punishment of death into imprisonment with enforced labour. It is generally expected that this atrocious murderer will be guillotined, notwithstanding the averseness of the government to capital punishment.

The circumstances are, indeed, hideous in all ways, and the more so from being mixed up with what is miscalled the tender passion. The cannibal fury which sets a man to kill his foe that he may eat him, has fully as much tenderness in it as this species of affection.

When "the passion is made up of nothing but the finest parts of love," it may, perhaps, deserve the epithet of tender; but we have heard of late of so many horrible and deliberate assassinations, originating in what newspapers are pleased to call "*une grande passion*" that the first idea which a love-story now suggests to me is, that the sequel will in all probability be murder "most foul, strange, and unnatural!"

Is there in any language a word that can raise so many shuddering sensations as "*La Morgue*?" Hatred, revenge, murder, are each terrible; but La Morgue outdoes them all in its power of bringing together in one syllable the abstract of whatever is most appalling in crime, poverty, despair, and death.

To the ghastly Morgue are conveyed the unowned dead of every description that are discovered in or near Paris. The Seine is the great receptacle which first receives the victims of assassination or despair; but they are not long permitted to elude the vigilance of the Parisian police: a huge net, stretched across the river at St. Cloud, receives and retains whatever the stream brings down; and anything that retains a trace of human form which is found amidst the product of the fearful draught is daily conveyed to La Morgue;—DAILY; for rarely does it chance that for four-and-twenty hours its melancholy biers remain unoccupied; often do eight, ten, a dozen corpses at a time arrive by the frightful caravan from "*les filets de St. Cloud.*"

I have, in common with most people, I believe, a very strong propensity within me for seeing everything connected directly or indirectly with any subject or event which has strongly roused my curiosity, or interested my feelings; but, strange to say, I never feel its influence so irresistible as when something of shuddering horror is mixed with the spectacle. It is this propensity which has now induced me to visit this citadel of death;—this low and solitary roof, placed in the very centre of moving, living, laughing Paris.

No visit to a tomb, however solemn or however sad, can approach in thrilling horror to the sensation caused by passing the threshold of this charnel-house.

The tomb calls us to the contemplation of the common, the inevitable lot; but this gathering place of sin and death arouses thoughts of all that most outrages nature, and most foully violates the sanctuary of life, into which God has breathed his spirit. But I was steadfast in my will to visit it, and I have done it.

The building is a low, square, carefully-whited structure, situated on the Quai de la Cité. It is open to all; and it is fearful to think how many anxious hearts have entered, how many despairing ones have quitted it.

On entering I found myself in a sort of low hall which contained no object whatever. If I mistake not, there is a chamber on each side of it: but it was to the left hand that I was led, and it was thither that about a dozen persons who entered at the same time either followed or preceded me. I do not too well remember how I reached the place where the bodies are visible; but I know that I stood before one of three large windows, through the panes of which, and very near to them, lighted also by windows in the roof, are seen a range of biers, sloping towards the spectator at an angle that gives the countenance as well as the whole figure of the persons extended on them fully to view.

In this manner I saw the bodies of four men stretched out before me; but their aspect bore no resemblance to death—neither were they swollen or distorted in any way, but so discoloured as to give them exactly the appearance of bronze statues.

Two out of the four had evidently been murdered, for their heads and throats gave frightful evidence of the violence that had been practised upon them; the third was a mere boy, who probably met his fate by accident: but that the fourth was a suicide, it was hardly possible to doubt; even in death his features held the desperate expression that might best paint the state of mind likely to lead to such an act.

It was past mid-day when we entered the Morgue; but neither of the bodies had yet been claimed or recognised.

This spectacle naturally set me upon seeking information, wherever I was likely to find it, respecting the average number of bodies thus exposed within the year, the proportion of them believed to be suicides, and the causes generally supposed most influential in producing this dreadful termination.

I will not venture to repeat the result of these inquiries in figures, as I doubt if the information I received was of that strictly accurate kind which could justify my doing so; yet it was quite enough so, to excite both horror and astonishment at the extraordinary number which are calculated to perish annually at Paris by self-slaughter.

In many recent instances, the causes which have led to these desperate deeds have been ascertained by the written acknowledgment of the perpetrators themselves, left as a legacy to mankind. Such a legacy might perhaps not be wholly unprofitable to the survivors, were it not that the motives assigned, in almost every instance where they have been published, have been of so frivolous and contemptible a nature as to turn wholesome horror to most ill-placed mirth.

It can hardly be doubted, from the testimony of these singular documents, that many young Frenchmen perish yearly in this guilty and deplorable manner for no other reason in the world than the hope of being talked of afterwards.

Had some solitary instance of so perverted a vanity been found among these records, it might perhaps have been considered as no more incredible than various other proofs of the enfeebling effects of this paltry passion on the judgment, and have been set down to insanity, produced by excessive egotism: but nothing short of the posthumous testimony of the persons themselves could induce any one to believe that scarcely a week passes without such an event, from such a cause, taking place in Paris.

In many instances, I am told that the good sense of surviving friends has led them to disobey the testamentary instructions left by the infatuated young men who have thus acted, requesting that the wretched reasonings which have led them to it should be published. But, in a multitude of cases, the "Constitutionnel" and other journals of the same stamp have their columns filled with reasons why these poor reckless creatures have dared the distant justice of their Creator, in the hope that their unmeaning names should be echoed through Paris for a day.

It is not long since two young men—mere youths—entered a *restaurant*, and bespoke a dinner of unusual luxury and expense, and afterwards arrived punctually at the appointed hour to eat it. They did so, apparently with all the zest of youthful appetite and youthful glee. They called for champagne, and quaffed it hand in hand. No symptom of sadness, thought, or reflection of any kind was observed to mix with their mirth, which was loud, long, and unremitting. At last came the *café noir*, the cognac, and the bill: one of them was seen to point out the amount to the other, and then both burst out afresh into violent laughter. Having swallowed each his cup of coffee to the dregs, the *garçon* was ordered to request the company of the *restaurateur* for a few minutes. He came immediately, expecting perhaps to receive his bill, minus some extra charge which the jocund but economical youths might deem exorbitant.

Instead of this, however, the elder of the two informed him that the dinner had been excellent, which was the more fortunate as it was decidedly the last that either of them should ever eat: that for his bill, he must of necessity excuse the payment of it, as in fact they neither of them possessed a single sous: that upon no other occasion would they thus have violated the customary etiquette between guest and landlord; but that finding this world, its toils and its troubles, unworthy of them, they had determined once more to enjoy a repast of which their poverty must for ever prevent the repetition, and then—take leave of existence for ever! For the first part of this resolution, he declared that it had, thanks to his cook and his cellar, been achieved nobly; and for the last, it would soon follow—for the *café noir*, besides the little glass of his admirable cognac, had been medicated with that which would speedily settle all their accounts for them.

The *restaurateur* was enraged. He believed no part of the rhodomontade but that which declared their inability to discharge the bill, and he talked loudly, in his turn, of putting them into the hands of the police. At length, however, upon their offering to give him their address, he was persuaded to let them depart.

On the following day, either the hope of obtaining his money, or some vague fear that they might have been in earnest in the wild tale that they had told him, induced this man to go to the address they had left with him; and he there heard that the two unhappy boys had been that morning found lying together hand in hand, on a bed hired a few weeks before by one of them. When they were discovered, they were already dead and quite cold.

On a small table in the room lay many written papers, all expressing aspirations after greatness that should cost neither labour nor care, a profound contempt for those who were satisfied to live by the sweat of their brow—sundry quotations from Victor Hugo, and a request that their names and the manner of their death might be transmitted to the newspapers.

Many are the cases recorded of young men, calling themselves dear friends, who have thus encouraged each other to make their final exit from life, if not with applause, at least with effect. And more numerous still are the tales recounted of young men and women found dead, and locked in each other's arms; fulfilling literally, and with most sad seriousness, the destiny sketched so merrily in the old song:—

Gai, gai, marions-nous—

Mettons-nous dans la misère;

Gai, gai, marions-nous—

Mettons-nous la corde au cou.

I have heard it remarked by several individuals among those who are watching with no unphilosophical eyes many ominous features of the present time and the present race, or rather perhaps of that portion of the population which stand apart from the rest in dissolute idleness, that the worst of all its threatening indications is the reckless, hard indifference, and gladiator-like contempt of death, which is nurtured, taught, and lauded as at once the foundation and perfection of all human wisdom and of all human virtue.

In place of the firmness derived from hope and resignation, these unhappy sophists seek courage in desperation, and consolation in notoriety. With this key to the philosophy of the day, it is not difficult to read its influence on many a countenance that one meets among those who are lounging in listless laziness on the Boulevards or in the gardens of Paris.

The aspect of these figures is altogether unlike what we may too often see among those who linger, sunken, pale, and hopeless, on the benches of our parks, or loiter under porticos and colonnades, as if waiting for courage to beg. Hunger and intemperance often leave blended traces on such figures as these, exciting at once pity and disgust. I have encountered at Paris nothing like this: whether any such exist, I know not; but if they do, their beat is distant from the public walks and fashionable promenades. Instead of these, however, there is a race who seem to live there, less wretched perhaps in actual want of bread, but as evidently thriftless, homeless, and friendless as the other. On the faces of such, one may read a state of mind wholly different,—less degraded, but still more perverted;—a wild, bold eye, that rather seeks than turns from every passing glance—unshrinking hardihood, but founded more on indifference than endurance, and a scornful sneer for any who may suffer curiosity to conquer disgust, while they fix their eye for a moment upon a figure that looks in all ways as if got up to enact the hero of a melodrame. Were I the king, or the minister either, I should think it right to keep an eye of watchfulness upon all such picturesque individuals; for one might say most truly,

"Yon Cassius hath a lean and hungry look;

He thinks too much: such men are dangerous."

The friend to whom I addressed myself on the subject of these constantly-recurring suicides told me that there was great reason to believe that the increase of this crime, so remarkable during the last few years, might be almost wholly attributed to the "light literature," as it is called, of the period:—dark literature would be a fitter name for it.

The total absence of anything approaching to a virtuous principle of action in every fictitious character held up to admiration throughout all the tales and dramas of the *décousu* school, while every hint of religion is banished as if it were treason to allude to it, is in truth quite enough to account for every species of depravity in those who make such characters their study and their model. "How oft and by how many shall they be laughed to scorn!"—yet believing all the while, poor souls! that they are producing a sensation, and that the eyes of Europe are fixed upon them, notwithstanding they once worked as a tailor or a tinker, or at some other such unpoetical handiwork; for they may all be described in the words of Ecclesiasticus, with a very slight alteration,—"They would maintain the state of the world, and all their desire is in (forgetting) the work of their craft."

# LETTER XXXVIII.

Opéra Comique.—"Cheval de Bronze."—"La Marquise."—Impossibility of playing Tragedy.—Mrs. Siddons's Readings.—Mademoiselle Mars has equal power.—*Laisser aller* of the Female Performers.—Decline of Theatrical Taste among the Fashionable.

The "Cheval de Bronze" being the *spectacle par excellence* at the Opéra Comique this season, we have considered it a matter of sight-seeing necessity to pay it a visit; and we have all agreed that it is as perfectly beautiful in its scenery and decorations as the size of the theatre would permit. We gazed upon it, indeed, with a perfection of contentment, which, in secret committee afterwards, we confessed did not say much in favour of our intellectual faculties.

I really know not how it is that one can sit, not only without murmuring, but with positive satisfaction, for three hours together, with no other occupation than looking at a collection of gewgaw objects, with a most unmeaning crowd, made for the most part by Nature's journeymen, incessantly undulating among them. Yet so it is, that a skilful arrangement of blue and white gauze, aided by the magic of many-coloured lights, decidedly the prettiest of all modern toys, made us exclaim at every fresh manœuvre of the carpenter, "Beautiful! beautiful!" with as much delight as ever a child of five years old displayed at a first-rate exhibition of Punch.

M. Auber's music has some pretty things in it; but he has done much better in days of yore; and the wretched taste exhibited by all the principal singers made me heartily wish that the well-appointed orchestra had kept the whole performance to themselves.

Madame Casimir has had, and indeed still has, a rich and powerful voice: but the meanest peasant-girl in Germany, who trims her vines to the sound of her native airs, might give her a lesson on taste more valuable than all that science has ever taught her.

I should like, could I do so with a conscience that should not reproach me with exaggeration, to name Miss Stephens and Madame Casimir as fair national specimens of English and French singing. And in fact they are so; though I confess that the over-dressing of Madame Casimir's airs is almost as much out of the common way here, as the chaste simplicity of our native syren's strains is with us: yet the one is essentially English, and the other French.

We were told that the manager of our London theatres had been in Paris for the purpose of seeing and taking a cast from this fine Chinese butterfly. If this be so, Mr. Bunn will find great advantage from the extent of his theatre: that of the Opéra Comique is scarcely of sufficient magnitude to exhibit its gaudy but graceful *tableaux* to advantage. But, on the other hand, I doubt if he will find any actress quite so *piquante* as the pretty Madame ——, in the last act, when she relates to the enchanted princess, her mistress, the failure she had made in attempting by her *agaceries* to retain the young female who had ventured into the magic region: and if he did, I doubt still more if her performance would be received with equal applause.

A *petite comédie* called "La Marquise" preceded this brilliant trifle. The fable must, I think, be taken, though greatly changed, from a story of George Sand. It has perhaps little in it worth talking about; but it is a fair specimen of one of that most agreeable of French nationalities, a natural, easy, playful little piece, at which you may sit and laugh in sympathy with the performers as much as with the characters, till you forget that there are such things as sorrow and sadness in the world.

The acting in this style is so very good, that the author's task really seems to be the least important part of the business. It is not at one theatre, but at all, that we have witnessed this extraordinary excellence in the performance of this species of drama; but I doubt if the chasm which seems to surround the tragic muse, keeping her apart on a pedestal sacred to recollections, be at all wider or more profound in England than in France. In truth, it is less impassible with us than it is here; for though I will allow that our tragic actresses may be no better than those of France, seeing that a woman's will in the one case, and the Atlantic Ocean in the other, have robbed us of Mrs. Bartley and the Fanny—who between them might bring our stage back to all its former glory,—still they have neither Charles Kemble nor Macready to stand in the place that Talma has left vacant.

I have indeed no doubt whatever that Mademoiselle Mars could read Corneille and Racine as effectively as Mrs. Siddons read Shakspeare in the days of Argyle-street luxury, and, like our great maga, give to every part a power that it never had before. I well remember coming home from one of Mrs. Siddons's readings with a passionate desire to see her act the part of Hamlet; and from another, quite persuaded that by some means the witch-scene in Macbeth should be so arranged that she should speak every word of it.

In like manner, were I to hear Mars read Corneille, I should insist upon it that she ought to play the Cid; and if Racine, Oreste would probably be the first part I should choose for her. But as even she, with all her Garrick-like versatility, would not be able to perform every part of every play, tragedy must be permitted to repose for the present in France as well as in England.

During this interregnum, it is well for them, considering how dearly they love to amuse themselves, that they have a stock of comedians, old, young, and middle-aged, that they need not fear should fail; for the whole French nation seem gifted with a talent that might enable them to supply, at an hour's warning, any deficiencies in the company.

I seldom return from an exhibition of this sort without endeavouring in some degree to analyse the charm that has enchanted me: but in most cases this is too light, too subtle, to permit itself to be caught by so matter-of-fact a process. I protest to you, that I am often half ashamed of the pleasure I receive from ... I know not what. A playful smile, a speaking glance, a comic tone, a pretty gesture, give effect to words that have often nothing in them more witty or more wise than may often be met with (especially here) in ordinary conversation. But the whole thing is so thoroughly understood, from the "*père noble*" to the scene-shifter—so perfect in its getting-up—the piece so admirably suited to the players, and the players to the piece,—that whatever there is to admire and enjoy, comes to you with no drawbacks from blunders or awkwardness of any kind.

That the composition of these happy trifles cannot be a work of any great labour or difficulty, may be reasonably inferred from the ceaseless succession of novelties which every theatre and every season produces. The process, for this lively and ready-witted people, must be pleasant enough—they must catch from what passes before them; no difficult task, perhaps—some *piquante* situation or ludicrous *bévue*: the slightest thread is strong enough to hold together the light materials of the plot; and then must follow the christening of a needful proportion of male and female, old and young, enchanting and ridiculous personages. The list of these once set down, and the order of scenes which are to bring forth the plot arranged, I can fancy the author perfectly enjoying himself as he puts into the mouth of each character all the saucy impertinences upon every subject that his imagination, skilful enough in such matters, can suggest. When to this is added an occasional touch of natural feeling, and a little popular high-mindedness in any line, the *petite comédie* is ready for the stage.

It is certainly a very light manufacture, and depends perhaps more upon the fearless *laisser aller* of both author and actor than upon the brilliancy of wit which it displays. That old-fashioned blushing grace too, so much in favour with King Solomon, and called in scripture phrase shamefacedness, is sacrificed rather too unmercifully by the female part of the performers, in the fear, as it should seem, of impairing the spirit and vivacity of the scene by any scruple of any kind. But I suspect these ladies miscalculate the respective value of opposing graces; Mademoiselle Mars may show them that delicacy and vivacity are not inseparable; and though I confess that it would be a little unreasonable to expect all the female vaudevillists of Paris to be like Mars, I cannot but think that, in a city where her mode of playing comedy has for so many years been declared perfect, it must be unnecessary to seek the power of attraction from what is so utterly at variance with it.

The performance of comedy is often assisted here by a freedom among the actors which I have sometimes, but not often, seen permitted in London. It requires for its success, and indeed for its endurance, that the audience should be perfectly in good-humour, and sympathise very cordially with the business of the scene. I allude to the part which the performers sometimes take not only in the acting, but in the enjoyment of it. I never in my life saw people more heartily amused, or disposed more unceremoniously to show it, than the actors in the "Précieuses Ridicules," which I saw played a few nights ago at the Français. On this occasion I think the spirit of the performance was certainly heightened by this license, and for this reason—the scene represents a group in which one party must of necessity be exceedingly amused by the success of the mystification which they are practising on the other. But I own that I have sometimes felt a little *English stiffness* at perceiving an air of frolic and fun upon the stage, which seemed fully as much got up for the performers as for the audience. But though the instance I have named of this occurred at the Théâtre Français, it is not there that it is likely to be carried to any offensive extent. The lesser theatres would in many instances do well to copy closely the etiquette and decorum of all kinds which the great national theatre exhibits: but perhaps it is hardly fair to expect this; and besides, we might be told, justly enough, to *look at home*.

The theatres, particularly the minor ones, appear to be still very well attended: but I constantly hear the same observations made in Paris as in London upon the decline of theatrical taste among the higher orders; and it arises, I think, from the same cause in both countries,—namely, the late dinner-hour, which renders the going to a play a matter of general family arrangement, and often of general family difficulty. The opera, which is later, is always full; and were it not that I have lived too long in the world to be surprised at anything that the power of fashion could effect, I should certainly be astonished that so lively a people as the French should throng night after night as they do to witness the exceeding dulness of this heavy spectacle.

The only people I have yet seen enjoying their theatres rationally, without abstaining from what they liked because it was unfashionable, or enduring what they did not, because it was the *mode*, are the Germans. Their genuine and universal love of music makes their delicious opera almost a necessary of life to them; and they must, I think, absolutely change their nature before they will suffer the silly conventional elegance supposed by some to attach to the act of eating their dinner late, to interfere with their enjoyment of it.

I used to think the theatre as dear to the French as music to the Germans. But what is a taste in France is, from the firmer fibre of the national character, a passion in Germany;—and it is easier to abandon a taste than to control a passion.

Perhaps, however, in England and France too, if some new-born theatrical talent of the first class were to "flame in the forehead of the morning sky," both Paris and London would submit to the degradation of dining at five o'clock in order to enjoy it: but late hours and indifferent performances, together, have gone far towards placing the stage among the popular rather than the fashionable amusements of either.

## LETTER XXXIX.

The Abbé de Lamennais.—Cobbett.—O'Connell.—Napoleon.—Robespierre.

I had last night the satisfaction of meeting the Abbé de Lamennais at a *soirée*. It was at the house of Madame Benjamin Constant; whose *salon* is as celebrated for the talent of every kind to be met there, as for the delightful talents and amiable qualities of its mistress.

In general appearance, this celebrated man recalls an original drawing that I remember to have seen of Rousseau. He is greatly below the ordinary height, and extremely small in his proportions. His countenance is very striking, and singularly indicative of habitual meditation; but the deep-set eye has something very nearly approaching to wildness in its rapid glance. His dress was black, but had certainly more of republican negligence than priestly dignity in it; and the little, tight, chequered cravat which encircled his slender throat, gave him decidedly the appearance of a person who heeded not either the fashion of the day, or the ordinary costume of the *salon*.

He, in company with four or five other distinguished men, had dined with Madame Constant; and we found him deep sunk in a *bergère* that almost concealed his diminutive person, surrounded by a knot of gentlemen, with whom he was conversing with great eagerness and animation. On one side of him was M. Jouy, the well-known "*Hermite*" of the Chaussée d'Antin; and on the other, a deputy well known on the benches of the *côté gauche*.

I was placed immediately opposite to him, and have seldom watched the play of a more animated countenance. In the course of the evening, he was brought up and introduced to me. His manners are extremely gentlemanlike; no stiffness or reserve, either rustic or priestly, interfering with their easy vivacity. He immediately drew a chair *vis-à-vis* to the sofa on which I was placed, and continued thus, with his back turned to the rest of the company, conversing very agreeably, till so many persons collected round him, many of whom were ladies, that not feeling pleased, I suppose, to sit while they stood, he bowed off, and retreated again to his *bergère*.

He told me that he must not remain long in Paris, where he was too much in society to do anything; that he should speedily retreat to the profound seclusion of his native Brittany, and there finish the work upon which he was engaged. Whether this work be the defence of the *prévenus d'Avril*, which he has threatened to fulminate in a printed form at the head of those who refused to let him plead for them in court, I know not; but this document, whenever it appears, is expected to be violent, powerful, and eloquent.

The writings of the Abbé de Lamennais remind me strongly of those of Cobbett,—not, certainly, from their matter, nor even from the manner of treating it, but from the sort of effect which they produce upon the mind. Had the pen of either of them been wholly devoted to the support of a good cause, their writings would have been invaluable to society; for they both have shown a singular power of carrying the attention, and almost the judgment, of the reader along with them, even when writing on subjects on which he and they were perfectly at issue.

Were there not circumstances in the literary history of both which contradict the notion, I should say that this species of power or charm in their writings arose from their being themselves very much in earnest in the opinions they were advocating: but as the Abbé de Lamennais and the late Mr. Cobbett have both shown that their faith in their own opinions was not strong enough to prevent them from changing them, the peculiar force of their eloquence can hardly be referred to the sincerity of it.

I remember hearing a lively young barrister declare that he would rather argue against his own judgment than according to it; and I am sure he spoke in all sincerity,—much as he would have done had he said that he preferred shooting wild game to slaughtering tame chickens: the difficulty made the pleasure. But we cannot presume to suppose that either of the two persons whose names I have so incongruously brought together have written and argued on the same principle; and even if it were so, they have not the less changed their minds,— unless we suppose that they have amused themselves and the public, by sometimes arguing for what they believed to be truth, and sometimes only to show their skill.

As to what Mr. Cobbett's principles might really have been, I think it is a question that must ever remain in uncertainty,—unless we adopt that easiest and most intelligible conclusion, that he had none at all. But it is far otherwise with M. de Lamennais: it is impossible to doubt that in his early writings he was perfectly sincere; there is a warmth of faith in them that could proceed from no fictitious fire. Nor is it easily to be imagined that he would have thrown himself from the height at which he stood in the opinion of all whom he most esteemed, had he not fancied that he saw truth at the bottom of that abyss of heresy and schism into which all good Catholics think that he has thrown himself.

The wild republicanism which M. de Lamennais has picked up in his descent is, however, what has probably injured him most in the general estimation. Some few years ago, liberal principles were advocated by many of the most able as well as the most honest men in Europe; but the unreasonable excesses into which the ultras of the party have fallen seem to have made the respectable portion of mankind draw back from it, and, whatever their speculative opinions may be, they now show themselves anxious to rally round all that bears the stamp of order and lawful authority.

It would be difficult to imagine a worse time for a man to commence republican and free-thinker than the present;—unless, indeed, he did so in the hope that the loaves and fishes were, or would be, at the disposition of that party. Putting, however, all hope of being paid for it aside, the period is singularly unpropitious for such a conversion. As long as their doctrine remained a theory only, it might easily delude many who had more imagination than judgment, or more ignorance than either: but so much deplorable mischief has arisen before our eyes every time the theory has been brought to the test of practice, that I believe the sound-minded in every land consider their speculations at present with as little respect as they would those of a joint-stock company proposing to colonize the moon.

That the Abbé de Lamennais is no longer considered in France as the pre-eminent man he has been, is most certain; and as it is easy to trace in his works a regular progression downwards, from the dignified and enthusiastic Catholic priest to the puzzled sceptic and factious demagogue, I should not be greatly surprised to hear that he, who has been spoken of at Rome as likely to become a cardinal, was carrying a scarlet flag through the streets of Paris, with a conical hat and a Robespierre waistcoat, singing "*Ça ira*" louder than he ever chanted a mass.

M. de Lamennais, in common with several other persons of republican principles with whom I have conversed since I have been in Paris, has conceived the idea that England is at this moment actually and *bonâ fide* under the rule, dictation, and government of Mr. Daniel O'Connell. He named him in an accent of the most profound admiration and respect, and referred to the English newspapers as evidence of the enthusiastic love and veneration in which he was held throughout Great Britain!

I waxed wroth, I confess; but I took wisdom and patience, and said very meekly, that he had probably seen only that portion of the English papers which were of Mr. Daniel's faction, and that I believed Great Britain was still under the dominion of King William the Fourth, his Lords and Commons. It is not many days since I met another politician of the same school who went farther still; for he gravely wished me joy of the prospect of emancipation which the virtue of the great O'Connell held out to my country. On this occasion, being in a gay mood, I laughed heartily, and did so with a safe conscience, having no need to set the enlightened propagandist right; this being done for me, much better than I could have done it myself, by a hard-headed doctrinaire who was with me.

"O'Connell is the Napoleon of England," said the republican.

"Not of England, at any rate," replied the doctrinaire. "And if he must have a name borrowed from France, let it be Robespierre's: let him be called magnificently the Robespierre of Ireland."

"He has already been the redeemer of Ireland," rejoined the republican gravely; "and now *he has taken England under his protection.*"

"And I suspect that ere long England will take him under hers," said my friend, laughing. "Hitherto it appears as if the country had not thought him worth whipping; ... mais si un chien est méchant, si même ce ne serait qu'un vilain petit hargneux, il devrait être lié, ou bien pendu."

Having finished this oracular sentence, the doctrinaire took a long pinch of snuff, and began discoursing of other matters: and I too withdrew from the discussion, persuaded that I could not bring it to a better conclusion.

## LETTER XL.

Which Party is it ranks second in the estimation of all?—No Caricatures against the Exiles.—Horror of a Republic.

I have been taking some pains to discover, by the aid of all the signs and tokens of public feeling within my reach, who among the different parties into which this country is divided enjoys the highest degree of general consideration.

We know that if every man in a town were desired to say who among its inhabitants he should consider as fittest to hold an employment of honour and profit, each would probably answer, "Myself:" we know also, that should it happen, after the avowal of this very natural partiality, that the name of the second best were asked for, and that the man named as such by one were so named by all, this second best would be accounted by the disinterested lookers-on as decidedly the right and proper person to fill the station. According to this rule, the right and proper government for France is neither republican, nor military, nor doctrinaire, but that of a legitimate and constitutional monarchy.

When men hold office, bringing both power and wealth, consideration will of necessity follow. That the ministers and their friends, therefore, should be seen in pride of place, and enjoying the dignity they have achieved, is natural, inevitable, and quite as it should be. But if, turning from this every-day spectacle, we endeavour to discover who it is that, possessing neither power nor place, most uniformly receive the homage of respect, I should say, without a shadow of doubt or misgiving, that it was the legitimate royalists.

The triumphant doctrinaires pass no jokes at their expense; no *bons mots* are quoted against them, nor does any shop exhibit caricatures either of what they have been or of what they are.

The republicans are no longer heard to name them, either with rancour or disrespect: all their wrath is now poured out upon the present actual power of the prosperous doctrinaires. This, indeed, is in strict conformity to the principle which constitutes the foundation of their sect; namely, that whatever exists ought to be overthrown. But neither in jest nor earnest do they now show hostility to Charles the Tenth or his family: nor even do the blank walls of Paris, which for nearly half a century have been the favourite receptacle of all their wit, exhibit any pleasantries, either in the shape of hieroglyphic, caricature, or lampoon, alluding to them or their cause.

I have listened repeatedly to sprightly and to bitter jestings, to judicious and to blundering reasonings, for and against the different doctrines which divide the country; but in no instance do I remember to have heard, either in jest or earnest, any revilings against the exiled race. A sort of sacred silence seems to envelope this theme; or if it be alluded to at all, it is far from being in a hostile spirit.

"H̲ᴇɴʀɪ!" is a name that, without note or comment, may be read *ça et là* in every quarter of Paris, that of the Tuileries not excepted: and on a wall near the Royal College of Henri Quatre, where the younger princes of the house of Orleans still study, were inscribed not long ago these very intelligible words:
—

"Pour arriver à Bordeaux, il faut passer par Orléans."

In short, whatever feelings of irritation and anger might have existed in 1830, and produced the scenes which led to the exile of the royal family, they now seem totally to have subsided.

It does not, however, necessarily follow from this that the majority of the people are ready again to hazard their precious tranquillity in order to restore them: on the contrary, it cannot be doubted that were such a measure attempted at the present moment, it would fail—not from any dislike of their legitimate monarch, or any affection for the kinsman who has been placed upon his throne, but wholly and solely from their wish to enjoy in peace their profitable speculations at the *Bourse*—their flourishing *restaurans*—their prosperous shops—and even their tables, chairs, beds, and coffee-pots.

Very different, however, is the feeling manifested towards the republicans. Never did Napoleon in the days of his most absolute power, or the descendants of Louis le Grand in those of their proudest state, contemplate this factious, restless race with such abhorrence as do the doctrinaires of the present hour. It is not that they fear them—they have no real cause to do so; but they feel a sentiment made up of hatred and contempt, which never seems to repose, and which, if not regulated by wisdom and moderation, is very likely eventually to lead to more barricades; though to none, I imagine, that the National Guards may not easily throw down.

It is on the subject of this unpopular *clique* that by far the greater part of the ever-springing Parisian jokes expends itself; though the doctrinaires get it "*pas mal*" in return, as I heard a national guardsman remark, as we were looking over some caricatures together. But, in truth, the republicans seem upon principle to offer themselves as victims and martyrs to the quizzing propensities of their countrymen. Harlequin does not more scrupulously adhere to his parti-coloured suit, than do the republicans of Paris to their burlesque costume. It is, I presume, to show their courage, that they so ostentatiously march with their colours flying; but the effect is very ludicrous. The symbolic peculiarities of their dress are classed and lithographed with infinite fun.

Drolleries, too, on the parvenus of the Empire are to be found for the seeking; and when they beset King Philippe himself, it should seem that it is done with all the enthusiasm so well expressed by Garrick in days of yore:—

"'Tis for my king, and, zounds! I'll do my best!"

The only extraordinary part of all this caricaturing on walls and in print-shops, is the license taken with those who have power to prevent it. The principle of legislation on this point appears, with a little variation, to be that of the old ballad:

"Thoughts, words, and deeds, the statute blames with reason;

But surely *jokes* were ne'er indicted treason."

In speaking of the parties into which France is divided, the three grand divisions of Carlists, Doctrinaires, and Republicans naturally present themselves first and foremost, and, to foreigners in general, appear to contain between them the entire nation: but a month or two passed in Paris society suffices to show one that there are many who cannot fairly be classed with either.

In the first place, the Carlist party by no means contains all those who disapprove of treating a crown like a ready-made shoe, which, if it be found to pinch the person it was intended for, may be disposed of to the first comer who is willing to take it. The Carlist party, properly so called, demand the restoration of King Charles the Tenth, the immediate descendant and representative of their long line of kings—the prince who has been crowned and anointed King of France, and who, while he remains alive, must render the crowning and anointing of any other prince an act of sacrilege. Wherefore, in effect, King Louis-Philippe has not received "*le sacre*:" he is not as yet the anointed King of France, whatever he may be hereafter. Henri Quatre is said to have exclaimed under the walls of the capital, "Paris vaut bien une messe;" and it is probable that Louis-Philippe Premier thinks so too; but hitherto he has been able to have this performed only in military style—being incapable, in fact, of going through the ceremony either civilly or religiously. The Carlists are, therefore, those only who *en rigueur* do not approve of any king but the real one.

The legitimate royalists are, I believe, a much more numerous party. As strictly attached to the throne and to the principle of regular and legitimate succession as the Carlists, they nevertheless conceive that the pressure of circumstances may not only authorise, but render it imperative upon the country to accept, or rather to permit, the abdication of a sovereign. The king's leaving the country and placing himself in exile, is one of the few causes that can justify this; and accordingly the abdication of Charles Dix is virtual death to him as a sovereign. But though this is granted, it does not follow in their creed, that any part of the nation have thereupon a right to present the hereditary crown to whom they will. The law of succession, they say, is not to be violated because the king has fled before a popular insurrection; and having permitted his abdication, the next heir becomes king. This next heir, however, choosing to follow his royal father's example, he too becomes virtually defunct, and his heir succeeds.

This heir is still an infant, and his remaining in exile cannot therefore be interpreted as his own act. Thus, according to the reasoning of those who conceive the abdication of the king and the dauphin to be acts within their own power, and beyond that of the nation to nullify, Henri, the son of the Duc de Berri, is beyond all doubt Henri Cinq, Roi de France.

Of this party, however, there are many, and I suspect their number is increasing, who, having granted the power of setting aside (by his own act) the anointed monarch, are not altogether averse to go a step farther, if so doing shall ensure the peace of the country; and considering the infancy of the rightful heir as constituting insufficiency, to confess Louis-Philippe as the next in succession to be the lawful as well as the actual King of the French.

It is this party who I always find have the most to say in support (or defence) of their opinions. Whether this proceed from their feeling that some eloquence is necessary to make them pass current, or that the conviction of their justice is such as to make their hearts overflow on the theme, I know not; but decidedly the sect of the "*Parcequ'il est Bourbon*" is that which I find most eager to discourse upon politics. And, to confess the truth, they have much to say for themselves, at least on the side of expediency.

It is often a matter of regret with me, that in addressing these letters to you I am compelled to devote so large a portion of them to politics; but in attempting to give you some idea of Paris at the present moment, it is impossible to avoid it. Were I to turn from this theme, I could only do so by labouring to forget everything I have seen, everything I see. Go where you will, do what you will, meet whom you will, it is out of your power to escape it. But observe, that it is wholly for your sake, and not at all for my own, that I lament it; for, however flat and unprofitable my report may be, the thing itself, when you are in the midst of it, is exceedingly interesting.

When I first arrived, I was considerably annoyed by finding, that as soon as I had noted down some piece of information as an undoubted fact, the next person I conversed with assured me that it was worth considerably less than nought; inasmuch as my informer had not only failed to give me useful instruction on the point concerning which I was inquiring, but had altogether deluded, deceived, and led me astray.

These days of primitive matter-of-factness are now, however, quite passed with me; and though I receive a vast deal of entertainment from all, I give my faith in return to very few. I listen to the Carlists, the Henri-Quintists, the Philippists, with great attention and real interest, but have sometimes caught myself humming as soon as they have left me,

"They were all of them kings in their turn."

Indeed, if you knew all that happens to me, instead of blaming me for being too political, you would be very thankful for the care and pains I bestow in endeavouring to make a digest of all I hear for your advantage, containing as few contradictions as possible. And truly this is no easy matter, not only from the contradictory nature of the information I receive, but from some varying weaknesses in my own nature, which sometimes put me in the very disagreeable predicament of doubting if what is right be right, and if what is wrong be wrong.

When I came here, I was a thorough unequivocating legitimatist, and felt quite ready and willing to buckle on armour against any who should doubt that a man once a king was always a king—that once crowned according to law, he could not be uncrowned according to mob—or that a man's eldest son was his rightful heir.

But, oh! these doctrinaires! They have such a way of proving that if they are not quite right, at least everybody else is a great deal more wrong: and then they talk so prettily of England and *our* revolution, and our glorious constitution—and the miseries of anarchy—and the advantages of letting things remain quietly as they are, till, as I said before, I begin to doubt what is right and what is wrong.

There is one point, however, on which we agree wholly and heartily; and it is this perhaps that has been the means of softening my heart thus towards them. The doctrinaires shudder at the name of a republic. This is not because their own party is regal, but is evidently the result of the experience which they and their fathers havehad from the tremendous experiment which has once already been made in the country.

"You will never know the full value of your constitution till you have lost it," said a doctrinaire to me the other evening, at the house of the beautiful Princess B———, formerly an energetic propagandiste, but now a very devoted doctrinaire,—"you will never know how beneficial is its influence on every hour of your lives, till your Mr. O'Connell has managed to arrange a republic for you: and when you have tasted that for about three months, you will make good and faithful subjects to the next king that Heaven shall bestow upon you. You know how devoted all France was to the Emperor, though the police was somewhat tight, and the conscriptions heavy: but he had saved us from a republic, and we adored him. For a few days, or rather hours, we were threatened again, five years ago, by the same terrible apparition: the result is, that four millions of armed men stand ready to protect the prince who chased it. Were it to appear a third time—which Heaven forbid!—you may depend upon it that the monarch who should next ascend the throne of France might play at *le jeu de quilles* with his subjects, and no one be found to complain."

## LETTER XLI.

M. Dupré.—His Drawings in Greece.—L'Eglise des Carmes.—M. Vinchon's Picture of the National Convention.—Léopold Robert's Fishermen.—Reported cause of his Suicide.—Roman Catholic Religion.—Mr. Daniel O'Connell.

We went the other morning, with Miss C——, a very agreeable countrywoman, who has however passed the greater portion of her life in Paris, to visit the house and atelier of M. Dupré, a young artist who seems to have devoted himself to the study of Greece. Her princes, her peasants, her heavy-eyed beauties, and the bright sky that glows above them,—all the material of her domestic life, and all the picturesque accompaniments of her classic reminiscences, are brought home by this gentleman in a series of spirited and highly-finished drawings, which give decidedly the most lively idea of the country that I have seen produced. Engravings or lithographs from them are, I believe, intended to illustrate a splendid work on this interesting country which is about to be published.

In our way from M. Dupré's house, in which was this collection of Greek drawings, to his atelier—where he was kind enough to show us a large picture recently commenced—we entered that fatal "Eglise des Carmes," where the most hideous massacre of the first revolution took place. A large tree that stands beside it is pointed out as having been sought as a shelter—alas! how vainly!—by the unhappy priests, who were shot, sabred, and dragged from its branches by dozens. A thousand terrible recollections are suggested by the interior of the building, aided by the popular traditions attached to it, unequalled in atrocity even in the history of that time of horror.

Another scene relating to the same period, which, though inferior to the massacre of the priests in multiplied barbarity, was of sufficient horror to freeze the blood of any but a republican, has, strange to say, been made, since the revolution of 1830, the subject of an enormous picture by M. Vinchon, and at the present moment makes part of the exhibition at the Louvre.

The canvass represents a hall at the Tuileries which in 1795 was the place where the National Convention sat. The mob has broken in, and murdered Feraud, who attempted to oppose them; and the moment chosen by the painter is that in which a certain "*jeune fille nommée Aspasie Migelli*" approaches the president's chair with the young man's head borne on a pike before her, while she triumphantly envelopes herself in some part of his dress. The whole scene is one of the most terrible revolutionary violence. This picture is stated in the catalogue to belong to the minister of the interior; but whether the present minister of the interior, or any other, I know not. The subject was given immediately after the revolution of 1830, and many artists made sketches in competition for the execution of it. One of those who tried, and failed before the superior genius of M. Vinchon, told us, that the subject was given at that time as one likely to be popular, either for love of the noble resolution with which Boissy d'Anglas keeps possession of the president's chair, which he had seized upon, or else from admiration of the energetic female who has assisted in doing the work of death. In either case, this young artist said, the popularity of such a subject was passed by, and no such order would be given now.

Finding myself again on the subject of pictures, I must mention a very admirable one which is now being exhibited at the "Mairie du Second Arrondissement." It is from the hand of the unfortunate Leopold Robert, who destroyed himself at Venice almost immediately after he had completed it. The subject is the departure of a partyof Italian fishermen; and there are parts of the picture fully equal to anything I have ever seen from the pencil of a modern artist. I should have looked at this picture with extreme pleasure, had the painter still lived to give hope of, perhaps, still higher efforts; but the history of his death, which I had just been listening to, mixed great pain with it.

I have been told that this young man was of a very religious and meditative turn of mind, but a Protestant. His only sister, to whom he was much attached, was a Catholic, and had recently taken the veil. Her affection for him was such, that she became perfectly wretched from the danger she believed awaited him from his heresy; and she commenced a species of affectionate persecution, which, though it failed to convert him, so harassed and distracted his mind, as finally to overthrow his reason, and lead him to self-destruction. This charming picture is exhibited for the benefit of the poor, at the especial desire of the unhappy nun; who is said, however, to be so perfect a fanatic, as only to regret that the dreadful act was not delayed till she had had time to work out the salvation of her own soul by a little more persecution of his.

There is something exceedingly curious, and, perhaps, under our present lamentable circumstances, somewhat alarming, in the young and vigorous after-growth of the Roman Catholic religion, which, by the aid of a very little inquiry, may be so easily traced throughout France. Were we keeping our own national church sacred, and guarded both by love and by law, as it has hitherto been from all assaults of the Pope and ... Mr. O'Connell, it could only be with pleasure that we should see France recovering from her long ague-fit of infidelity,—and, as far as she is concerned, we must in Christian charity rejoice, for she is unquestionably the better for it; but there is a regenerated activity among the Roman Catholic clergy, which, under existing circumstances, makes a Protestant feel rather nervous,—and I declare to you, I never pass within sight of that famous window of the Louvre, whence Charles Neuf, with his own royal and catholic hand, discharged a blunderbuss amongst the Huguenots, without thinking how well a window at Whitehall, already noted in history as a scene of horror, might serve King Daniel for the same purpose.

The great influence which the religion of Rome has of late regained over the minds of the French people has, I am told, been considerably increased by the priests having added to the strength derived from their command of pardons and indulgences, that which our Methodist preachers gain from the terrors of hell. They use the same language, too, respecting regeneration and grace; and, as one means of regaining the hold they had lost upon the human mind, they now anathematize all recreations, as if their congregations were so many aspirants to the sublime purifications of La Trappe, or so many groaning fanatics just made over to them from Lady Huntingdon's Chapel. That there is, however, a pretty strong force to stem this fresh spring-tide of moon-struck superstition, is very certain. The doctrinaires, I am told, taken as a body, are not much addicted to this species of weakness. I remember, during the prevalence of that sweeping complaint called the influenza, hearing of a "good lady," of the high evangelical *clique*, who said to some of the numerous pensioners who flocked to receive the crumbs of her table and the precepts of her lips, that she could make up some medicine that was very good for all POOR people that were seized with this complaint.

"What can be the difference, ma'am," said the poor body who told me this, "between us and Madame C—— in this illness? Is not what is good for the poor, good for the rich too?"

The same pertinent question may, I think, be asked in Paris just now respecting the medicine called religion. It is administered in large doses to the poor, to which class a great number of the fair sex of all ranks happily seem to have joined themselves, intending, at least, to rank themselves as among the poor in spirit; nay, parish doctors are regularly paid by authority; yet, if the tale be true, the authorities themselves take little of it. "It is very good for poor people;" but, like the hot-baths which Anstie talks of,

"No creature e'er view'd

Any one of the government gentry stew'd."

Whether the returning power of this pompous and aspiring faith will mount as it proceeds, and embrace within its grasp, as it was wont to do, all the great ones of the earth, is a question that it may require some years to answer; but one thing is at least certain,—that its ministers will try hard that it shall do so, whether they are likely to succeed or not; and, at the worst, they may console themselves by the reflection of Lafontaine:—

"Si de les gagner je n'emporte pas le prix,

J'aurais au moins l'honneur de l'avoir entrepris."

One great one they have certainly already got, besides King Charles the Tenth,—even the immortal Daniel; and however little consequence you may be inclined to attach to this fact, it cannot be considered as wholly unimportant, since I have heard his religious principles and his influence in England alluded to in the pulpit here with a tone of hope and triumph which made me tremble.

I heartily wish that some of those who continue to vote in his traitorous majority because they are pledged to do so, could hear him and his power spoken of here. If they have English hearts, it must, I think, give them a pang.


## LETTER XLII.

Old Maids.—Rarely to be found in France.—The reasons for this.

Several years ago, while passing a few weeks in Paris, I had a conversation with a Frenchman upon the subject of old maids, which, though so long past, I refer to now for the sake of the sequel, which has just reached me.

We were, I well remember, parading in the Gardens of the Luxembourg; and as we paced up and down its long alleys, the "miserable fate," as he called it, of single women in England was discussed and deplored by my companion as being one of the most melancholy results of faulty national manners that could be mentioned.

"I know nothing," said he with much energy, "that ever gave me more pain in society, than seeing, as I did in England, numbers of unhappy women who, however well-born, well-educated, or estimable, were without a position, without an *état* and without a name, excepting one that they would generally give half their remaining days to get rid of."

"I think you somewhat exaggerate the evil," I replied: "but even if it were as bad as you state it to be, I see not why single ladies should be better off here."

"Here!" he exclaimed, in a tone of horror: "Do you really imagine that in France, where we pride ourselves on making the destiny of our women the happiest in the world,—do you really imagine that we suffer a set of unhappy, innocent, helpless girls to drop, as it were, out of society into the *néant* of celibacy, as you do? God keep us from such barbarity!"

"But how can you help it? It is impossible but that circumstances must arise to keep many of your men single; and if the numbers be equally balanced, it follows that there must be single women too."

"It may seem so; but the fact is otherwise: we have no single women."

"What, then, becomes of them?"

"I know not; but were any Frenchwoman to find herself so circumstanced, depend upon it she would drown herself."

"I know one such, however," said a lady who was with us: "Mademoiselle Isabelle B*** is an old maid."

"Est-il possible!" cried the gentleman, in a tone that made me laugh very heartily. "And how old is she, this unhappy Mademoiselle Isabelle?"

"I do not know exactly," replied the lady; "but I think she must be considerably past thirty."

"C'est une horreur!" he exclaimed again; adding, rather mysteriously, in a half-whisper, "Trust me, she will not bear it long!"

I had certainly forgotten Mademoiselle Isabelle and all about her, when I again met the lady who had named her as the one sole existing old maid of France. While conversing with her the other day on many things which had passed when we were last together, she asked me if I remembered this conversation. I assured her that I had forgotten no part of it.

"Well, then," said she, "I must tell you what happened to me about three months after it took place. I was invited with my husband to pay a visit at the house of a friend in the country,—the same house where I had formerly seen the Mademoiselle Isabelle B*** whom I had named to you. While playing *écarté* with our host in the evening, I recollected our conversation in the Gardens of the Luxembourg, and inquired for the lady who had been named in it.

"'Is it possible that you have not heard what has happened to her?' he replied.

"'No, indeed; I have heard nothing. Is she married, then?'

"'Married!... Alas, no! she has *drowned herself*!'"

Terrible as this dénouement was, it could not be heard with the solemn gravity it called for, after what had been said respecting her. Was ever coincidence more strange! My friend told me, that on her return to Paris she mentioned this catastrophe to the gentleman who had seemed to predict it; when the information was received by an exclamation quite in character,—"God be praised! then she is out of her misery!"

This incident, and the conversation which followed upon it, induced me to inquire in sober earnest what degree of truth there might really be in the statement made to us in this well-remembered conversation; and it certainly does appear, from all I can learn, that the meeting a single woman past thirty is a very rare occurrence in France. The arranging *un mariage convenable* is in fact as necessary and as ordinary a duty in parents towards a daughter, as the sending her to nurse or the sending her to school. The proposal for such an alliance proceeds quite as frequently from the friends of the lady as from those of the gentleman: and it is obvious that this must at once very greatly increase the chance of a suitable marriage for young women; for though we do occasionally send our daughters to India in the hope of obtaining this much-desired result, few English parents have as yet gone the length of proposing to anybody, or to anybody's son, to take their daughter off their hands.

I have not the least doubt in the world that, were the custom otherwise—were a young lady's claim to an establishment pointed out by her friends, instead of being left to be discovered or undiscovered as chance will have it,—I have no doubt in the world that in such a case many happy marriages might be the result: and where such an arrangement infringes on no feeling of propriety, but is adopted only in conformity to national custom, I can well believe that the fair lady herself may deem her having nothing to do with the business a privilege of infinite importance to her delicacy. But would our English girls like, for the satisfaction of escaping the chance of being an old maid, to give up the dear right of awaiting in maiden dignity till they are chosen—selected from out the entire world—and then of saying yes or no, as may please their fancy best?

If I do not greatly mistake the national character of Englishwomen, there are very few who could be found to exchange this privilege for the most perfect assurance that could be given of obtaining a marriage in any other way. As to which is best and which is wisest, or even which is likely to produce, ultimately and generally, the most happy *ménage*, I will not pretend to say; because I have heard so much plausible, and indeed, in some respects, substantial reasoning in favour of the mode pursued here, that I feel it may be considered as doubtful: but as to which is and must be most agreeable to the parties chiefly concerned at the time the connexion is formed, herein I own I think there can be no question whatever that English men and English women have the advantage.

With all the inclination in the world to believe that France abounds with loving, constant, faithful wives, and husbands too, I cannot but think that if they are so, it is in spite of the manner in which their marriages are made, and not in consequence of it. The strongest argument in favour of their manner of proceeding undoubtedly is, that a husband who receives a young wife as totally without impressions of any kind, (as a well-brought-up French girl certainly is,) has a better chance—or rather, has more *power* of making her heart entirely his own, than any man can have that falls in love with a beauty of twenty, who may already have heard as tender sighs as he can utter breathed in her ear by some one who may have had no power to marry her, but who might have had a heart to love her, and a tongue to win her as well as himself.

But against this how much is to be placed! However dearly a Frenchwoman may love her husband, he can never feel that it is a love which has selected him; and though it may sometimes happen that a pretty creature is applied for because of her prettiness, yet if the application be made and answered, and no question asked as to her will or wish in the affair, she can feel but little gratification even to her vanity—and certainly nothing whatever approaching to a feeling of tenderness at her heart.

The force of habit is ever so inveterate, that it is not likely either nation can be really a fair and impartial judge of the other in a matter so entirely regulated by it. Therefore, all that I, as English, will venture to say farther on the subject is, that I should be sorry on this point to see us adopt the fashion of our neighbour France.

I have reason to believe, however, that my friend of the Luxembourg Gardens exaggerated a good deal in his statement respecting the non-existence of single women in France. They do exist here, though certainly in less numbers than in England,—but it is not so easy to find them out. With us it is not unusual for single ladies to take what is called *brevet rank*;—that is, Miss Dorothy Tomkins becomes Mrs. Dorothy Tomkins—and sometimes *tout bonnement* Mrs. Tomkins, provided there be no collateral Mrs. Tomkins to interfere with her: but upon no occasion do I remember that any lady in this predicament called herself the widow Tomkins, or the widow anything else.

Here, however, I am assured that the case is different; and that, let the number of spinsters be great or small, no one but the near connexions and most intimate friends of the party know anything of the matter. Many a *veuve respectable* has never had a husband in her life; and I have heard it positively affirmed, that the secret is often so well kept, that the nieces and nephews of a family do not know their maiden aunts from their widowed ones.

This shows, at least, that matrimony is considered here as a more honourable state than that of celibacy; though it does not quite go the length of proving that all single women drown themselves.

But before I quit this subject, I must say a few words to you concerning the old maids of England. There are few things which chafe my spirit more than hearing single women spoken of with contempt because they are such, or seeing them treated with less consideration and attention than those who chance to be married. The cruelty and injustice of this must be obvious to every one upon a moment's thought; but to me its absurdity is more obvious still.

It is, I believe, a notorious fact, that there is scarcely a woman to be found, of any rank under that of a princess of the blood royal, who, at the age of fifty, has not at some time or in some manner had the power of marrying if she chose it. That many who have had this power have been tyrannically or unfortunately prevented from using it, is certain; but there is nothing either ridiculous or contemptible in this.

Still less does a woman merit scorn if she has had the firmness and constancy of purpose to prefer a single life because she has considered it best and fittest for her: in fact, I know nothing more high-minded than the doing so. The sneering which follows female celibacy is so well known and so coarsely manifested, that it shows very considerable dignity of character to enable a woman to endure it, rather than act against her sense of what is right.

I by no means say this by way of running a-tilt against all the ladies in France who have submitted, *bon gré, mal gré,* to become wives at the command of their fathers, mothers, uncles, aunts, and guardians: they have done exactly what they ought, and I hope all their pretty little quiet-looking daughters will do the same; it is the custom of the country, and cannot discreetly be departed from. But being on the subject, I am led, while defending our own modes of proceeding in the important affair of marriage, to remark also on the result of them. In permitting a young woman to become acquainted with the man who proposes for her before she consents to pass her whole life with him, I certainly see some advantage; but in my estimation there is more still in the protection which our usage in these matters affords to those who, rather than marry a man who is not the object of their choice, prefer remaining single. I confess, too, that I consider the class of single women as an extremely important one. Their entire freedom from control gives them great power over their time and resources, much more than any other woman can possibly possess who is not a childless widow. That this power is often—very often—nobly used, none can deny who are really and thoroughly acquainted with English society; and if among the class there be some who love cards, and tattle, and dress, and slander, they should be treated with just the same measure of contempt as the married ladies who may also occasionally be found to love cards, and tattle, and dress, and slander,—but with no more.

It has been my chance, and I imagine that it has been the chance of most other people, to have found my dearest and most constant friends among single women. Of all the Helenas and Hermias that before marriage have sat "upon one cushion, warbling of one song," even for years together, how few are there who are not severed by marriage! Kind feelings may be retained, and correspondence (lazily enough) kept up; but to whom is it that the anxious mother, watching beside the sick couch of her child, turns for sympathy and consolation?—certainly not to the occupied and perhaps distant wedded confidante of her youthful days, but to her maiden sister or her maiden friend. Nor is it only in sickness that such friends are among the first blessings of life: they violate no duty by giving their time and their talents to society; and many a day through every house in England has probably owed some of its most delightful hours to the presence of those whom no duty has called

"To suckle fools or chronicle small beer,"

and whose talents, therefore, are not only at their own disposal, but in all probability much more highly cultivated than any possessed by their married friends.

Thus, spite of him of the Luxembourg, I am most decidedly of opinion, that, in England at least, there is no reason whatever that an unmarried woman should consign herself to the fate of the unfortunate Mademoiselle Isabelle.

END OF THE FIRST VOLUME.